IS FOR ELVIS

By the same authors:

THE KENNEDY ENCYCLOPEDIA: An A-to-Z Illustrated Guide to America's Royal Family

THE ROYALS: An Intimate Look at the Lives and Lifestyles of Britain's Royal Family

IS FOR ELVIS

An A-to-Z Illustrated Guide to the King of Rock and Roll

Caroline Latham
and
Jeannie Sakol

NAL BOOKS

NAL BOOKS
Published by the Penguin Group
Penguin Books USA Inc., 375 Hudson Street New York, New York, 10014 U.S.A.
Penguin Books Ltd, 27 Wrights Lane, London W8 5TZ, England
Penguin Books Australia Ltd. Ringwood, Victoria, Australia
Penguin Books Canada, 2801 John Street, Markham, Ontario, Canada L3R 1B4
Penguin Books (N.Z.) Ltd., 182-190 Wairau Road, Auckland 10, New Zealand

Penguin Books Ltd, Registered Offices:
Harmondsworth, Middlesex, England

First published by NAL Books, an imprint of New American Library, a division of Penguin Books USA Inc.
Published simultaneously in Canada.

First Printing, June, 1990
10 9 8 7 6 5 4 3 2 1

REGISTERED TRADEMARK—MARCA REGISTRADA

Library of Congress Cataloging-in-Publication Data

Latham, Caroline.
  "E" is for Elvis : an A-to-Z illustrated guide to the king of rock
and roll / Caroline Latham and Jeannie Sakol.
     p.   cm.
  ISBN 0-453-00732-5
  1. Presley, Elvis, 1935-1977—Miscellanea. 2. Presley, Elvis,
1935-1977—Dictionaries, indexes, etc. I. Sakol, Jeannie.
II. Title.
ML420.P96L37   1990
782.42166'092—dc20   89-13590
                                                              CIP

Printed in the United States of America
Set in ITC Bookman
Designed by Nissa Knuth

For Elvis, who left behind his magic and his music, and gave the world memories we continue to cherish

IS FOR ELVIS

The Aron/Aaron Controversy

Elvis Presley's birth certificate clearly gives his middle name as "Aron," whereas on his tombstone it is "Aaron." This discrepancy has been cited as evidence to support the possibility that Elvis faked his own death. According to this theory, "Aron" was the version of the name selected by Elvis's parents to match the middle name they gave his stillborn twin, Jesse Garon, but superstitious dread kept Elvis from using his real full name on his grave.

However, Marty Lacker, in his book written in 1978, says that "Aron" was just a misspelling by Vernon Presley when he filled out the papers for his surviving son's birth certificate, and that Elvis had frequently teased his father about the error. To correct it, Elvis had legally changed his middle name to the conventional spelling of "Aaron," which then became the official version of his name and was naturally used at the time of his death.

Jean and Julian Aberbach

Jean and Julian Aberbach were the brothers who owned Hill & Range, the country music publishers. They were Jewish refugees who left Germany on the eve of World War II and brought their music publishing skills to America, where they quickly spotted the growth potential of the country music business and entered the field.

They were the publishers of Eddy Arnold's recorded music, and thus became friendly with the manager he hired in late 1944, Colonel Tom Parker. Because of their friendship with Parker, the Aberbachs were to become the publishers of the entire catalog of Elvis Presley's recorded music.

Acupuncture for Elvis

According to Elvis Presley's personal physician, Dr. George "Nick" Nichopoulos, the star's first serious illness was caused by the action of an unscrupulous acupuncturist in California. The man injected Elvis with Novocain, Demerol and cortisone, telling him that the injections were a form of acupuncture. This is how Elvis got started taking such drugs by injection.

Nick Adams

Actor Nick Adams was one the first friends Elvis Presley made in Hollywood when he went there in 1956 to film *Love Me Tender*. Nick had been a close pal of actor James Dean ever since the two appeared in a Pepsi-Cola commercial in 1951, and he also hit it off well with Elvis, another rebel. In 1957, Nick accepted an invitation to visit Elvis at Graceland. Then just another struggling young actor, Nick Adams went on to become the star of the TV series "The Rebel," playing the role of Johnny Yuma. He died of a drug overdose on February 1, 1968, the day Elvis's daughter Lisa Marie was born.

Nick Adams was one of the first good friends Elvis made in Hollywood. Here they pretend to spar in a picture taken before Elvis went into the Army. (Photo from Neal Peters Collection)

Alabama Avenue

In Elvis Presley's senior year of high school, his family moved out of the tiny apartment on Cypress Street in the center of Memphis and into a slightly nicer one at 462 Alabama Avenue. Their new home was right across from Lauderdale Court and their old friends in the housing project where they had previously lived. The Presleys' landlady there was a Mrs. Dubrovner. The house on Alabama Avenue has since been pulled down to make way for an access road to the Hernando Desoto Bridge.

Alberta "V05"

When the Presleys moved into their house on Audubon Avenue in 1956, they hired their first maid, a black woman named Alberta. Alberta continued to work for the Presley family when they relocated to Graceland. She was always a favorite with Elvis, who nicknamed her "Alberta V05," often affectionately shortening it to "05." When Elvis discovered that Alberta's home was a mile from the place she had to catch the bus to Graceland, he gave her a car.

Albums That Hit Number One

During his recording career, Elvis Presley issued nine LP albums that made it to the number one position on the pop charts. They were:

Elvis—Aloha from Hawaii via Satellite
Blue Hawaii
Elvis
Elvis Presley
Elvis's Christmas Album
G.I. Blues
Loving You
Roustabout
Something for Everyone

Albums That Went Gold

Elvis, Vol. 1 (45 rpm), 1956
Elvis Presley, 1956
Jailhouse Rock (45 rpm), 1957
Loving You, 1957
Elvis, 1957
Elvis's Christmas Album, 1957
Elvis's Golden Records, 1958
King Creole, 1958
50,000,000 Can't Be Wrong: Elvis's Gold Records, Vol. 2, 1959
Elvis Is Back, 1960
G.I. Blues, 1960
His Hand in Mine, 1960
Elvis By Request: Flaming Star (EP), 1961

Something for Everybody, 1961
Blue Hawaii, 1961
Girls! Girls! Girls!, 1962
Pot Luck, 1962
Elvis's Golden Records, Vol. 3, 1963
Fun in Acapulco, 1963
It Happened at the World's Fair, 1963
Kissin' Cousins, 1964
Roustabout, 1964
Girl Happy, 1965
Elvis for Everyone, 1965
Harum Scarum, 1965
Paradise, Hawaiian Style, 1966
How Great Thou Art, 1967
Elvis (TV Special), 1968
Elvis Sings Flaming Star, 1969
From Elvis in Memphis, 1969
From Memphis to Vegas/
    From Vegas to Memphis, 1969
Elvis: Worldwide 50 Gold Award Hits,
    Vol. 1, 1970

That's the Way It Is, 1970
On Stage, February, 1970, 1971
Elvis Country, 1971
Elvis Sings the Wonderful World of
    Christmas, 1971
Elvis as Recorded at Madison Square
    Garden, 1972
Elvis—Aloha from Hawaii via Satellite,
    1973
Elvis—A Legendary Performer, Vol. 1,
    1974
Promised Land, 1975
Pure Gold, 1975
Welcome to My World, 1977
From Elvis Presley Boulevard, Memphis,
    Tennessee, 1977
Elvis—A Legendary Performer, Vol. 2,
    1977
His Hand in Mine, 1977
Moody Blue, 1977
Elvis in Concert, 1977

Ginger Alden

Near the end of 1976, Elvis Presley began dating Ginger Alden. She was the runner-up in the Miss Tennessee beauty pageant that year (the same pageant that Linda Thompson had won four years earlier) and a former Miss Memphis Traffic Safety. Ginger and her sister Terry (herself a former Miss Tennessee) were introduced to Elvis by his old Memphis friend George Klein when they were visiting Las Vegas. Elvis's favorite nickname for Ginger was "Gingerbread."

Ginger remained with the star for about a year, until his death; in fact, Ginger was the one who found Elvis's body on the floor of his bathroom at Graceland in the early hours of August 16, 1977. After his death, she told the press that Elvis had planned to marry her that year at Christmas, and she displayed the engagement ring he had given her, which had as its center stone the eleven-and-a-half-carat diamond Elvis had previously worn in his own TCB ring. Some members of Elvis's inner circle dispute that claim and point out that Elvis frequently gave women diamonds.

Ginger recorded a song about her affair with Elvis, "I'd Rather Have a Memory Than a Dream," in 1980. In the same year she also appeared, playing herself, in a movie called The Living Legend, considered by many a tasteless exploitation of Elvis (although of course he had been tastelessly exploited throughout his entire career). She countered the criticism by explaining that Elvis had communicated with her from the beyond after his death and told her to accept the role. Ginger has gone on to a minor career in TV commercials and is reported to be writing a book about her relationship with Elvis.

A

Ginger's mother sued the Presley estate for $40,000 after the star's death, demanding continued payment of the mortgage on her house as Elvis had promised her. She lost the suit and had to make the remaining payments by herself. Ginger was luckier: The house Elvis had bought for her, at 4152 Royal Crest Place, was fully paid for.

Alias "Dr. John Carpenter"

Elvis's enormous fame made it necessary for him to use various aliases to keep his movements a secret from his fans. Before he bought his own planes, he occasionally traveled on commercial airlines. His staff routinely made the reservations in the name of "Dr. John Carpenter."

All-Elvis Radio Station

In August 1988 a country radio station in Cincinnati, Ohio, announced that it was switching to a new format. WCVG henceforth would play nothing but the songs of Elvis Presley twenty-four hours a day. Since the singer recorded more than seven hundred songs and released over ninety albums, the station ought to be able to fill up the airwaves. The first record played on the station after the change was "Heartbreak Hotel." Elvis's music was supplemented with special features such as interviews with Elvis insiders and syndicated programming about the star. The station's general manager, John Stolz, explained, "There is so much depth to the artist that we feel it's a viable format." On the first day of the new format, the station received more than six hundred enthusiastic calls from happy listeners. A year later, the all-Elvis format was replaced by the Business Radio Network.

Also in 1988 station WHOS in Decatur, Alabama, followed suit and switched from a gospel format to all-Elvis broadcasting. It dropped the new format in February, 1989.

"All Shook Up"

Otis Blackwell wrote and recorded the song called "All Shook Up," supposedly in response to a challenge from a friend who was shaking up his bottle of Pepsi at the time. Elvis recorded it in January 1957, and RCA released it soon thereafter. Within three weeks, the song was number one on the pop charts, where it remained for eight weeks. Although "All Shook Up" was for a time Elvis's best-selling single, it was later surpassed by other hits. To date, it has sold more than two million copies worldwide. It was always one of the most popular songs in Elvis's live performances.

"The Steve Allen Show"

In 1956 a key Elvis Presley television appearance came on the "Steve Allen Show," the forerunner of "The Tonight Show," with Steve Allen pioneering the role of host now filled by Johnny Carson. In the show that was broadcast on July 1, Elvis appeared with Steve, Imogen Coca, and Andy Griffith in a skit that had a Western theme; Elvis played a character called "Tumbleweed." The highlight of the show, though, was the moment when Steve introduced "the new Elvis" and the star walked out on stage wearing a tuxedo. After he sang "I Want You, I Need You, I Love You," Steve arranged for him to croon "Hound Dog" to a real—and very morose—hound. The whole thing was so silly that the following day Elvis fans picketed the network offices carrying signs that protested, "Give Us the Real Elvis." In fact, many viewers assumed that Allen had intended to make a fool out of his guest. If that was his intention, he certainly failed. Elvis responded without any visible sign of irritation, performed in a way that made the studio audience shout itself hoarse, and politely thanked his host as he departed. That TV appearance made the singer more popular than ever.

Aloha from Hawaii: The Concert

In 1973 Elvis Presley gave a live concert at the Honolulu International Center, which was televised and transmitted by satellite to stations around the world. A percentage of the gate was donated to the Kuiokolani Lee Cancer Fund, in memory of a popular figure in Hawaiian music. A double album of the live performance was later released and became a quick million-seller.

For several months before the concert, Elvis had been on a diet and fitness regime, and he was looking and feeling his best by the time of the concert date. As Sonny West put it, he was "thin as a rake and handsomer than ten movie stars." He sang twenty-three songs and gave the show a dramatic finish by hurling his heavily jeweled cape into the audience.

Aloha from Hawaii via Satellite: The Album

The last album by Elvis Presley to go gold during his lifetime was the 1973 two-record soundtrack of his Hawaiian TV special, "Aloha from Hawaii via Satellite." Released in February, the RCA album made it to the top spot for just one week, but remained in the Top 100 for more than a year. It gave fans a complete package of

A

the tunes Elvis favored for live performances, including opener "Also Sprach Zarathustra," "See See Rider," "My Way," "Blue Suede Shoes," "Hound Dog," "Fever," "American Trilogy," and his usual closing number, "Can't Help Falling in Love."

"Also Sprach Zarathustra"

The symphonic piece "Also Sprach Zarathustra," by Richard Strauss, was the music Elvis Presley always used to open his live shows in the last decade of his performing career. The music is instantly recognizable as the theme from the movie *2001*.

Alviss

Experts on the derivation of proper names suggest that the name Elvis comes from the old Norse name "Alviss," meaning all-wise.

Always Elvis

After Elvis Presley died, his manager, Colonel Tom Parker, came up with a marketing slogan to carry on the work of selling his "merchandise," the term he used to refer to Elvis. The slogan was "Always Elvis." A year after the star's death, the Colonel staged the first Always Elvis convention in Las Vegas, with special appearances by Vernon Presley and Priscilla Presley.

Some years later, Parker made a deal with the Italian winemakers Frantenac to market a wine in the United States under the label "Always Elvis." Elvis, of course, was not a wine drinker.

The American Royal Show

Colonel Tom Parker's apprenticeship in show business began with his ten-year stint working for the American Royal Show, which he joined in mid-1935. At that time, the American Royal was the biggest and best carnival in the country. It employed more than a thousand people and traveled on its own train with seventy red and white cars to hundreds of local fairs, where it set up the midway and provided the entertainment. The American Royal wintered in Tampa, Florida, which was also the winter home of the Johnny J. Jones Exposition, for which Parker had worked since the time he was discharged from the army, around 1931.

Parker quickly made himself at home with the midgets, the fire-eaters, and the hustlers of all kinds, and was in fact one of the best of the hustlers himself. Among his fabled exploits during this period were his attempt to sell sparrows as canaries by painting them yellow, and his impromptu invention of the "dancing chicken" act, which involved setting the poor bird down on a concealed hot plate. He left the American Royal around 1940.

The American Studios in Memphis

In early 1969, after Elvis Presley's triumphant TV special that heralded his return to making music instead of movies, Elvis went into the recording studio to cut some new material. Instead of going to the RCA studio in Nashville, he worked in the American Studios in Memphis. The result, critics agreed, was an exceptionally strong performance. Located at 827 Danny Thomas Street, the American studio, established in 1964, had recently been used by the Boxtops, Dusty Springfield, and Neil Diamond.

The producer of Elvis's session was Chips Moman, a studio founder who had also produced hits for such artists as Dionne Warwick and Wilson Pickett. Moman credits much of the freshness and energy of the recordings made during that Memphis session to the band he assembled for the occasion. Elvis knew most of the guys—all of them local musicians—personally and felt comfortable with them. They were able to urge him on to some of his own best work.

"An American Trilogy"

"An American Trilogy" was a medley of three familiar American songs: "Dixie," "The Battle Hymn of the Republic," and "All My Trials." The medley was arranged for Elvis Presley by Mickey Newbury and released as a single in 1971. Thereafter, the star frequently performed "An American Trilogy" in his concert appearances.

Ursula Andress

Ursula Andress, born in Switzerland on March 19, 1936, costarred with Elvis Presley in the 1963 Hal B. Wallis movie, *Fun in Acapulco*, playing a hotel social director named Margarita Dauphine. It was her second movie released in the U.S., coming on the heels of her success in the James Bond film, *Dr. No*. For a time, rumors linked the sultry foreign actress with the king of rock and roll, even though she was at the time married to former actor John Derek, who had photographed her in the nude for *Playboy*. According to Elvis's secretary, Becky Yancy, Ursula frequently telephoned Elvis at Graceland, but Yancy believes that Elvis was too straitlaced to have had an affair with a married woman. Elvis himself commented when he returned from making *Fun in Acapulco* that Ursula had shoulders bigger than his. "I was embarrassed to take my goddam shirt off next to her," he complained.

Sultry Ursula Andress co-starred with Elvis in *Fun in Acapulco*, but their personal relationship never got off the ground. (Photo from Neal Peters Collection)

Ann-Margret

Ann-Margret, who had been called by the press the "female Elvis Presley," met the very male Elvis Presley when they costarred in the movie *Viva Las Vegas* in 1964, in which she played a character named Rusty Martin. The Swedish-born actress, whose birthday is April 28, 1941, and whose real name is Ann-Margret Olssen, had worked in Las Vegas as part of comedian George Burns's act, appeared as a singer and dancer on television, and attracted favorable attention for her performance in the film *Bye-Bye Birdie* in 1963.

The immediate magnetism between the two stars blossomed into a Hollywood romance that was chronicled by the media. The two rode motorcycles together and shared evenings at Elvis's house. About six weeks after *Viva Las Vegas* was finished, while Elvis was still in Hollywood about to start the shooting of *Kissin' Cousins*, Ann-Margret told the press she and Elvis were engaged. Elvis's reaction apparently spelled the end of their romantic relationship, but they continued to be friends for the rest of his life. Ann-Margret later married actor Roger Smith, with whom she lives in the Benedict Canyon house that once belonged to Humphrey Bogart and Lauren Bacall. Elvis always sent Ann-Margret guitar-shaped floral arrangements on her opening nights. She never visited Graceland until she and her husband went there for Elvis's funeral.

Because her romance with Elvis occurred after Priscilla Beaulieu had moved into Graceland, Ann-Margret used the code name "Bunny" when she telephoned Elvis there; she also called herself "Scoobie," a name taken from one of her hit records. The "guys," the members of Elvis's entourage, called her "Rusty Ammo," a nickname derived from the name of her character in *Viva Las Vegas*.

The Anniversary of Elvis's Death

It is a daily occurrence for fans at Graceland to pass by Elvis Presley's grave and place flowers and other tributes on it. The biggest commemoration, though, comes each year on the anniversary of his death, August 16. Thousands usually gather at his home to mark the somber event. Innumerable floral tributes, including such fanciful creations as guitars and teddy bears, cover the grave, and at night there is a candlelight procession by weeping fans. On the most recent anniversary, more than four thousand fans toured Graceland and remained that evening to commemorate the date on which their idol left them.

Ann-Margret and Elvis do "the climb" in a scene from *Viva Las Vegas* (1964). (Photo from Neal Peters Collection)

Answering the First Question About Priscilla

Sharp-eyed members of the press noticed that when Elvis Presley left Germany to return to the United States, there was a young lady who seemed to be saying a tearful goodbye to him. They discovered that she was the daughter of an American Air Force officer stationed in Germany, fifteen-year-old Priscilla Beaulieu. At Elvis's first press conference after his return home, a reporter asked the star about Priscilla. "She is very mature, very intelligent, and the most beautiful girl I've ever seen," answered Elvis. "But," he added, "there's no romance. It's nothing serious."

"Are You Lonesome Tonight?"

One of Elvis Presley's biggest hits was "Are You Lonesome Tonight?" written by Roy Turk and Lou Handman. The ballad was originally sung by Al Jolson, then covered by Jaye P. Morgan in 1959. Elvis recorded his tender version of the song in his first major recording session after his discharge from the army, in the RCA studios in Nashville on April 4, 1960. In its first release in November of that year, the single, backed with "I Gotta Know," sold nearly four million copies and occupied the number one spot on the charts for six weeks. Elvis received three Grammy nominations for the recording, but failed to win the award in any of the categories in which he was nominated.

The Army Career

Elvis Presley received his draft notice on December 10, 1957. Ten days later he was sent word that he had been called up and should report to the Memphis draft board on January 10, 1958. That date conflicted with the scheduled filming of his fourth movie, *King Creole*, so he asked for and received a postponement of his induction date, which actually took place on March 25, 1958. Private Presley was bussed to Fort Chaffee, Arkansas, for processing and then was sent to Fort Hood, Texas.

After six months of training, Elvis, along with the rest of his unit, the Second Medium Tank Battalion, was sent to Weisbaden, Germany; on September 19, the eve of his departure, he was promoted to private first class. Overseas he was assigned to duty with the Fourth Armored Division as a jeep driver. On June 14, 1959, he was promoted to corporal. On March 1, 1960, he was promoted to sergeant as he completed his required military service. Elvis returned to the United States in late February 1960, and was officially discharged at Fort Dix, New Jersey, on March 5, 1960.

The Army Jeep

When Elvis Presley was posted by the army to Germany, he was given the job of driving a jeep. It was a perfect assignment for a man who loved vehicles of any sort, and Elvis even enjoyed the work of maintaining his jeep. According to the recollections of one of his fellow soldiers, "He was one of five who got a perfect rating after an inspection of over three hundred of the vehicles." Another G.I. remembers that Elvis would get down on his hands and knees and sandpaper the exhaust pipe to make it sparkle.

A

Elvis adopts a suitable martial attitude. His badge identifies his unit, a tank battalion. (Photo from Neal Peters Collection)

The Army Uniform

When Elvis Presley left the service, he saved his old army uniform, which eventually made its way to the Graceland attic. In 1981, during the making of the docudrama *This Is Elvis*, the Presley estate lent the uniform to the film's producers, to be worn by actor David Scott, who played Elvis as a young man. Estate trustees were so impressed by Scott's performance that they gave him the uniform.

In 1988 the actor was offered a sum "in the six figures" to sell the uniform to a chicken-and-ribs restaurant in Montreal that wanted to use it for promotion purposes. Scott is still mulling over the offer.

A

Eddy Arnold

Country music great Eddy Arnold was born in 1918 in Henderson, Tennessee. In late 1944, he signed a management contract with Colonel Tom Parker, whom he had met when Parker was working as an advance man for the Grand Ole Opry. Arnold, the "Tennessee Plowboy," already had a recording contract with RCA, but he was not yet the big star he would eventually become. Parker not only promoted Arnold's recording career, he also got him a two-picture contract in Hollywood. "The movies will be lean on artistic quality," Parker warned Arnold, "but they will be acceptable as movies."

Undoubtedly, Arnold's career prospered under Parker's managership, but Arnold became increasingly annoyed by Parker's heavy-handed style and by his constant presence in Arnold's office, dressing room, and home. For example, when Parker decided to relocate from Tampa to Tennessee, the center of the country music business, he simply moved himself and his wife into Arnold's home in Madison, near Nashville. In self-defense, Arnold gave Parker a house he owned in the town, which became the Parkers' first permanent home. Arnold once asked Parker why he didn't get himself a hobby to take up some of his time, and Parker replied by looking him straight in the eye and saying, "You're my hobby." In 1953, Eddy Arnold fired Parker.

Arnold was elected to the Country Music Hall of Fame in 1966. His records have sold more than seventy million copies worldwide, and thirteen of them have hit the number one position on the country charts. Colonel Parker's last client, Elvis Presley, recorded several of Arnold's hits, including "I Really Don't Want To Know," and "You Don't Know Me."

As the World Turns

Elvis Presley's grandmother, Minnie Mae Presley, was a big fan of the daytime soap opera "As the World Turns," which she watched regularly. She often compared the Hughes family, the central characters of the program, with the Presleys. She believed that both families possessed the admirable trait of sticking together through good times and bad.

Edward Asner

Ed Asner, who created the beloved television character Lou Grant, featured on the "Mary Tyler Moore" show and the "Lou Grant" show, appeared in two movies with Elvis Presley—*Kid Galahad* and *Change of Habit*, which also costarred Mary Tyler Moore. Asner wrote superfan Sue Wiegert that he remembered Elvis as "a very polite, proper young man—friendly in some ways, but I remember that he was rather shy and did not hang around with the cast or crew too much."

An Assault on Elvis

On November 23, 1956, an unemployed steelworker in Toledo, Ohio, took a swing at Elvis Presley because his wife's love for Elvis had broken up their marriage. The man, Louis John Balint, was fined $19.60 for his assault on the young star.

The Assembly of God Church Music

Elvis Presley's first exposure to music came in East Tupelo, Mississippi, when he went with his parents to the nearby Assembly of God church. He later recalled, "We used to go to these religious singings all the time. There were these singers, perfectly fine singers, but nobody responded to them. Then there were the preachers, and they cut up all over the place, jumping on the piano, moving ever' which way. The audience liked them." The fire and energy of the preachers and the beauty of the hymns sung in church were to be important influences on Elvis's performing style.

The Astrodome Concerts

In February 1970, Elvis Presley gave a series of concerts at the Houston Astrodome, which seats forty-five thousand people. More than two hundred thousand people bought tickets, and by the time the concert series was over, Elvis had earned a paycheck of about $1.2 million.

Chet Atkins

Chester Burton "Chet" Atkins, the legendary guitarist, was both the producer of many of Elvis Presley's recordings at the RCA studio in Nashville and a session musician who played on the tracks. Chet was born in Luttrell, Tennessee, in 1924 and started out playing the fiddle before he switched to guitar, an instrument of which he is one of the acknowledged masters. The Atkins guitar can be best heard on such Presley classics as "Heartbreak Hotel" and "I Want You, I Need You, I Love You." Chet produced Elvis's recordings for nearly a decade, until Felton Jarvis took over the job in 1966. He also produced records for such artists as Perry Como, Floyd Cramer, and Hank Snow, and helped pioneer what became known as the Nashville sound. Atkins became a division vice president of RCA in 1968.

Audubon Drive

In 1956, when Elvis Presley first began to make money from his recordings, he bought a home for himself and his parents in Memphis, at 1034 Audubon Drive. It was a brand-new $40,000 ranch house, painted green with a gray roof and red-brick trim. There was a big patio in the back of the house, and it was located in one of Memphis's best areas.

The Presleys bought all new furniture when they moved into the house on Audubon Drive. Among the more memorable of the selections made by Gladys and Elvis were a red phone studded with rhinestones, three-dimensional ceramic plaques for all the walls depicting leaping minstrels, and a collection of huge stuffed animals (including the teddy bears that would soon be the inspiration for a hit song) for Elvis's bed. The walls were papered in gaudy splashy prints. Elvis later installed a pool, which his friend and employee Red West concluded was "there for show, because Elvis really ain't that keen on swimming." That house on curving Audubon Drive was a big step up from the little brick house on Getwell Street in which the Presley family had been living.

Fans soon discovered the address of Elvis's new home, and in their search for souvenirs even stole the wash hanging out on the line. The Presleys put up a brick and iron fence to protect their privacy but still found themselves continually invaded by fans in search of their idol. Neighbors in the once-quiet area began to complain. Within a year, Elvis used that house on Audubon Drive as a down payment on the thirteen-acre property at Graceland, which provided all the privacy a superstar needed.

James Ausborn

James Ausborn was the younger brother of the country-and-western singer from Tupelo, Mississippi Slim (born Carvel Ausborn). During the time young Elvis Presley was hanging around Slim at the Tupelo radio station, he also became friendly with James, and the friendship intensified when Elvis transferred to James's school in town.

Gene Austin

According to the thorough research of Dirk Vellenga and Mick Farren, published in their book *Elvis and the Colonel*, the first singer Tom Parker ever had as a client was Gene Austin. Austin had made one hit record in the thirties, a version of "My Blue Heaven," but by the time he met Parker, he no longer had a recording contract and was pulling only small crowds for his live performances. In 1939, Parker acted as an advance man for the singer in small towns throughout the South, drawing audiences through the methods that he had learned with the carnival—and that he was later to use with his last client, Elvis Presley. One of the Colonel's favorite devices was the use of elephants as walking billboards; another was employing midgets as hucksters outside the performance site.

.

The Avon Lady Calls at Graceland

When Priscilla Presley was first married to Elvis, she bought most of her cosmetics from the Avon lady, who called at Graceland every few weeks. In those days Priscilla wore a ton of makeup, keeping her Avon lady very busy indeed.

Baba

Baba was the name of Elvis Presley's pet collie, a long-time companion. Baba went to Hollywood with Elvis and can be seen in the movie *Paradise, Hawaiian Style* (1966). As a boy, Elvis never had a dog, but he made up for the lack when he became a star, owning a number of different dogs over the years.

Baby Talk

Elvis Presley never outgrew his fondness for baby talk. He and his mother employed it frequently as a mode of expressing their affection, and he also used it in his intimate relationships with women. Among Elvis's favorite baby-talk expressions were:

- *butch* (milk)
- *toophies* (teeth)
- *yittle* (little)
- *yuv* (love)
- *duckling* (water)
- *sooties* (feet)
- *boocups* (a lot; a common Southern expression derived from the French word *beaucoup*)

Bad Nauheim

When Elvis Presley was sent by the army to Weisbaden, Germany, he arranged for his father and his grandmother to live with him there. The Presleys rented a simple three-story house surrounded by a white picket fence at 14 Goethestrasse in the nearby small town of Bad Nauheim, and it was there that Elvis resided for the eighteen months he was in Germany. Outside the house, someone had posted a sign that said in German, "Autographs Between 7:00 and 8:00 PM Only."

Lucy de Barbin

In 1987, Lucy de Barbin, collaborating with writer Dary Matera, published a book entitled *Are You Lonesome Tonight?* It told her story of her romance with Elvis Presley, which she said began in 1953 when they both were hired to entertain guests at a party given in Monroe, Louisiana, by former state governor James Noe. According to Lucy, she gave birth to Elvis's daughter on August 23, 1958, but she never told Elvis of the existence of their child, whom she named Desiree, because she didn't want to complicate his life or expose him to the danger of an attack by her ex-husband. The details of Lucy's story seem to confirm the fact that she did indeed know Elvis and that he stayed in touch with her on and off for a number of years. Whether Desiree is or is not his daughter is probably a question that will never be answered.

A Basic Elvis Library

For a basic library of books about Elvis Presley, fans should consider the following selections:

- Elaine Dundy, *Elvis and Gladys.* New York: Macmillan, 1985.
- Albert Goldman, *Elvis.* New York: McGraw-Hill, 1981.
- Jerry Hopkins, *Elvis.* New York: Simon & Schuster, 1971.
- Greil Marcus, "Elvis Presliad" in *Mystery Train.* New York: E.P. Dutton, 1976
- Priscilla Beaulieu Presley with Sandra Harmon, *Elvis and Me.* New York: G.P. Putnam's Sons, 1985.
- Red West, Sonny West, Dave Hebler, and Steve Dunleavy, *Elvis: What Happened?* New York: Ballantine Books, 1977.
- Fred L. Worth and Steve D. Tamerius, *Elvis: His Life from A to Z.* Chicago: Contemporary Books, 1988.

The Battered Old Guitar

When Elvis Presley first began performing live, everyone noticed how battered his guitar was. According to Chet Atkins, Elvis used an old Gibson. It was the young singer's custom never to keep it in a case. He kept it slung over his shoulder and when he was ready to play he just pulled it around to the front and hit a few chords.

The way Elvis played also contributed to his guitar's battered look—he hit it so hard that he routinely broke several strings at a time.

Interestingly, a 1989 charity auction in Memphis featured a battered black guitar case, which sold for $3000. The question is: When was it ever used?

Beale Street

Beale Street in Memphis, immortalized in Memphis resident W.C. Handy's wonderful "Beale Street Blues," was the site of the large Orpheum Theatre (built in 1928) as well as many small clubs where the best of the black musicians from the South performed throughout the twenties, thirties, forties, and fifties. They primarily sang the blues, a form they both pioneered and per-fected. Beale Street was only about a mile away from Elvis Presley's home, and according to fellow rockabilly singer Johnny Burnette, he and Elvis sometimes went to Beale Street to listen to the music. Blues singer B.B. King also recalls meeting Elvis in Beale Street hangouts. The blues, as performed by southern blacks, were a big influence on Elvis's own musical style.

The Beatles Are Nervous in the Presence of Elvis

On August 27, 1965, the Beatles paid a visit to Elvis Presley at his leased Italian-style villa on Perugia Way, in the Bel Air section of Los Angeles. Although the media had tried to create a story of rivalry between Elvis and the new pop stars, Elvis openly expressed his affinity for the Beatles and their music. When the "Fab Four" appeared on the Ed Sullivan Show the previous year, Elvis sent them a good-luck telegram. Later he arranged for their visit to his home, which lasted about four hours.

John Lennon said the Beatles all felt nervous: "This was the guy we had all idolized for years—from way back when we were just starting out in Liverpool. He was a legend in his own lifetime, and it's never easy meeting a legend for the first time." Initially it seemed that the visit was going to be a failure because the Brits were collectively paralyzed by the strength of their hero worship. Finally Elvis said, in tones of mock disgust, "Look, guys, if you're just going to sit there and stare at me, I'm going to bed." That broke the ice, and soon Elvis was calling for some guitars and an impromptu jam session got under way. Lennon recalled that they also talked about their similar experiences in being mobbed by crowds of fans. Talking about it among themselves later, the Beatles wondered how Elvis could handle the full brunt of such adulation all on his own.

When reporters later asked the Beatles to comment on their visit to the living legend, they were uncharacteristically reticent. Paul McCartney was the only one to voice an opinion, saying simply that Elvis was "odd." It was not until years later that they each talked openly about the hours they spent with Elvis and their nervousness in his presence.

Becoming Elvis

In 1978, Elvis Presley impersonator Herbert Baer legally changed his name to Elvis Presley.

Bellagio Road

During the 1960s, Elvis Presley's movie career dictated that he must spend much of his time in Hollywood. Since he considered Graceland his real home, he leased houses in California for a number of years before finally deciding to buy. The second house Elvis leased in Los Angeles, an Italian-style villa on Bellagio Road in Bel Air, was a Hollywood mansion with all the clichés, including a huge marble-paved entrance and a bowling alley in the basement. He moved into the house in 1963, after deciding that his leased house on Perugia Road was too small for all the friends and relatives who stayed with him when he was making movies in Hollywood. But he stayed in the Bellagio Road house only a few months, returning to Perugia, which he found more comfortable and congenial.

"The Milton Berle Show"

On April 3, 1956, when "Heartbreak Hotel" was at the top of the singles charts, Elvis Presley made his first appearance on "The Milton Berle Show," a televised comedy-variety program. He sang "Blue Suede Shoes" and "Heartbreak Hotel," and appeared in a comedy sketch in which Milton played his twin brother Melvin. On his second appearance on the show, June 5 of the same year, which happened to be Berle's last show, Elvis sang his new release, "Hound Dog." His performance created a swirl of controversy because of his on-stage gyrations and the fact that his every movement was greeted with screams of delight from the teenage girls in the studio audience. Elvis was hurt by the criticism and defended his performance. "I wouldn't do anything vulgar in front of anybody, especially children. My folks didn't bring me up that way. I don't do anything bad when I work, I just move with the music, it's the way I feel."

Kodak is currently marketing tapes of the old Milton Berle shows, including the Elvis appearance.

Bear

Bear was the name of Elvis Presley's prize-winning Tennessee walking horse. Elvis bought the black horse fully trained, and loved to gather an audience of his buddies to watch him put Bear through his high-stepping paces. Bear had one peculiarity: In order to get him to perform, he had to be ridden along a fence line.

"Beau"

"Beau" was one of the nicknames Elvis Presley used for his wife, Priscilla Beaulieu Presley.

Ann Wagner Beaulieu

Ann Wagner Beaulieu was Priscilla Beaulieu Presley's mother. Born in 1927, Ann worked as a photographer's model before she married her first husband, air force lieutenant James Wagner, in 1944. When their daughter Priscilla was only six months old, Wagner was killed in a plane crash in 1945. About two years later, Ann married career army officer Paul Beaulieu, who adopted young Priscilla. Ann and Paul had five children of their own—Donald, Michelle, Jeffrey, and twins Tim and Tom. The Beaulieus now live in New Jersey; they travel frequently to California to visit their daughter Priscilla, granddaughter Lisa Marie, and great-granddaughter Danielle.

Joseph Paul Beaulieu

Joseph Paul Beaulieu was Priscilla Beaulieu Presley's stepfather. He was an army lieutenant at the time he met and married Priscilla's mother Ann Wagner, who had been widowed when her daughter was only six months old. Paul Beaulieu adopted young Priscilla and was always a devoted and concerned parent to the girl.

Paul and Ann Beaulieu had five children—Donald, Michelle, Jeffrey, and twins Tim and Tom. Paul Beaulieu eventually made colonel before retiring from the service. He and his wife now live in New Jersey. Despite some ups and downs in their relationship with Priscilla during her years with Elvis, she—and her daughter Lisa Marie as well—has remained close to the Beaulieus.

"Big E"

"Big E" was a nickname that members of Elvis Presley's entourage often used to refer to him.

"Big Hunk of Love"

Elvis Presley went into the RCA recording studio just before he entered the army to create some new material that could be released while his performing career was on hold. One of the songs from that session was "Big Hunk of Love," written by the team of Aaron Schroeder and Sid Wyche and released late in 1958. It was another huge hit single for Elvis, rising to the number one spot and selling more than a million copies.

Delta Mae Presley Biggs

Delta Mae Presley was Elvis Presley's aunt, the sister of his father Vernon. She married Pat Biggs, but the couple had no children of their own. They always lavished attention on their young nephew Elvis, a kindness which he remembered later when he was a famous star. In 1966, Pat Biggs died of a heart attack at the wheel of the family car while the couple was on vacation. Elvis sent some of his entourage to take care of the funeral arrangements and to bring his aunt Delta to Memphis. She was promptly put on the Graceland payroll to act as housekeeper and companion to her mother, Minnie Mae Presley, who was already living at the mansion. Delta had a sharp tongue and a tendency to feud with some of Elvis's entourage.

Steve Binder

Steve Binder was the producer of the Elvis TV special that aired on December 3, 1968, and came to be known as the "comeback special." Colonel Tom Parker, who had approached NBC-TV with the idea of an Elvis Christmas show, had envisioned it as the traditional production featuring Christmas carols, a full orchestra and choir backing

B

Elvis as he sang, a few celebrity guests, and the usual manufactured holiday nostalgia.

Steve Binder had a different idea. He had been a teenager when Elvis first became a national star in the mid-1950s and he remembered the thrill of the music and the energy of the young singer's performance. Steve wanted to present the Elvis he remembered and idolized—energetic, raw, sexy, rebellious, the star that parents warned their children not to watch. After a few confrontations with the Colonel (who kept calling him "Bindle") about the unexpected direction the special was taking, Steve took his case to Elvis. Elvis immediately grasped what Steve intended to do, and although he was clearly anxious about putting himself on the line as a performer in the way Steve intended, he agreed to do it Steve's way, and overrode the Colonel's objections.

For the opening sequence of the special, Steve chose to show Elvis dressed in a black leather jacket and pants with huge leather cuffs. He looked dangerous, ready to erupt all over the small home screen. Then he sang "Trouble Man," and it was clear that the king of rock and roll still lived.

In the 1980s, Steve Binder produced the TV special on Graceland that was hosted by Priscilla Presley.

The Birth of Lisa Marie

For the last month of Priscilla Presley's pregnancy, Elvis remained home at Graceland with her, anxiously awaiting the big event. On the morning of February 1, 1968, Priscilla awoke Elvis and told him it was time to go to the hospital. That's when he put his carefully rehearsed hospital departure plan into action. First, several decoy cars left, in case the press was standing by, as usual, outside the Music Gate of Graceland. Then Elvis and Priscilla hopped into the back seat of a brand-new Cadillac, driven by Charlie Hodge, to make the four-mile trip to the hospital. They were followed by another brand-new Cadillac, driven by Joe Esposito, which Elvis had ordered to serve as a backup, in case anything happened to the first car during the trip. There was only one hitch in the arrangements: Charlie started to drive to Methodist Hospital, forgetting that the plans had been changed in favor of Memphis's Baptist Hospital. Eventually, both cars succeeded in arriving safely at the right place.

During the long wait throughout the day, Elvis was kept company by Hodge and Esposito, as well as Richard Davis, Jerry Schilling and his wife, Patsy Presley and her husband Gee Gee Gambill, Marty Lacker, Lamar Fike, George Klein, and grandfather-to-be Vernon Presley and his wife Dee. Uniformed Memphis policemen guarded the access to Priscilla's room in the maternity ward. The baby, named Lisa Marie Presley, was born at 5:01 that afternoon; the delivery, with Priscilla under sedation, was uneventful. An excited Elvis told the press his daughter was perfect, that Priscilla was fine, and that he himself was "a little shaky."

Bis and Beau

Bis and Beau was the name of the Beverly Hills clothing boutique opened by Priscilla Presley in 1974, after her divorce from Elvis, in partnership with professional designer Olivia Bis. Olivia had made clothes for Priscilla in the past, often working from rough designs that Priscilla had sketched according to her own ideas. Their small but prestigious shop, located at 9650 Santa Monica Boulevard, was a success with the Hollywood community, and sold eye-catching trendy clothes to such show-biz notables as Cher, Cybill Shepherd, Natalie Wood, Suzanne Pleshette, and Barbara Eden. Priscilla sold her interest in the business in 1976 when she felt she no longer had the necessary time to devote to it.

Elvis plays with the back-up band that helped make him famous. Drummer D. J. Fontana is on the far left, bassist Bill Black next to him. Scotty Moore is on the far right. (Photo from Neal Peters Collection)

Bill Black

Bill Black was a bass player who frequently backed up Elvis Presley in live performances and studio recordings at the beginning of the star's career. Elvis met "Blackie" in 1951 at Lauderdale Courts in Memphis, a housing project where both Elvis and Blackie's mother lived. At that time, Blackie, about a decade older than Elvis, was a member of a group called Doug Poindexter's Starlight Wranglers. The country-and-western band played regularly in clubs in the Memphis area and worked as a backup band for Sam Phillips at the Memphis Recording Studio. Blackie and Elvis used to hang out and make music together in the Lauderdale courtyard, and Blackie often urged Elvis to spend the $4 it took to make a record of himself at Sam's studio.

Three years later, Sam put Elvis together with Blackie and another musician from the Starlite Wranglers, Scotty Moore. Blackie played bass on Elvis's first record and for a time he appeared with Elvis live in the Memphis area. He can be seen in the Elvis movie *Jailhouse Rock*, backing Elvis up during one of the production numbers. Like Scotty Moore, Blackie quit playing with Elvis, except for an occasional studio session, after Colonel Tom Parker began to manage the star's career. Blackie was paid only $200 a week to play with Elvis; out of that sum he was expected to pay his own touring expenses.

Bill Black died of a brain tumor on October 21, 1965. The bass he used when he played with Elvis is now owned by former Beatle Paul McCartney.

Joan Blackman

Joan Blackman costarred in two movies with Elvis Presley—*Blue Hawaii*, (1961) and *Kid Galahad* (1962). Elvis's former secretary Becky Yancy said that Elvis told her he didn't get along with Blackman, although he never explained why.

Malessa Blackwood

Malessa Blackwood dated Elvis Presley immediately after his divorce from Priscilla. At the time, she was eighteen and held the title of Miss Memphis Southmen, queen of the city's professional football team. Elvis called her "Brown Eyes," and gave her a white Pontiac Grand Prix on their first date. After a very brief acquaintance, he asked her to move into Graceland so she would always be near him. When she refused, he was kind and understanding, walked her to the door—and never saw her again.

The Blackwood Brothers

The Blackwood Brothers were a popular white male gospel group in Memphis when Elvis was a teenager there. Like Elvis, the singers were originally from Mississippi and were members of the First Assembly of God church. They performed many of the songs Elvis had heard as a boy at church. Elvis got into the habit of hanging around Ellis Auditorium, where the Blackwoods hosted all-night gospel sings, and he was usually in the audience every time they performed. In 1954, one of the Blackwood brothers, R.W., was killed in a plane crash; his place was filled by younger brother Cecil. Others in the quartet were leader James Blackwood, Bill Lyles, and William Snow. The Blackwoods sang at Gladys Presley's funeral.

Blue Hawaii: The Album

The soundtrack from Elvis Presley's movie *Blue Hawaii* was released by RCA as an album in 1961. It was the most successful of all his soundtrack albums, selling more than five million copies and remaining in the number one spot on the album charts for twenty straight weeks. The title song was written by Leo Robin and Ralph Rainger in 1937 and was a hit for Billy Vaughn in 1959. For the most part, the soundtrack album was full of forgettable Hawaiian numbers, but it did contain one of Elvis's classic ballads and the song with which he was thereafter identified, "Can't Help Falling in Love."

Blue Hawaii: The Movie

The film *Blue Hawaii*, starring Elvis Presley as the wealthy son of a pineapple plantation owner, was released in 1961. The Paramount picture had been tentatively titled first *Hawaiian Beach Boy* and then *Beach Boy Blues*. Part of the movie was shot on location, after Elvis went to Hawaii to make a benefit concert appearance; as producer Hal B. Wallis put it, "Once again we tried to parallel his own life with his screen personality." One of Elvis's costars was Angela Lansbury of "Murder She Wrote," who played his domineering mother, although she was only nine years older than Elvis; other members of the supporting cast included love interests Joan Blackman (in a role originally intended for Juliet Prowse) and Jenny Maxwell. *Blue Hawaii* was Elvis's top-grossing movie. The soundtrack, featuring Elvis backed by the Jordanaires, was released by RCA and became the best-selling album of the year, staying in the number one spot for twenty weeks and eventually selling more than five million copies—a surprising success for such an unmemorable collection of songs, including "Ito Fats," "Ku-U-I-Po," and "The Hawaiian Wedding Song."

The Blue Moon Boys

When Elvis Presley first began performing in the Memphis area, he was accompanied by the two musicians who had backed him up on his first Sun recording, Scotty Moore on guitar and Bill Black on bass. They felt they should have a group identity, so they called themselves the Blue Moon Boys, after the B side of their first record, "Blue Moon of Kentucky." Soon, however, it was clear that Elvis was the star who overshadowed the other two musicians, and the Blue Moon Boys turned into Elvis Presley and his backup group, Scotty and Bill.

The first time Elvis appeared in Las Vegas he was still considered little more than a teen sensation by the mature audiences in attendance. That's when he welcomed the encouragement of friends like Bobby Darren. (Photo from Neal Peters Collection)

B

Bombing in Vegas

In the summer of 1956, Colonel Tom Parker booked the new teen sensation, Elvis Presley, into the Frontier Hotel in Las Vegas for six weeks. Elvis was the opener for comedian Shecky Green and the music of the Freddy Martin Orchestra. That Vegas appearance was one of the few times in Elvis's career when he really bombed. Bass player Bill Black said the audience was so quiet that the musicians could, for the first time since they'd been playing with Elvis, hear their own mistakes. After a week, it was mutually agreed to tear up the contract for subsequent appearances. Elvis remained bitter about the Vegas crowd for more than a decade, until he appeared there again in 1969 and enjoyed a tremendous success.

Jon Bon Jovi

Jon Bon Jovi, star of the rock group Bon Jovi, is a big fan of Elvis Presley. He has toured Graceland several times, and guides later reported that he burst into tears of emotion. Even his wedding was a form of homage to the King. On May 4, 1989, he was married in Las Vegas in front of the Graceland Wedding Chapel.

Books Elvis Loved

Elvis Presley liked to read, and there were certain books that he read over and over. These included:

• *Siddartha*, by Hermann Hesse
• *The Prophet*, by Khalil Gibran
• *The Impersonal Life*, by Joseph Benner
• *Autobiography of a Yogi*, by Paramahansa Yogananda
• *The Mystical Christ*, by Manley Palmer Hall
• *The Life and Teachings of the Master of the Far East*, by Baird Spalding
• *Book of Numbers*, by Cheiro

Bootleg Elvis

One sure tribute to the popularity of Elvis Presley's music is the fact that so many bootleg Elvis records exist. Some of them are recordings of live performances or broadcast specials that were never recorded by Elvis's own label, RCA. Others are alternate versions of songs released by RCA, of interest to fans who want to hear all the different ways Elvis tried a song in a recording session. A few are privately made tapes that capture Elvis in a relaxed mood. And then, of course, many are simply rip-offs of songs already available under the RCA label, made by entrepreneurs who hoped to join the long list of people who are selling Elvis. All told, there are literally hundreds of bootleg Elvis recordings.

Boppin' Hillbilly

In his very early performance career, Elvis Presley was occasionally called the "Boppin' Hillbilly." Later, his own name was all that was needed.

The Boring Institute

In December, 1988, the Boring Institute of Maplewood, New Jersey, issued its tongue-in-cheek list of the Most Boring Celebrities of the Year. Number five on the list was Elvis Presley, about whom the Institute said firmly (and using the words of Monty Python) "Okay, let's get this straight. Elvis is *dead*. Buried. Croaked. Kicked the bucket. Pushing up daisies. Deceased." Boring Institute founder Alan Caruba says the list is based on "massive media overexposure."

The Boss Sings Elvis

Several years ago, a regular highlight of every Bruce Springsteen concert was his rendition of the Elvis Presley hit "Can't Help Falling in Love." Usually, he sang it looking offstage, to the spot where his wife was standing. Now that Springsteen and his wife are divorced, the song has been dropped from the act. It is no secret that Bruce Springsteen, who has also performed the title song from the 1962 movie *Follow That Dream* at concerts, is a big fan of Elvis Presley. Bruce once tried to enter Graceland by climbing over the fence, getting as far as the front door before he was turned away by the guards.

The Bottom Line

According to one informed estimate, passed along by Elvis biographer Jerry Hopkins, the total amount of money Elvis Presley earned during his lifetime was about $18 billion.

Boxcar Records

By the end of his life, Elvis Presley didn't even own the rights to his own face. In the 1970s, Colonel Tom Parker set up a record label called Boxcar, based in his hometown of Madison, Tennessee (near Nashville). Originally, the company was to have been a joint venture with Elvis that would extend to issuing records by new young performers. As it turned out, Elvis's only real involvement with Boxcar came on August 15, 1974, when he signed an agreement that transferred all of his own commercial rights to the corporation, giving the Colonel the lion's share of the profit from his own personality. Until a court decision in the 1980s changed the situation, Colonel Parker controlled all licensing agreements and all rights to the image of Elvis.

Boy

Boy was the first dog Elvis Presley owned, acquired shortly after he began to achieve stardom.

The Boys Get Elvis into Trouble

On the night of May 20, 1974, Elvis Presley was the featured performer at the Sahara Tahoe, a prestigious hotel in the mountain resort of Lake Tahoe, Nevada. As usual, he was accompanied by some of the "Memphis Mafia," who also acted as his bodyguards. One night, as they all sat in Elvis's suite after the second show, the lights went out. Red West, David Stanley, and Dick Grob rushed out the door and found a man standing there. He was Edward L. Ashley, a land developer from California, who later claimed he had paid a stagehand from the show $60 for admission to what the man said would be a party in Elvis's suite that night. Ashley knocked at the door, and when he got no answer, he threw some breaker switches he had noticed on the wall.

Ashley claimed he was then beaten up by Elvis's bodyguards, with the star looking on approvingly. He sued both Elvis and the hotel for a total of $6.6 million in damages. Eventually, both of Ashley's suits were dismissed by the court.

A Brawl at the Gas Station

On October 18, 1956, Elvis Presley stopped at a Memphis gas station to fill up the tank of his $10,000 Cadillac. His presence immediately drew crowds of gawkers, and station attendant Ed Hopper became annoyed when he observed that the fans were blocking the gas pumps and preventing any other sales. Hopper told Elvis to leave, and then, as he told the story, he slapped the star lightly on the back of the head. Elvis responded to what he perceived as an assault by leaning out of the car and punching Hopper. A second attendant witnessed the punch and came to Hopper's aid, and he too got a fist in the face. A Memphis court subsequently found Elvis the innocent victim of this incident and fined the two station attendants for assault and battery.

"Bring the Boy"

Jimmy Savile, a famous British disc jockey, reminisced after Elvis Presley's death about his first meeting with the star. It was 1960, and Elvis was in Hollywood filming *Wild in the Country*. Savile, who had brought Elvis a gold record from Britain, managed to get an appointment with manager Colonel Tom Parker, who was obviously sizing up the Englishman. After some conversational sparring, the Colonel called to one of his minions, "Bring the boy." That was the way Parker referred to the twenty-five-year-old idol of millions.

British "Gold"

British deejay Jimmy Savile remembers how Elvis Presley reacted when he brought the star a gold record from England. The year was 1960, and the gold record was for sales of "It's Now or Never" in Great Britain. Savile knew from his research that Elvis already possessed at least thirty-four gold records, so he didn't expect "the King" to be particularly thrilled with one more for his collection. To his great surprise, however, Elvis hugged the gold record to his chest and spent the rest of the day showing it proudly to everyone on the set.

Browning Automatics

Elvis Presley's gun collection included two Browning automatic rifles, capable of firing more than thirty rounds a minute. The star and his buddies used the guns for target practice around Graceland.

Brushing with Colgate

Elvis Presley always used Colgate toothpaste.

Brut

Elvis Presley's favorite cologne was Brut, by Fabergé.

"Bunny" or "Thumper"?

When friends and associates of Elvis Presley called Graceland to speak to him, they generally used code names so staff members could verify their identity and put the call through to the star. During Ann-Margret's romance with Elvis, she used the code name "Bunny." Secretary Becky Yancy says the staff at Graceland thereafter jokingly nicknamed the redhead "Thumper."

"Bunting"

"Bunting" was one of the nicknames girlfriend Linda Thompson used as a term of endearment for Elvis Presley.

Carol Burnett

One of Elvis Presley's favorite television programs was "The Carol Burnett Show." He especially enjoyed the take-offs of classic Hollywood movies and the antics of costars Harvey Korman and Tim Conway. Coincidentally, when Elvis Presley appeared on "The Ed Sullivan Show" in 1956, one of his fellow guests was the young comedienne Carol Burnett.

Johnny Burnette

Johnny Burnette was a rockabilly singer from Memphis who sometimes performed with Doug Poindexter's Starlite Wranglers in the early 1950s. Through band member Bill Black, Elvis Presley met Johnny, who was a few years older. For a time Johnny seemed to be Elvis's role model—a graduate of Humes High, which Elvis then attended, and former Golden Gloves boxer, Johnny was driving a truck for Crown Electric in the day and singing in local bars and clubs at night. Johnny, his brother Dorsey, and Paul Burlison formed a group that not only appeared locally but also made it to the finals of Ted Mack's Amateur Hour program; the group eventually sang in the 1957 movie *Rock, Rock, Rock*. Johnny was to become a successful singer and composer. He wrote the classic "You're Sixteen" and he also wrote "The Fool," which Elvis Presley recorded in 1971. Johnny Burnette drowned in a boating accident on August 1, 1964.

B
33

"Burning Love"

"Burning Love" was a song written by Dennis Linde that was recorded by Elvis Presley in early 1972. It features guitar work by James Burton and John Wilkinson, supporting Elvis's heavily echoed vocal. The song was released as a single in August of that year, backed with "It's a Matter of Time." It immediately climbed to the number two spot on the charts. The fact that it stayed on the charts for fifteen weeks was a shot in the arm for Elvis's career, since he hadn't had a solid hit single in several years.

James Burton

In the late 1960s, after Elvis Presley began once again to make live appearances, the singer needed a regular guitar player to tour with him—something Scotty Moore, who had played with Elvis from the very beginning, was unwilling to do. Elvis found what he needed in guitarist James Burton. Burton had played with Ricky Nelson for many years, and then briefly with Hoyt Axton and Randy Newman. He had the range of styles and experience Elvis needed, and he was able to produce a smooth and polished sound that fitted with the type of music Elvis performed in the last decade of his life. Late in 1970, James Burton made a solo recording, an endeavor greatly helped by Elvis. The star had booked five days of expensive studio time to make a new album, but found he was not feeling well enough to continue after the first day. So he generously gave the other four days to Burton, who had been offered a contract by A&M unaccompanied by sufficient funds to make a decent recording. Thanks to Elvis, Burton got his chance to make a good solo album.

"Button"

Linda Thompson's nickname for Elvis Presley was "Button." Elvis, who loved to use nicknames, sometimes copied her and called her "Button" too.

"Buttonhead"

"Buttonhead" was one of Elvis Presley's nicknames for his daughter Lisa Marie.

Buying Firecrackers

Drummer D.J. Fontana, who toured with Elvis Presley in the early days of the singer's performing career, remembers that when the group traveled, the car stopped frequently to allow Elvis to buy more Pepsi and a new supply of firecrackers. "He got the biggest kick out of trying to hit billboards and roadside signs with them. That's why we had to stop so much—he'd run out of firecrackers!"

Buying His First Car

The first car Elvis Presley ever bought for himself was a secondhand, four-year-old Lincoln Continental that he purchased in 1955 with some financial help from his manager at the time, Bob Neal. Elvis and his backup musicians, Scotty Moore and Bill Black, had to drive to the places all around the South where they were booked to perform. One night on the road, with "Blackie" at the wheel, the car was wrecked. Elvis replaced it with a used 1954 Cadillac that he had painted pink.

The Buy-Out Agreement

In 1973, Colonel Tom Parker negotiated with RCA to obtain a deal in which RCA bought from Elvis Presley all his rights to the more than seven hundred songs that he had recorded on the RCA label. The deal gave Elvis $2.8 million in a flat payment and an additional $2 million in various other payments to companies in which he owned a share. The Colonel did even better than his client. He got $2.6 million in immediate cash and nearly $4 million more in fees and payments to companies he owned, for a total of $6.2 million. The deal gave RCA the entire Elvis catalog with no further royalties to be paid out, saving the company millions of dollars in future payments.

In 1980, a probate court raised questions about the wisdom and propriety of this agreement. The following year, the Presley estate, no longer managed by the Colonel's ally, Vernon Presley, sued both Colonel Parker and RCA over the agreement, which they claimed had not been in Elvis's best interests. The matter was eventually settled out of court, and the rights to royalties produced by sales of RCA records reverted to the Presley estate.

Bye-Bye Birdie

The Broadway musical *Bye-Bye Birdie*, which opened in 1961, was based on the legend of Elvis Presley, then out of the army for about a year and enjoying even greater career success than he'd had before he went in. The central character of the play was teen idol Conrad Birdie (a role originated by Dick Gautier) who resembled Elvis in many ways. *Bye-Bye Birdie* was later made into a movie starring Janet Leigh, Dick Van Dyke, and young singer-dancer Ann-Margret; Jesse Pearson played the Elvis-based role. The movie's producers asked Elvis to sing several songs for the soundtrack but Colonel Parker turned down the request.

The Cadillac Goes on Tour

In the mid-1960s, Colonel Tom Parker decided to hype Elvis Presley's sagging career by sending one of the star's most extravagant cars out on tour. It was a gold Cadillac, customized by Barris Kustom City, which the Colonel managed to sell outright to RCA for $24,000. RCA then sent the car on the road to promote Elvis's *Frankie and Johnny*, both the movie and the album. Hundreds of thousands of people paid money to look at the gold Cadillac and millions bought picture postcards of the vehicle.

Calling "John Burrows"

Any telephone caller who reached Graceland and asked for "John Burrows" was immediately put through to Elvis Presley with no questions asked. That was the code name he gave to close friends so they would always be able to reach him. The code was also used for mail: Inside an envelope addressed to Elvis a second envelope with the inscription "John Burrows" would be given to Elvis unopened.

Camden Records

Camden was a subsidiary of RCA that specialized in discount albums. Between 1969 and 1973, ten Elvis Presley albums were issued on the Camden label:

- *Elvis Sings Flaming Star*
- *Let's Be Friends*
- *Elvis's Christmas Album*
- *Almost in Love*

- *You'll Never Walk Alone*
- *C'mon Everybody*
- *I Got Lucky*
- *Elvis Sings Hits from His Movies*, Vols. 1 and 2
- *Separate Ways*

In 1975, RCA sold the rights to these Camden recordings to Pickwick Records, which has since reissued them.

Campaign '88

A strange moment of the 1988 presidential campaign came just a few days before the election. Candidate Dan Quayle traveled to Memphis, where he was greeted by an Elvis impersonator—a "photo opportunity" that led to innumerable newspaper pictures the following day. Afterward, Quayle's staff toured Graceland.

Can Lisa Sing?

Rumor has it that Lisa Marie Presley has been offered $1 million to make a record. Presumably, the mere fact that she is Elvis Presley's daughter could be expected to send fans to the record store. The question is, Can Lisa actually sing? Some insiders say she has her father's musicality, although not, of course, his voice.

"Can't Help Falling in Love"

One of Elvis Presley's most popular love songs was "Can't Help Falling in Love," written by Hugo Peretti, Luigi Creatore, and George Weiss and based on a melody by the eighteenth-century composer Giovanni Martini. The song was originally recorded for the movie *Blue Hawaii* and released as a single in the spring of 1961. It stayed in the number one spot on the pop charts for six weeks. "Can't Help Falling in Love" later appeared on a number of live albums. Elvis always used the song to close his concerts.

Capricorn

Elvis Presley's birthday was on January 8, making him a Capricorn, born under the sign of the goat. Here's the way astrologer Linda Goodman describes the Capricorn male in her best-selling book, *Sun Signs*:

He has a self-made brick wall around him. He's shy, but he's strong and tough. He's pleasant, but he's fiercely ambitious. Like the legendary silent, earthy cowboy, the Capricorn man seems to prefer to be alone. He doesn't. Not really.

Secretly, Capricorn yearns for adulation. He'd love to thrill the crowd on a flying trapeze. In his private dreams, the goat is an incurable romantic, but Saturn chains his nature. The stern planet of discipline de-

C

mands of him calm behavior, practical actions and serious intent . . . Many Capricorn men live at home long past the age when their friends are out enjoying the delights of a bachelor pad. They usually fall in love later than most men too—and they seldom marry before they're settled in a career . . . As a father, he'll be a Father—the literal personification of the word. He'll always be at the head of the table.

Captain Marvel Jr.

Author and biographer Elaine Dundy has concluded that Elvis Presley adopted his lightning bolt motif from the comic books of Captain Marvel Jr., created in 1942 when Elvis was seven years old. Dundy also draws fans' attention to the fact that Elvis to a great extent modeled his appearance on the way the character of Captain Marvel Jr. was drawn. She points to young Marvel's stance with legs spread wide apart, palms turned flat, fingers outstretched and thumbs extended; and to the sideburns, the lock of hair over the forehead, and the shiny look of the hair. Elvis was known to have been a big fan of both Captain Marvel and Captain Marvel Jr., who in ordinary life was the crippled newsboy Freddy Freeman.

The Car-Buying Sprees

In a single month, Elvis Presley's secretary revealed, the star bought thirty-three vehicles, more than one a day. Some were for himself, but most of them were given away to buddies, girlfriends, employees, and even total strangers.

In January 1976, Elvis gave away three Cadillacs and two Lincoln Continentals to people he met on a skiing trip in Vail, Colorado.

One of Elvis's favorite cars was the big Mercedes-Benz, and most of the people who worked for him eventually received a Mercedes as a gift. When he gave his personal Mercedes to Shelby County Sheriff Richard Morris, there was unfavorable publicity in local papers about Elvis's purchase of foreign cars rather than American-made models.

One of Elvis's most notable buying sprees came when he bought the Circle G ranch in Mississippi. He wanted all of his buddies to drive around the ranch with him, so he bought about thirty new Ford Rancheros with four-wheel drive for his entourage.

Johnny Cash

Johnny Cash, the legendary country singer, was recording on the Sun label at the same time as Elvis Presley. The two were members of Sam Phillips' so-called "Million-Dollar Quartet" that also included Jerry Lee Lewis and Roy Orbison. Johnny was three years older than Elvis, born in 1932 in Kingsland, Arkansas. Like Elvis, he spent two years in the army, most of the time stationed in Germany. Johnny moved to Nashville in 1954 and soon thereafter was signed by Sun records. Sun released his big hit "I Walk the Line," which became his signature tune. Elvis often played

Cash's records at Graceland and also performed several of his songs in concert. According to one report, it was Elvis who introduced Johnny to his wife June Carter, who was, like Elvis, touring with the Hank Snow road show in 1955. At the time, Elvis was interested in dating June's sister Anita.

Chai

Chai is the Hebrew word for life, and also a letter of the Hebrew alphabet. Elvis Presley frequently wore a gold *Chai* on a chain around his neck.

Change of Habit

Change of Habit was the last movie Elvis Presley made, except for the two documentaries of the 1970s about his real life and his performances. In *Change of Habit* (1970), he played a doctor (!) who falls in love with a nun(!!), played by Mary Tyler Moore(!!!). Naturally, Dr. Elvis still gets to sing a couple of numbers—"Rubberneckin' " and a gospel song, "Let's Pray Together." Ed Asner, who was later to costar with Moore in her highly acclaimed TV sitcom, played a cop in this movie.

The Chapel of Inspiration

On May 18, 1979, the Elvis Presley Memorial Chapel was opened in East Tupelo, Mississippi, to honor its most famous citizen. Elvis once commented that if he was to have a permanent memorial, he'd like it to be a church. So in his memory one was built, with funds from the community where he was born, augmented by contributions from fans all over the world. The chapel was erected on the grounds of the Elvis Presley Youth Center, located behind the house where Elvis was born, itself now a museum and state historical site. One of the treasured relics at the chapel is Elvis's own personal Bible, presented by his father Vernon only weeks before his own death.

Charro!

Charro!, released in 1969, is noteworthy among Elvis Presley films because it's the only one in which he didn't perform a song. Although he sings the title tune over the opening credits (a fact prominently advertised on the movie posters), there is no singing production number within the film itself. Shot on location in the Arizona desert, *Charro!* stars Elvis as a man on the run from both American and Mexican authorities because of a frame-up that he is out to avenge. He wears a beard and cowboy clothes in this 1870 period piece, one of the last films he made. A weak script, hurried production, and noticeable lack of continuity all contributed to the movie's lack of success at the box office.

Elvis never looked more handsome than in this close up from *Charro!* (Photo from Neal Peters Collection)

The *Christina*

The *Christina* was the name of the Learjet owned by Frank Sinatra, which Elvis Presley borrowed on his wedding day to take him and his bride from Las Vegas back to Palm Springs, where they spent the first night of their honeymoon. The *Christina* crashed in 1976, killing the pilot and the passenger, Frank Sinatra's mother.

Christmas at Graceland

Elvis Presley always loved Christmas, and during the holiday season the mansion became an enchanted place dedicated to the spirit of giving—and getting. The yard-men searched far and wide to find a tree deemed large enough for Graceland's living room, and there were usually a number of smaller trees outside the house. The huge main tree was always completely covered with ornaments and surrounded by an immense pile of presents at the base. The grounds of Graceland were filled with lights, and the entire house was decorated with holly, wreaths, and colored lights. Christmas music recorded by Elvis echoed throughout.

Elvis liked to give people presents, and he spent large sums every year at Christmas. Employees received bonuses and generous gifts. He might send out dozens of television sets, expensive clocks, and watches to colleagues, friends, and acquaintances. The spirit of giving also extended to charitable contributions, particularly to local Memphis organizations. Family members could expect to receive jewelry, or maybe even a car. Lisa Marie's pile of presents was always bigger than anyone else's.

Of course, Elvis also received thousands of Christmas presents too. Fans sent everything from hand-knitted sweaters to homemade cookies to framed photos of themselves. Shirts, ties, shaving lotion, and billfolds came in by the hundreds. Friends and employees also gave him presents, sometimes pooling their money to get him something lavish for Graceland. On Christmas Eve, Elvis and his family and friends gathered in the big living room, Christmas music was put on the stereo, and hot drinks and snacks were served. Elvis then spent hours opening his huge pile of presents. His ability to buy himself anything he wanted didn't prevent his utter enjoyment of the occasion, and he was as enthusiastic about receiving as he was about giving.

Today there are still special Christmas festivities at Graceland, which fans can share. The mansion is decorated just as it was in Elvis's lifetime and twinkling lights still turn the house and grounds into fairyland. For information about visiting Graceland at Christmas time, write Graceland, 3797 Elvis Presley Blvd., Memphis TN 38116.

The Church of Scientology

Priscilla Presley first became interested in the Church of Scientology during a lunchtime conversation with John Travolta. She was so impressed with the helpfulness of the Scientology philosophy that she also encouraged her daughter Lisa Marie to become involved. Lisa Marie was married by a minister of the Church of Scientology, and her husband Danny is also a Scientologist.

Cigars

Elvis Presley, who never smoked in his youth, grew to love smoking cigars. His preference was for the long fat kind, and in the 1970s he never traveled without his own private stock.

"Cilla"

"Cilla" was the nickname by which Elvis Presley most frequently referred to his wife, Priscilla Beaulieu Presley. He also liked to call her "Priscilla-Illa."

Circle G Ranch

The Circle G was the ranch in Mississippi that Elvis Presley bought from rancher Jack Adams in February 1967, at the height of his interest in horses. The ranch, which cost about $300,000, consisted of 163 acres, some barns to house a herd of Santa Gertrudis cattle, and a white one-bedroom house. It was located near the little town of Walls, Mississippi, just over the Tennessee state line, only about ten miles from Graceland. Priscilla had spotted the property one day while out for a drive and thought it would make a cozy getaway for herself and Elvis. As usual, he brought the whole entourage along with them.

Besieged by fans, Elvis put a big fence around the ranch and tried to buy more land to expand, but nothing in the vicinity was for sale. So he moved out of the modest house that came with the ranch and was too near the entrance, and bought a huge trailer, with a king-sized bed and a brick fireplace, to serve as his own headquarters. Elvis's friend Alan Fortas was hired as ranch manager, and eight other members of the Elvis entourage were put on the ranch payroll as well.

Elvis kept his own eighteen horses at the ranch, and he acquired good purebred cattle to improve his herd of Santa Gertrudis. He bought horses for all his buddies, so they could ride around the ranch with him, as well as their own trailers, which were installed around the ranch on concrete foundations. He gave most of the guys their personal Ford Rancheros, four-wheel drive vehicles to take them over the dirt roads and paths at the ranch; he spent more than $100,000 on the vehicles in a single month.

Elvis's enthusiasm for the life of a rancher lasted less than a year. In the spring of 1967, he went to Hollywood to make the movie *Clambake*. Then he married Priscilla, and the couple soon began to look forward to parenthood. Graceland, with its full staff of servants and wide range of creature comforts, was once again the focus of Elvis's life. Some of the equipment he had bought for the Circle G was auctioned, and then the place itself was sold for $440,100. The prizewinning cattle were sold to another gentleman farmer, Winthrop Rockefeller.

The Circle G has recently changed hands again, and there are reports that the new owner intends to turn it into a resort with a Presley theme.

Clambake

Early in 1967, Elvis Presley was scheduled to start shooting his twenty-fifth movie, *Clambake*. When he reported to the set of the United Artists film, director Arthur Nadel was distressed to see that his leading man weighed more than two hundred pounds, the result of a months-long eating spree. Elvis dieted as a wardrobe of concealing jackets was hastily concocted. Then the star tripped over a wire in his room in the middle of the night, suffering a mild concussion. The filming had to be delayed, and the movie was not completed until after Elvis got married on May 1 of that year. He and Priscilla had just a few days to themselves in Palm Strings before he reported back to the set. *Clambake*, which costarred Elvis's old love interest, Shelley Fabares, had Elvis singing enough songs to release a soundtrack album; cuts included the title track, "How Can You Lose What You Never Had?" and "Singing Tree." The album, which also offered fans a bonus color photo of Elvis and Priscilla at their wedding, never climbed higher than the number fourteen spot on the charts.

Frank C. Clement

Frank C. Clement ran for governor of Tennessee in 1953, and he hired Tom Parker, who had just been fired by former client, country-and-western singer Eddy Arnold, as an advance man during his campaign. When Clement won the election, he showed his gratitude by making Parker an honorary colonel of the state of Tennessee.

Clothes Sizes

Elvis Presley wore a size 16-35 shirt. His shoe size was 11D.

Collectibles

According to one story, in 1980 Elvis memorabilia was one of the most important industries in America, with annual sales only slightly less than those of Coca-Cola. Fans of Elvis Presley collect practically everything associated with their favorite star. Top on the list, of course, are the records—the hundreds of singles and albums issued by RCA in the course of Elvis's career, as well as the even larger number of bootleg records that contain alternate takes never released by RCA, badly recorded live performances, and virtually every word Elvis ever uttered in public.

Elvis videos are also popular. They include videotapes of all his movies and many of his live performances. Fans collect Elvis autographs and photos. A few of the lucky ones have a piece of clothing worn by Elvis, or a scrap thereof. Every now and then a lock of his hair turns up for sale or on exhibition somewhere.

Another category is the commemorative item. One popular type is the Elvis decanter, most often made by McCormick, often with a music box in the base. A typical example is the gold decanter with Elvis lounging against an amp, microphone in hand, that plays "My Way," in the collection of the author. A complete set of McCormick decanters runs in the thousands of dollars.

The Danbury Mint has produced a porcelain Elvis doll in its lines of collectibles. Their eighteen-inch Elvis is wearing the jumpsuit from the *Aloha* TV special. It is covered with more than three-hundred rhinestones as well as a multitude of gold stars, studs, and chains.

For more information on Elvis collectibles and their value, see *The Official Price Guide to Memorabilia of Elvis Presley and the Beatles*, published in 1988 by House of Collectibles.

The Colon Problem

In the last years of his life, Elvis Presley suffered serious problems with his colon. For a long time, he had regularly consumed large quantities of laxatives, especially during the periods he was dieting by virtually fasting, which produced irregularity. Probably because of the long-term use of laxatives, his colon lost its ability to contract and became quite enlarged. This made his abdomen distended and led to chronic discomfort. Elvis was tested for various colon ailments, and treated to try to return some degree of normal function to the colon. But his erratic eating habits and continued use of drugs made it difficult to get the colon problem under control.

Colonel Elvis

In 1961, the governor of Tennessee, Buford Ellington, made Elvis Presley an honorary colonel of the state, the same title bestowed on his manager, Colonel Tom Parker. Perhaps to avoid competing with Parker, Elvis never used the title.

Colonel Midnight

Colonel Midnight was a horse given to Vernon Presley by his son Elvis, during the period between 1966 and 1967 when Elvis was at the height of his craze for riding. Vernon never quite shared his son's enthusiasm for the sport.

C

"Colonel Snow"

All of the people close to Elvis Presley had code names they used when they telephoned Graceland, a step that was necessary because so many fans called and pretended to be relatives or business associates of the star. Elvis's manager, Colonel Tom Parker, chose the ironic code name "Colonel Snow."

The Colonel Stays Home

Colonel Tom Parker had stuck close by the side of his client Elvis Presley from the minute he met him in 1955 until the day Private Presley left for Germany. The Colonel stage-managed Elvis's induction into the army, visited him often when he was stationed in Arkansas and Texas, and sat by his side at a farewell press conference in New York in September 1958, before Elvis embarked on the troop ship that took him overseas. Then, most surprisingly, the Colonel didn't see Elvis again until he returned to the United States to be discharged in February 1960.

The official reason for the long separation was that the Colonel had to attend to Elvis's business affairs back in the States. It later came to light, however, that the real reason was that Parker was a Dutch citizen and an illegal alien in the U.S., who couldn't produce a passport to get back into his adopted country.

The Colonel's Musical Clients

Colonel Tom Parker broke into the country-and-western music business when he was hired in the mid-1940s by the Grand Ole Opry to do advance publicity for their shows, first in Tampa, where he was working for the local Humane Society, and later in other towns throughout the South. Soon the Colonel was signed as manager by one of the singers traveling with the Opry, the young Eddy Arnold. Parker managed Arnold for nine years, as Arnold rose to the top of the country-and-western business. When Arnold fired him in 1953, the Colonel promptly signed up the singer Hank Snow.

While touring with Hank in the summer of 1955, the Colonel met a young singer who was appearing on the same bill, Elvis Presley. Parker immediately recognized Elvis's enormous potential and signed him to a management contract. Originally, the Colonel signed the contract as an agent for Hank Snow Jamboree Attractions, but somehow, when real stardom came to Elvis, Hank Snow discovered he no longer had a piece of the action.

C

The 1968 TV special featured Elvis at his best: lean, mean, dressed in black leather, and sexy enough to set the stage on fire. It may have been the best performance of his life. (Photo from Neal Peters Collection)

"The Comeback Special"

By 1968, Elvis Presley's career was obviously suffering from too many mediocre movies and soundtrack albums, however profitable they might have been. The star hadn't appeared in front of an audience since a Hawaiian concert in 1961 and a whole generation of teenagers knew him only from the silly songs written for his movies and from an occasional ballad heard on the radio. The Beatles were the latest craze, and the Rolling Stones were poaching on Elvis's territory, fusing black blues and soul music with the hard beat of rock. And the antics of such performers as Mick Jagger and Jim Morrison of the Doors made Elvis's gyrations of the 1950s look like a Sunday school picnic.

Elvis's career was rescued in a most unlikely manner, through a Christmas television special. His manager, Colonel Tom Parker, had approached NBC with the idea, and a deal was quickly worked out. The Colonel had a stereotyped conception of the special, with Elvis singing some familiar holiday music, introducing a few wholesome guests, and wishing his audience a merry Christmas as artificial snow fell over the final credits. But the hip young producer chosen by NBC, Steve Binder, had a different idea. He turned the special into a show that focused on Elvis the rock-and-roll legend.

The resulting production revitalized Elvis's career. Rock critic Greil Marcus wrote that the special contained the finest music of Elvis's life. "If there was ever music that bleeds, this was it. Nothing came easy that night and he gave everything that he had—more than anyone knew he had." Thereafter, fans referred to the program as the "comeback special." Under the title "Elvis Presley's 1968 Comeback," the TV show is still being rebroadcast today.

Compact Disc Releases

As of October 1988, thirty-three Elvis Presley albums have been rereleased in compact disc form. That makes him number one in terms of albums available in CD—a tribute to the big sales RCA has racked up with the new releases, and to Elvis's continuing popularity with music lovers.

Competing in the Jimmie Rodgers Festival

In May 1953, Meridian, Mississippi, held its first annual Jimmie Rodgers Festival, in honor of the country-and-western star who had been born there and died of tuberculosis at 36. Flushed with his success at a high school variety show, Elvis Presley decided to hitchhike to Meridian to compete in the Festival's talent show. He arrived with only ten cents, but a reporter for the paper that sponsored the contest lent him the money for a room and meals. (Elvis never paid the reporter back.) Elvis came in second in the contest, and won a new guitar.

Concert Appearances

All those who ever saw him on stage agree that Elvis Presley was a consummate live performer; it was perhaps his most notable talent. At the beginning of his career, his onstage appearances were the fuel that propelled him to stardom, and those who had the chance to see the young Elvis's effect on an audience never forgot the spectacle. The star returned to concert appearances in the last years of his career, once again displaying a total mastery of his audiences. Even when he was obviously overweight and out of shape, he could still perform the old Elvis magic. And he did it often. The statistics regarding Elvis's live appearances are staggering.

In 1954, Elvis Presley made about thirty live appearances. Most were in his hometown of Memphis; there were other appearances in various towns in Texas, and one in Nashville.

In 1955, the number of appearances jumped to about 140. Most of them were in the nearby states of Texas, Louisiana, Mississippi, Alabama, and Arkansas, with a few swings through North Carolina and some scattered appearances in Georgia and Virginia.

In 1956, the year he catapulted to national stardom, the number dropped to sixty-one, as Elvis, by then managed by Colonel Tom Parker, became more selective about his venues. He was booked into large auditoriums, such as the Olympic Theater in Miami, the University of Nebraska Coliseum in Lincoln, the Veterans' Memorial Auditorium in Columbus, and the Cotton Bowl Stadium in Dallas. He traveled as far away as Long Beach, California; St. Paul, Minnesota; and Lacrosse, Wisconsin.

In 1957, the number of appearances dropped again, to just twenty-two, as part of Colonel Parker's strategy of always leaving them asking for more. Nearly all the appearances were at huge arenas and only a very few of them in Elvis's native South. He performed in Seattle, Ottawa, Detroit, Philadelphia, Spokane, San Francisco, and Honolulu—and at the Mississippi-Alabama Fair and Dairy Show in Tupelo.

In 1958, there was just one live appearance, in Memphis, during a weekend leave from the army. Elvis's next live concert did not come until 1961, when he played

two dates—Memphis in February and Pearl Harbor in March.

There followed a long hiatus from public performances. The next time Elvis appeared on a stage came in 1969, when he was booked for four weeks at the Las Vegas International Hotel for fifty-seven shows.

In 1970, he returned again to live concerts. In addition to two four-week bookings in Vegas, he gave concerts in seventeen other venues, ranging from the Houston Astrodome to the San Francisco Cow Palace.

The pattern was much the same in 1971. Elvis did his usual two four-week stints in Vegas and also two weeks in Tahoe, and then he made twelve concert appearances in large venues, such as the Boston Garden and the Salt Palace in Salt Lake City.

The year 1972 saw the usual two long bookings in Vegas and more touring than before. Elvis appeared in thirty-seven venues, some of them as large as Madison Square Garden in New York, and some of them smaller, such as the Coliseum in Richmond, Virginia, and the Tingley Coliseum in Albuquerque.

In 1973, he was booked in twenty-four different locations for live performances, in addition to working twice in Vegas and once in Tahoe for extended engagements.

The pace picked up in 1974 with forty-five bookings for concerts, two appearances in Vegas, and two appearances in Tahoe.

The following year started out even busier. In 1975, Elvis traveled to forty-three venues by the middle of July, and was booked for two appearances at the Hilton Hotel in Vegas. The second engagement, which started in August, was cut short by Elvis's illness, and he made no more live appearances the rest of the year.

In 1976, he seemed to be trying to make up for lost time. Although he didn't get out on the road until nearly the middle of March, there was an amazing total of

C

eighty-eight bookings for concerts in the last full year of Elvis's career, along with two extended engagements in Vegas.

By the time of Elvis's death in mid-August 1977, he had already made fifty-five appearances all over the country, and ten more concerts, scheduled for late August, had to be canceled.

Elvis's smile, with its hint of a sneer, was his second most famous trademark. First was the undulation of his hips! (Photo from Neal Peters Collection)

The Controversial Gyrations

In 1956, as soon as the public began to see Elvis Presley perform, rather than merely hear his records on the radio, a controversy arose about the way he moved his body while he sang. Today, of course, all rock and pop stars gyrate around the stage and strike provocative poses, and after the lewd antics of such popular stars as Jim Morrison, who exposed himself on the stage, and Mick Jagger, with his overtly sexual movements, audiences are virtually shock proof. But in the 1950s, when Elvis first gained national attention, white singers simply stood at the microphone and sang; the only body parts they ever moved were their arms. Can you imagine the Four Freshman, Pat Boone, or Perry Como acting obscene?

Elvis modeled his onstage antics after the preachers he had seen in the Assembly of God churches, and after black performers, who were then limited to performing in black clubs. Elvis bopped, he rocked, he swung his hips in a way that was distinctly sexual. To the teenagers who watched him, he was both exciting and rebellious, but to some of their parents and grandparents, he was obscene (which of course merely made him more appealing). Church bulletins denounced Presley's gyrations, one local judge was ready to serve him with a warrant for corrupting the morals of youth, and a big-city vice squad ordered him to clean up his act.

The controversy, of course, was a definite boost to Elvis's career. His manager, Colonel Tom Parker, defended the singer somewhat disingenuously: "If I'd thought he was doing it on purpose, I'd have been against it; but he honestly just gets overexcited when he sings." Elvis himself always denied that his movements were vulgar. "I know that I get carried away with the music and the beat sometimes. And I don't know quite what I'm doing. But it is all rhythm and the beat—it's full of life. I enjoy it." He also confessed, "You take the wiggle out of it, it is finished."

Eventually the controversy waned, partly because by the mid-1960s, Elvis seemed tame compared to the new group of performers idolized by teens, and partly because Elvis lost that sense of life and enjoyment that made the movements come naturally to him. When we look at the man who played Vegas so successfully, it's hard to remember that skinny baby-faced youth whose hips seemed to lead a life of their own. Another legend of the fifties recently put the whole controversy into perspective. Said Carl Perkins, the composer of "Blue Suede Shoes," "How beautiful it was to see a leg that couldn't stand still."

Coping with Overnight Success

In one interview in 1956, Elvis Presley revealed that he felt unable to keep up with the changes that were happening so fast as his career took off, and said his sleep was affected. In another interview that same year, Elvis commented, "My dad and I were laughing about it the other day. He looked at me and said, 'What happened, Elvis? The last thing I remember is, I was working in a factory and you were driving a truck.'"

Elvis Costello

British pop star Elvis Costello was born Declan MacManus. In 1977, at the urging of his manager Jake Riviera, he gave himself the name Elvis in homage to one of his idols, Elvis Presley.

C

"Crazy"

"Crazy" was one of the nicknames frequently used for Elvis Presley by members of his entourage.

Crown Electric Company

In the fall of 1953, the year Elvis Presley graduated from L.C. Humes High School in Memphis, he quit the job he had held during the summer on the assembly line at the Precision Tool Company in Memphis, and got a job driving a truck for the Crown Electric Company. The business was located at 353 Poplar Avenue in downtown Memphis, and the owners, Jim and Gladys Tipler, were used to the ways of aspiring musicians—one of their previous drivers had been Johnny Burnette, a local rockabilly singer of Elvis's acquaintance. Elvis made deliveries all over the city for Crown in a battered but reliable Ford truck. His salary was only $41 a week; though it was less than he'd been paid on the assembly line, he found the freedom of the road more congenial than the deadly routine of the factory. Elvis later claimed he had always wanted to be a truck driver, and had thus achieved his ambition. It was not until several of his Sun recordings had been released and he was getting regular bookings for live performances that Elvis finally relinquished the security of his job at Crown Electric.

Arthur "Big Boy" Crudup

Arthur "Big Boy" Crudup was one of Elvis Presley's early influences. Born in Virginia in 1905, Crudup was a classic delta blues singer who wrote most of his own material. Typically, he sang soulfully and kept the instrumentation sparse. His song "That's All Right" was the first commercially released Elvis Presley recording. In 1956 Elvis recorded two more of Big Boy's songs, "So Glad You're Mine" and "My Baby Left Me." In recognition of his musical debt to Crudup, Elvis later financed several of the bluesman's recording sessions. Big Boy Crudup died in 1974.

George Cukor Comments on Elvis Presley the Actor

Veteran movie director George Cukor, whose credits include *Little Women* and *The Philadelphia Story*, spent a day on the set of an Elvis Presley movie in the early 1960s. He left that evening convinced that the pop star was one of the major acting talents of his time. "He can do *anything!*," exclaimed Cukor excitedly. "He would be a dream to direct. His comedy timing is faultless." What a pity Cukor never worked with Elvis on a film.

The Cultural Phenomenon of Elvis Presley: The Making of a Folk Hero

"The Cultural Phenomenon of Elvis Presley: The Making of a Folk Hero" is a college course about Elvis Presley and his career that was first offered for credit at the University of Tennessee in 1980.

Tony Curtis

When Elvis Presley was a teenager in Memphis, he went to the movies as often as possible, and one of his favorite screen heroes was Tony Curtis. Elvis was especially impressed by Curtis's image in *City Across the River* and he did his best to imitate the way the star looked and acted. Tony Curtis was one source of the greasy pompadour Elvis adopted, and his screen character was also the basis of the early Elvis's defiant performing persona, such an odd contrast to his nice farm-boy manners when he stepped off the stage.

Customized Touring Bus

Elvis Presley had the customizing firm of George Barris, in California, create a touring bus extravaganza for him, starting with a standard Greyhound. The interior was done in red plush and included all the comforts of home—a kitchen, a TV set, and an excellent stereo system.

C

Customized Van

In the 1970s, Elvis Presley fell in love with the customized Dodge van belonging to country-and-western singer Conway Twitty (like Elvis, a Sun Records alumnus) and decided to order one just like it. The work was done at Van Mann in Elkhart, Indiana. The brown van, painted on the sides with pictures of horses, was equipped with a comfortable double bed, television set and tape deck, air conditioning, sink, refrigerator, and burglar alarm. The cost of the customization was between $15,000 and $20,000.

Cypress Street

About the time Elvis Presley was in his senior year of high school, the Presley family was evicted from their apartment in Lauderdale Court, reportedly because they had been unable to keep up with their rent. The four Presleys (Elvis's grandmother, Minnie Mae Presley, lived with them at this time) moved to a smaller, less comfortable two-room apartment on Cypress Street. Vernon had hurt his back and was unable to work for a while, and Gladys was beginning to slip into the chronic illness that would end her life when she was only forty-six. Within a few months, the Presleys left Cypress Street when they found another apartment back in the neighborhood of Lauderdale Court, at 462 Alabama Avenue. With Elvis finishing school and thus soon able to work full time, the family's economic picture looked a little brighter.

Dallas

From the fall of 1983 through the spring of 1988, Priscilla Presley was one of the stars of the prime-time dramatic TV series *Dallas*. She played the role of Jenna Wade, an early girlfriend of Bobby Ewing who reappeared years later with his daughter. Eventually she married Bobby's brother Ray, and they went to live in Europe—thus removing them from the show.

The Dancing Talent of Gladys

According to those who knew Elvis Presley's mother when she was young, Gladys Smith was a wonderful dancer—the kind who made everyone else on the floor stop and watch as she soloed.

The Dangers of Capped Teeth

While Elvis Presley was in Hollywood in 1957, working on the dance number for the movie *Jailhouse Rock*, he danced so wildly that he knocked a cap off one of his front teeth and accidentally inhaled it. The star had to be taken to Los Angeles's Cedars of Lebanon Hospital to have the cap removed.

A Date with Elvis

A Date with Elvis was an LP issued by RCA in August 1959, while Elvis Presley was still in the army and stationed in Germany. He hadn't been able to record any new material for a year and a half, but RCA kept his fans happy by collecting some of the songs from his films that had never been released and adding some songs from the early Sun recordings, to which they had purchased the rights in 1955. Inside the album was a signed telegram from Elvis, written from Germany; the original back cover had a calendar with the expected date of his release from the army circled in red. Although the album really had no new material on it, it moved up as high as number thirty-two on the album charts.

Richard Davis

Richard Davis met Elvis Presley when they played touch football together in Memphis. The two men became buddies and in 1962 Davis was given the official post of valet. Vernon Presley fired him seven years later, reportedly in one of his attempts to save his son's money. In 1988, Davis was arrested on drug charges. Friend George Klein, another former Elvis associate in Memphis, organized a legal defense fund for Davis, asking Elvis fans to contribute.

The Death of Elvis Presley

Sometime in the early hours of the morning of August 16, 1977, Elvis Presley's girlfriend Ginger Alden became concerned when she realized Elvis had been in the bathroom for an extended period. She went to the door and called to him; when there was no answer she pushed open the door to see him lying motionless on the floor. She immediately summoned help. Elvis's financial manager, Joe Esposito, and his physician, Dr. Nichopoulos, got to the Graceland master bedroom soon thereafter. Dr. Nick, although privately convinced that Elvis was already dead, used all his skill and training to revive his famous patient, continuing his efforts all the way to Baptist Hospital in the ambulance. On the star's arrival in the well-equipped emergency room, a team of doctors tried all possible resuscitation measures, but Elvis Presley was officially pronounced dead at 3:30 A.M.

The Death of Gladys Presley

Gladys Presley had been ailing for several years by the time her son Elvis entered the army in March 1958. She had sought medical treatment for problems with her gall bladder, obesity, and the mysterious fatigue and malaise that would later turn out to be early symptoms of liver problems, possibly due to heavy alcohol consumption. In June of 1958, she and her husband Vernon drove four hundred miles to join Elvis at Fort Hood, Texas, where they lived off base in a three-bedroom trailer under the army regulation that allowed soldiers to live with their families if they were nearby. But by the end of July it was obvious that Gladys was seriously ill; she was losing her motor coordination and her mental faculties also seemed affected.

On a weekend pass Elvis drove his parents to Fort Worth, where they caught the train back to Memphis, returning on August 9. Gladys immediately entered Methodist Hospital, where doctors diagnosed hepatitus, a liver infection that Gladys didn't seem to have the strength to fight. She was suffering from severe liver damage and her condition was critical. Elvis managed to obtain leave on August 12 and arrived at his mother's bedside that night. He stayed there for twenty-four hours, until she urged him to go home to Graceland and get some sleep. A few hours after he had left, Gladys suffered a heart attack and died. Vernon, who was with his wife when she died, later told his son, "She woke me up struggling. She was suffering for breath. I got to her as quick as I could and the nurse and doctor put her in an oxygen tent. But it was too late." Elvis, awakened by the telephone call that his mother was gone, rushed to the hospital, where he wept and prayed at her bedside for hours.

Debasing the Merchandise

Elvis Presley's manager, Colonel Tom Parker, often spoke about his philosophy of managing the star's career. "A sure way to debase your merchandise is to give it away. I don't believe in overexposure of an artist. I think one of the reasons Elvis is a star is that he hasn't appeared too much in person or on television. Make the fans clamor for a view of the product." Of course, as writer Elaine Dundy has pointed out, a sure way to debase your star is to refer to him as a piece of merchandise.

Debut of Raquel Welch

The first time Raquel Welch appeared on the movie screen was as a walk-on in the 1964 film *Roustabout*, starring Elvis Presley.

D

The Decision to Marry

Priscilla Beaulieu moved into Graceland in 1963, and she was for years Elvis's unofficial steady girlfriend—although that didn't keep him from having other girlfriends, many of them celebrities. Elvis did not decide to marry Priscilla until late 1966, when he finally gave her an engagement ring and told her the wedding would be soon. Priscilla herself could not account for either the long delay in making the commitment or the timing of it when it did come.

Some biographers have suggested that the impetus for the marriage actually came from Colonel Parker. As Elvis became more and more bored with his movie career and lacked the challenge of live performances, his behavior became erratic. He started to go on the eating binges that caused him to gain thirty or forty pounds at a time; he took an interest in some of the more bizarre aspects of spiritualism; and his rowdy exploits with "the guys" were beginning to be talked about. According to one theory, the Colonel decided that Elvis needed marriage to "settle him down," and so he pushed his client into taking the long-deferred step. Another writer has pointed to the 1966 wedding of Frank Sinatra to Mia Farrow in a private ceremony in Las Vegas as the inspiration for the Elvis–Priscilla wedding. The Colonel supposedly hoped such a marriage might revive Elvis's sagging career in the same way it helped Frank's. A third theory suggests that the Colonel was worried that the well-kept secret of Priscilla's long residence at Graceland would become public knowledge and possibly destroy Elvis's career.

In her book, *Elvis: Precious Memories*, Sue Wiegert quotes a fellow Elvis fan, who says Elvis told her he didn't love Priscilla and never would, but that he felt responsible for her. Wiegert also quotes Elvis's housekeeper as saying that Elvis told her on the eve of the wedding that he didn't want to get married but was being pressured into it. A certain reluctance on Elvis's part would be easy to understand. He already had all the love any man could want from his fans, his friends, and a variety of attractive women. Marriage could easily have a negative effect on the devotion of his fans, and thus on his career. On the other hand, Elvis wanted and needed that one special someone in his life, and his relationship with Priscilla seemed a stable and happy one.

The Deputy

Because of occasional threats on his life, often from men whose wives or girlfriends had become infatuated with the nation's idol, Elvis Presley wanted to carry a gun for his protection. In Tennessee, it was against the law for private citizens to carry guns, but the problem was solved when Shelby County Sheriff Roy Nixon swore Elvis in as a special deputy on September 1, 1970, giving the star the right to carry a handgun. Photos of Elvis in his later years indicate that he frequently availed himself of his privilege.

The "Designing Women" Episode

A November 1988 episode of the CBS sit-com "Designing Women" featured a plotline that sends Charlene, a long-time Elvis fan, on a visit to Graceland, accompanied by the other three stars of the show. The four women encounter a fan who once took her twin daughters to an Elvis concert and was thrilled when Elvis told her the babies were "almost as pretty as their momma" and kissed all three of them. Another fan paying homage at Graceland is a truck driver whose son, dying of leukemia, was visited by Elvis in the hospital; Elvis gave the child his belt buckle, which the father later buried with the boy. As Julie Banhart, president of the Suspicious Minds Fan Club, said, "This was the first time I've seen a show built around Elvis which caught the essence of both the man and his talent, capturing not only Elvis but us, and the relationship between Elvis and his fans."

The script was sent to the Presley estate for approval, which was withheld. According to business manager Joseph Rascoff, "They presented a script to us that we felt was not something we would be proud of or that fans would appreciate." Although the estate threatened to sue, the Graceland episode of "Designing Women" was taped and aired anyway. Afterward, the lawsuit threat was dropped and another estate spokesperson, C. Barry Ward, commented that "on balance, we viewed the show as positive."

Dexedrine

According to published reports, Elvis Presley was first introduced to Dexedrine, a stimulant that is sold only by prescription, while he was in the army. While he was stationed in Germany his unit was often dispatched on maneuvers that lasted for several days. To keep the men in his unit awake and alert, a sergeant gave them all Dexedrine pills. Elvis, who had always liked to stay up all night, found the pills helped him maintain his preferred life-style. He got into the habit of taking them regularly—a habit which he continued when he got back to Graceland.

Did Elvis Have Bone Cancer?

Three separate sources, in their respective autobiographies, have claimed that they were told that Elvis Presley was dying of bone cancer. The stories come from Kathy Westmoreland, Charlie Hodge, and Larry Geller, but it appears all three received their information from the same source, Dr. George Nichopoulos. According to the sources quoting Dr. Nick, it was the reason he was prescribing so many pain-killers for the star. The doctor has never himself commented publicly on this issue and there was nothing in the autopsy report to confirm the story. At this point, it seems unlikely that the report can be either proved or disproved.

The Divorce

On February 23, 1972, Priscilla Beaulieu Presley moved out of the Presley home in Los Angeles's Holmby Hills section and into her own apartment in another area of the city. On January 8, 1973, his birthday, Elvis filed for a California divorce, citing "irreconcilable differences" that had caused the breakdown in the marriage. The divorce was granted in Santa Monica on October 11, 1973. Priscilla was granted full custody of the couple's daughter Lisa Marie and received a financial settlement reported to be worth about $2 million, half paid at the time of the divorce and half in a ten-year period thereafter. She also received $4,000 a month in child support.

In order to get that settlement, Priscilla had hired the law firm of Tanker, Toll and Leavitt to repudiate an earlier settlement to which she had informally agreed with Elvis. That called for just $100,000 in cash, plus $1,000 a month in alimony and $500 in child support. Priscilla's lawyers told the court that she had been unaware of the extent of Elvis's assets, and had not been informed by the lawyer he selected for her (who was also his lawyer) that she might have a right to half of his total net worth. The new settlement was quickly reached.

"Do You Know How to Wiggle?"

In the last few years of Elvis Presley's life, he was often tired and ill and he showed little of the sexy sparkle and raw energy on which his career had been based. One day when Elvis was in the kitchen asking for a snack, one of the recently hired cooks was teasing her employer. "Mr. P.," she joked, "do you know how to wiggle?" Elvis shot back, "How the hell do you think I got this big house on this hill?"

The Doctor Discusses His Patient

After Elvis Presley died, Dr. George "Nick" Nichopoulos gave an interview in which he described some of the problems of his most famous patient.

There were a couple of tours, one Vegas tour and maybe a couple of other tours, where the shows didn't go too well because he was oversedated . . . He always wanted to keep

D

something there by his bed in case he'd wake up. He'd wake up and think he wasn't going back to sleep. He'd be half asleep, and he'd reach over and take whatever was there. Maybe three or four or five sleeping pills. Then next day, try to get him up, no way to get him up. There were several times when he was a robot onstage.

"Dodger"

Elvis Presley nicknamed his grandmother, Minnie Mae Presley, "Dodger." The genesis of the name lay in one of Elvis's childhood temper tantrums. In the course of it, he threw a baseball at his grandmother's head. He was impressed by the way his grandmother agilely managed to dodge the ball, so he started calling her "Dodger."

Dogcatcher

In about 1940, Tom Parker left the American Royal Show. For a time he worked as country singer Gene Austin's advance man, but Austin wanted to go back to Tennessee and Parker wanted to stay in Tampa, Florida, where he had married a local woman, Marie Mott. So Parker found himself a new job there—he was appointed the dogcatcher for the Hillsborough County Humane Society. The job carried the perk of a rent-free apartment upstairs, as well as unlimited access to such items as tires, sugar, meat, and gasoline, which were rationed at the start of World War II. Some- how Parker also managed to get himself classified as 3-A in the draft, deferred "by reason of extreme hardship to dependents."

Parker turned a personal profit from his days as dogcatcher, not only by pocketing some of the money he collected on behalf of the homeless animals, but also by starting a pet cemetery in the Humane Society's backyard, charging Tampa residents $100 for a sentimental send-off for their departed animal companions. When the war was over, Parker left the Humane Society to act as manager of country-and-western singer Eddy Arnold.

Domino

Domino was a black quarterhorse with one white stocking that Elvis Presley gave to Priscilla Beaulieu before they were married. Like many teenage girls, she had always loved horses and was thrilled to have one of her own. After watching Priscilla ride, Elvis decided he wanted a horse of his own so he could go out with her, and he bought a palomino named Rising Sun. Soon he and his whole entourage were riding everywhere; he even bought the Circle G Ranch in Mississippi to pursue the horsy life that was his momentary craze. After Elvis and Priscilla were divorced, Priscilla took Domino with her to her new home in California.

D

"Don't"

"Don't" was written for Elvis Presley by Jerry Leiber and Mike Stoller, and he recorded it in the fall of 1957. Advance orders for the single topped one million copies before its release, and it climbed all the way to the number one position on the pop charts.

"Don't Be Cruel"

Elvis Presley's rendition of the classic Otis Blackwell song "Don't Be Cruel" was one of the biggest-selling singles of all time. Elvis recorded the song in his July 1956 session for RCA; it features Scotty Moore on guitar, Bill Black on bass, and backup vocals by the Jordanaires. The recording was released as the flipside of "Hound Dog." "Don't Be Cruel" rose to the number one spot on the pop, country, and rhythm-and-blues charts all at the same time, and it stayed at the top of the pop charts for seven weeks. The record sold at least nine million copies.

In 1988, the hit song associated with Elvis was covered by the rock group Cheap Trick, and it rose to number four on the pop charts.

Morton Downey Jr.

A journalist asked controversial talk-show host Morton Downey Jr. what he would ask Elvis Presley if he could have the singer on his show today. Downey shot back, "My first question would have been, 'Why did it take you more than three days to rise from the dead?' "

Draft Notice

On December 10, 1957, Elvis A. Presley received his official draft notice from the Memphis draft board. It was announced at that time that the star had already been given his physical exam and had been found fit for active duty. Elvis was not expected to be called to enter the army until sometime in late 1958, but ten days later he was told to report for duty on January 20, 1958. The movie studio to which he was then under contract, Paramount, sent a letter to the draft board, asking for a delay so Elvis could complete the filming of *King Creole*, then about to start shooting. Postponing the movie for two years would have dealt the studio a severe economic loss. The draft board held that the request for a delay must come from Elvis himself; although the star told friends that he wanted to go immediately so he could get his required service behind him, he agreed to write a second letter, and his request was granted. It was not until March 24, 1958 that Elvis Presley reported for his induction into the army.

The Drawing Room at Graceland

Although Graceland was redecorated several times, the drawing room was always done in red and gold. In its final version, the furniture is carved and gilded fake Louis XVI with red velvet upholstery. There is a huge paneled fake fireplace surrounded by bookshelves filled with fake books, as well as a real white marble fireplace embedded in a wall of gold-streaked mirrored glass. Some critics have labeled the decor "early whorehouse," and others have called it suitable for the residence of a Mafia chieftain. Whatever else it may be, the room is a monument to Elvis Presley's delight in his ability to buy anything he wanted.

The Drug Problem

Elvis Presley began relying on drugs as early as 1959. When he was in the army he was given Dexedrine, an amphetamine, to stay awake during all-night maneuvers. Later he started taking other amphetamines as well as tranquilizers and barbiturates to help him relax and go to sleep. His pharmacological problem increased as the years went by, complicated by the prescription of other medicines for the various health problems he developed. For example, he often took a drug prescribed to relax his colon, in order to help his digestive difficulties, and medication for hypertension, to control his glaucoma.

Dying at Forty-two

Elvis Presley was forty-two years old when he died. That was also the age Gladys Presley claimed to be at her death, and some people made much of the coincidence. In reality, she was forty-six, because she had shaved four years off her age at the time she married Vernon, who was just seventeen to her twenty-one.

The Dylan Connection

Elvis Presley was greatly perplexed by Bob Dylan's vocal style, but he recognized the genius of Bob's lyrics and recorded two of Dylan's songs: "Tomorrow Is a Long Time" (1966) and "Don't Think Twice, It's All Right" (1971). The late rock writer, Lester Bangs, once published an amusing imaginary conversation between Presley and Dylan, in which Dylan decides to go to Vegas with Elvis and sing protest songs "with arrangements that sound like a lounge band in the Catskills." The Dylan–Presley equation has not escaped Bob Dylan's fans, who talk about turning the house where the former Bobby Zimmerman grew up in Hibbing, Minnesota, into the "Graceland of the Far North." Dylan himself once commented about Elvis, "Elvis recorded a song of mine; that's the record I treasure most."

D

The Eagle's Nest

A popular nightclub in Memphis in the 1950s was the Eagle's Nest. Elvis Presley liked to hang out there and occasionally he managed to sing for the audience. According to Lucy de Barbin's book, *Are You Lonesome Tonight?*, the Eagle's Nest was where he met her in the fall of 1953, spark-ing a long-term romance and eventually, she claims, producing a child, her daughter Desiree. In 1954, Elvis made several professional appearances at the Eagle's Nest, along with Bill Black and Scotty Moore, and he also sang there with local musical celebrity Tiny Dixon.

Ear Music

Although Elvis Presley eventually learned to read music, he didn't like to play sheet music, complaining that it never sounded the way it looked. He picked tunes up by ear and liked to play with other musicians who had the same approach. "For my re-cording sessions," he once explained, "I like to work with ear musicians and not sheet musicians. They're great. You just hum or whistle or sing a tune for them twice and then they get to work, and in-side a minute or two, the joint is jumping."

An Early Elvis Concert

Bob Luman, a country singer who per-formed in the Memphis area in the 1950s, later recalled his first sight of Elvis on stage. "This cat came out in red pants and a green coat and a pink shirt and socks, and he had this sneer on his face and he stood behind the mike for five minutes, I'll bet, before he made a move. Then he hit his guitar a lick and broke two strings! I'd been playing ten years and I hadn't bro-ken a total of two strings. He made chills run up my back."

East Tupelo Consolidated School

Elvis Presley began his education at the East Tupelo Consolidated School, a few minutes' walk from his home in that small Mississippi town. Housing over seven hundred students from East Tupelo and the surrounding agricultural communities, the rural school, built in 1926, was unusual in that it had electricity, heat, and plumbing. For the time and place, East Tupelo Consolidated School had high standards for academic excellence and student deportment. Gladys Presley walked her young son back and forth to the school every single day—a tradition that was to continue until his graduation from high school.

Edmund

Edmund was a Pomeranian that was one of Elvis Presley's favorite pets at the time of his death.

Michael Edwards

Michael Edwards is a model and would-be actor who was romantically involved with Priscilla Presley from 1978 to 1986. Edwards, born in 1945, accompanied Priscilla to the Church of Scientology, which both she and Lisa Marie still attend. In 1988 Edwards published a kiss-and-tell book about his life with Priscilla and his secret attraction to the young Lisa Marie.

El Vez

One of the more amusing Elvis impersonators is a man who calls himself "El Vez," the Latino version of the King. Backed up by a female trio he calls the El Vettes, he sings such favorites as "Ain't Nothing but a Chihuahua," "That's All Right, Mamacita," and "In the Barrio." El Vez, in real life an art gallery curator named Robert Lopez, says, "Elvis is universal and crosses all cultures. My dream is to have a rainbow coalition of Elvises."

"El's Angels"

A nickname given Elvis Presley's entourage, in recognition of their generally rowdy behavior, was "El's Angels."

"Ma" Elliott

Elvis Presley tended to collect relatives at Graceland—even when they weren't his own. A case in point was the frequent months-long visits of "Ma" Elliott, the step-mother of Elvis's own stepmother, Dee Presley. Ma and Elvis got along well, and he treated her with the courtly behavior he always displayed toward elderly females.

Jimmy Ellis

Jimmy Ellis is a singer who can sound remarkably like Elvis Presley. Shortly after Elvis's death, under the pseudonym Orion Eckley Darnell, Jimmy recorded an album entitled *Reborn*, which was issued by Sun Records. Immediately rumors began to spread that the singer was actually Elvis Presley, who had faked his own death and then decided to return to making records under an assumed name. A whole biography for "Orion" was whipped up, which included a manager born in Tennessee named Colonel Mac Weiman. All the publicity helped get nine of Orion's singles on the country charts. Today Ellis is emphatic in saying that he, not Elvis Presley, is the real voice of Orion.

Elvis: The Album

The second Elvis Presley album released was called *Elvis*. Most of the cuts were recorded in September 1956, just a few weeks before the album's issue date of October 19. So great was the interest in Elvis at that point that the album hit the charts at the number six position and quickly rose to number one. Among the songs included on the album, which had a portrait of Elvis on the front cover, were "Long Tall Sally," "When My Blue Moon Turns to Gold," "Ready Teddy," and "Old Shep."

E

Elvis: The Musical

In late 1977, a musical based on the life of Elvis Presley was staged in London and won an award for best musical production of the year. Originally the play starred three different actors in the role of Elvis—Tim Whitnall, Shakin' Stevens, and P.J. Proby.

Elvis: The TV Movie

Elvis was a 1979 TV movie based on the life of Elvis Presley, produced by Dick Clark, of "American Bandstand" fame, and directed by John Carpenter, the master of schlock horror films. It starred Kurt Russell as Elvis (a role for which he received an Emmy nomination), Kurt's father Bing Russell as Elvis's father Vernon Presley, Pat Hingle as Colonel Parker, and in a piece of inspired casting, Shelley Winters as Gladys Presley. Ronnie McDowell dubbed the Elvis vocal numbers, which were produced by Felton Jarvis, for many years Elvis's producer at RCA, and the Jordanaires sang backup. Appearing as themselves were Charlie Hodge, Larry Geller, and Kathy Westmoreland. Sam Phillips of Sun Records was a consultant for the production. *Elvis* debuted on February 11, 1979 and drew the lion's share of the television audience that night.

Elvis: The TV Special

At the urging of manager Colonel Tom Parker, Elvis Presley agreed to tape a television special to be aired on December 3, 1968. It was an attempt to shore up his sagging career, which had begun to sink under the weight of innumerable bad movies and a spate of soundtrack albums that all sounded exactly alike.

The Colonel seemed to feel that the special should be modeled after the typical Elvis movie. Luckily for Elvis fans, the young director, Steve Binder, had different ideas, wanting to focus the show not on the superstar but on the talented musician who changed the musical tastes of a generation. Said Binder, "I felt very strongly that the TV special was Elvis's moment of truth . . . If he could do a special and prove he was still number one, then he could have a whole rejuvenation thing going." The special was to be taped before a live audience, the first time Elvis had been in front of real people since a benefit concert in Hawaii in 1961.

The special did contain some of the expected production numbers, with dancers and a large backup orchestra. But the highlight of the show came when Elvis sat on a small stage, relaxed and casual with musicians he had played with for years, including Scotty Moore and D.J. Fontana, and chatted, joked, and sang. He looked good, trim and stylish in black leather jacket and pants, and he sang with the old Elvis magic. The critic for *The New York Times*, Jon Landau, wrote, "There is something magical about watching a man who has lost himself, find his way home. He sang

E

with the kind of power people no longer expect from rock'n'roll performers. And while most of the songs were ten or twelve years old, he performed them as freshly as though they were written yesterday." Others were equally laudatory, and Elvis fans were in utter ecstasy.

Elvis: An American Musical

In July 1988, Elvis: An American Musical opened in Las Vegas before heading out for a long tour on the road. The musical production, which cost $3 million to mount and features more than 550 songs from the Presley repertoire, was an immediate hit. Portraying the Elvis legend on stage was such a big job that it took not one but three actors for the role of the King. Terry Mike Jeffrey played the young Elvis, Johnny Seaton the star in all his glory, and Julian Whitaker the mature Elvis of Vegas days. Whitaker spoke about the special experience of impersonating Elvis night after night. "There are moments when I get chills. I feel somebody beside me or standing behind me. It spooks me out."

Eventually retitled Elvis: A Rockin' Remembrance, the musical achieved both critical and box office success.

"Elvis '56"

"Elvis '56" was a TV special first seen on Cinemax in August 1987. The show, created by Alan and Susan Raymond, was a collection of clips from the early movies, montages of publicity stills, and some personal movies. The focus of the program was the year 1956, when Elvis became a superstar. "Elvis '56" was later released on videocassette.

"Elvis: Good Rockin' Tonight"

A pilot made for the 1989-90 TV season was "Elvis: Good Rockin' Tonight" It starred Michael St. Gerard as Elvis and Millie Perkins (with whom the real Elvis once co-starred in Wild in the Country) as his mother Gladys. Billy Green Bush was cast as Vernon. The plot hinged on events that happened to the Presley family before Elvis became a big star. The producer, Rick Husky, mentioned the appeal of such early Elvis stories as Vernon's imprisonment at Parchman Farm, the time little Elvis won the talent contest, and the time his pink car caught fire and burned as he drove to another one-night gig. The executive producer of the pilot was Priscilla Presley. She described the concept of the series: "This will be Elvis and the guys on the road, going from town to town, and the lives they touched, the shows they did, the human interest." The new show was scheduled to start in early 1990 on ABC-TV, according to co-producer Jerry Schilling.

E

Elvis—That's the Way It Is

In 1970, as Elvis Presley prepared his stage shows for the summer season in Las Vegas, the star was followed everywhere by a movie crew, shooting a documentary called *Elvis—That's the Way It Is.* The documentary, released in theaters later that year by MGM, showed Elvis, just eighteen months after the comeback of 1968 and still in great physical and vocal shape, rehearsing with the musicians and the backup vocal group, the Sweet Inspirations. All the musical performances in this film were vintage Elvis. Fans rejoiced as they watched him sing twenty-seven numbers, including his classics "That's All Right," "Blue Suede Shoes," "Suspicious Minds," "Heartbreak Hotel," "Can't Help Fallin' in Love with You," and "Mystery Train." The movie also gave audiences a glimpse of Elvis at his hardworking professional best. Elvis himself was very happy with the film, rightly calling it the best he had made in years.

Elvis: What Happened?

The first inside look at the dark side of Elvis Presley's life came with the publication of the book *Elvis: What Happened?* It was written by former Memphis Mafia members Red West, Sonny West, and Dave Hebler, with the aid of journalist Steve Dunleavy. The book shocked fans by speaking openly about Elvis's use of prescription drugs, his temper tantrums, and his occasional near-psychotic responses to emotional problems in his life. The book was published just a few weeks before Elvis's death and some insiders said the star was depressed and unhappy over the betrayal by old friends, as well as the negative impact of the book. The tell-all writers explained that they wrote the book as a way to reach Elvis and try to make him confront his problems. At the time the book appeared, there was much controversy over its accuracy. As other eyewitness accounts have subsequently appeared, confirming the general outlines of the book, the controversy has dwindled into mere carping over the authors' motives.

After Elvis died in 1977, some adoring fans pointed a finger of blame at the book and its authors in the belief that sorrow over the betrayal by friends is what killed Elvis. Others were angry that such a negative book existed at a time they wanted to remember all the good things about their hero. Many took positive action—stores reported that people were ripping out pages or gluing them together to make the books unsalable. It became almost a personal vendetta for the faithful fans, who still bristle over what they see as the Wests' disloyalty.

Elvis and the Beauty Queen

Elvis and the Beauty Queen was a 1981 made-for-TV movie that fictionalized the real-life relationship between Elvis Presley and Linda Thompson, which started after the star separated from Priscilla and lasted until a year and a half before his death. The role of Linda was played by Stephanie Zimbalist, and Don Johnson appeared as Elvis—putting on forty pounds to look like the singer in his later years. Ronnie McDowell sang the soundtrack. Linda Thompson, who served as a consultant during production, was much criticized by Elvis fans for authorizing the tell-all TV movie.

Elvis and Me

Elvis and Me was the title of the book Priscilla wrote (with coauthor Sandra Harmon) about her life with Elvis Presley. Published in 1985, the book was excoriated by many Elvis fans. It revealed the inside details that could be known only to Priscilla of Elvis's long courtship of the teenager who was to become his wife and the problems of their marriage. It became a bestseller in both hardcover and paperback and sparked the appearance of many other books about Elvis within the next few years. In 1988, Priscilla's personal story was aired as a TV movie. The movie version starred Dale Midkiff as Elvis and Susan Walters as Priscilla. Priscilla herself served as executive producer of the movie, along with Bernard Schwartz and Joel Stevens. Songs were performed by Ronnie McDowell. *Elvis and Me* was the highest-rated TV movie of the 1987-1988 season.

An Elvis Bibliography

It's been nearly thirty-five years since Elvis Presley first became a national star, and in that time a huge number of books and articles have been written about him. Here is a list of the books that were most useful to the writers of the present volume.

- de Barbin, Lucy, with Dary Matera, *Are You Lonesome Tonight?* New York: Villard Books, 1987.
- Cocke, Marian J., *I Called Him Babe.* Memphis: Memphis State University Press, 1979.
- Cotten, Lee, *All Shook Up.* London: Pierian Press, 1985.
- Dundy, Elaine, *Elvis and Gladys.* New York: Macmillan, 1985.
- Edwards, Michael, *Priscilla, Elvis and Me.* New York: Random House, 1988.
- Ehrenstein, David and Bill Reed, *Rock on Film.* New York: Delilah Books, 1982.
- Farren, Mick and Pearce Marchbank, *Elvis in His Own Words.* New York: Omnibus Press, 1977.
- Fitzgerald, Jim and Al Kilgore, *Elvis—The Paperdoll Book.* New York: St. Martin's Press, 1982.
- Gibson, J. Robert and Sid Shaw, *Elvis.* New York: McGraw-Hill, 1985.
- Goldman, Albert, *Elvis.* New York: McGraw-Hill, 1981.

- Haining, Peter, ed., *Elvis in Private*. New York: St. Martin's Press, 1987.
- Hanna, David, *Elvis: Lonely Star at the Top*. New York: Leisure Books, 1977.
- Hopkins, Jerry, *Elvis*. New York, Simon & Schuster, 1971.
- Hopkins, Jerry, *Elvis: The Final Years*. New York: St. Martin's Press, 1980.
- Lacker, Marty, Patsy Lacker, and Leslie S. Smith, *Elvis: Portrait of a Friend*. New York: Bantam Books, 1980.
- Latham, Caroline, *Elvis and Priscilla*. New York: NAL, 1985.
- Love, Robert, *Elvis Presley*. New York: Franklin Watts, 1986.
- Mann, May, *Elvis and the Colonel*. New York: Drake Publishing, 1975.
- Mann, Richard, *Elvis*. Van Nuys, CA: Bible Voice, 1977.
- Nelson, Peter, *King: When Elvis Rocked the World*. London: Proteus Books, 1985.
- Noland, Hal and Sean Shaver, *The Life of Elvis Presley*. London: Timur Publishing Company, 1979.
- Presley, Davada, Rick Stanley, David Stanley, Billy Stanley, and Martin Torgoff, *Elvis, We Love You Tender*. New York: Delacorte, 1981.
- Presley, Priscilla Beaulieu, with Sandra Harmon, *Elvis and Me*. New York: G.P. Putnam's Sons, 1985.
- Sakol, Jeannie, *The Wonderful World of Country Music*. New York: Delilah Communications, 1979.
- Stern, Jane and Michael Stern, *Elvis World*. New York: Alfred A. Knopf, 1987.
- Tharpe, Jac. L, ed., *Elvis: Images and Fancies*. Oxford, MS: The University of Mississippi Press, 1981.
- Torgoff, Martin, ed., *The Complete Elvis*. New York: Perigee Books, 1981.
- Vellenga, Dirk, with Mick Farren, *Elvis and the Colonel*. New York: Delacorte Press, 1988.
- West, Red, Sonny West, Dave Hebler, and Steve Dunleavy, *Elvis: What Happened?* New York: Ballantine Books, 1977.
- Westmoreland, Kathy, with William G. Quinn, *Elvis and Kathy*. Glendale, CA: Glendale House, 1987.
- Wootton, Richard, *Elvis!* New York: Random House, 1985.
- Worth, Fred L. and Steve D. Tamarius, *Elvis: His Life from A To Z*. Chicago: Contemporary Books, 1988.
- Yancy, Becky and Cliff Linedecker, *My Life with Elvis*. New York: St. Martin's Press, 1977.
- Zmijewsky, Steven and Boris Zmijewsky, *Elvis: The Films and Career of Elvis Presley*. Secaucus, NJ: Citadel Press, 1976.

Elvis in Concert

In June 1977, RCA recorded two live performances by Elvis Presley, in conjunction with the CBS TV special scheduled to appear later in the year. When Elvis died, the company decided to release the two-record set even before the telecast. Titled *Elvis in Concert* and packaged with an ad for all the Elvis albums in the RCA catalog, it was issued in October and almost immediately sold more than one million copies, going platinum. It stayed on the charts for seventeen weeks.

Elvis in Doonesburyland

In 1988, amidst increasing numbers of reports of Elvis sightings, cartoonist Garry Trudeau introduced an aging, fat, and nearly bald Elvis Presley into his comic strip, *Doonesbury*. The strip shows Elvis hiding aboard Donald Trump's yacht while he receives beautiful cellophane-wrapped baskets of drugs.

Elvis Is Back

In April 1960, Elvis Presley recorded the album *Elvis Is Back*. It was his first major studio date since early 1958, when he entered the army. Among the songs on the album are "Fever," the Peggy Lee hit; "Soldier Boy" and "I Will Be Home Again," thematically related to his army service; and the old Clyde McPhatter song, also covered by Johnny Ray, "Such a Night." The album, the first in two years to contain all new material, went gold and rose to the number two position on the album charts.

Elvis Lives

The year after Elvis Presley's death, a tribute to him appeared in the form of a Broadway show, *Elvis Lives*. It closed after very few performances.

"Elvis Memories"

"Elvis Memories" was a syndicated TV special produced by Elvis Presley's old friend, George Klein. It was first aired in 1981 and contained Elvis interviews and film clips.

The Elvis Monthly

The Elvis Monthly is a British fan magazine founded in 1959 by the president of an Elvis Presley fan club, Albert Hand, and distributed internationally by the Elvis Presley Fan Club.

Elvis on Tour

In 1973, Elvis Presley starred in his thirty-third movie, also to be his last, called *Elvis on Tour*. Like the 1970 success, *Elvis—That's the Way It Is*, the MGM movie was a documentary about the life of Elvis Presley; Elvis had become such a star that fans would rather see a movie about him than some fictional character he played. The movie followed Elvis as he went on tour with a concert performance, so audiences were able to see some of the highlights of his concerts, as well as the preparation for the performances. Also of special interest to Elvis fans was the fact that several sequences were shot on location at Graceland, providing a look at the fabled mansion (then strictly off limits to fans), as well as the "normal" everyday life of the superstar. There was enough footage shot at Graceland for Elvis's father Vernon to be listed in the credits as a cast member.

Elvis, often backed up by the Sweet Inspirations, who were with him on the tour, sings twenty-nine numbers in this film, including some of his classics, such as "That's All Right," "Mystery Train," "Burnin' Love," and "Suspicious Minds," and his popular covers of other performers' hits as well, such as Ray Charles's "I Got a Woman." The comedian who opened for him on the tour, Jackie Kahane, is also featured, and there are cameo appearances by some celebrities who attend the concerts and go backstage to say hello. The movie, along with a soundtrack album, was released in the summer of 1973.

The two young men who made *Elvis on Tour* were Bob Abel and Pierre Adidge. Abel had worked on a film about Robert F. Kennedy, and Abel and Adidge together had created a documentary of a Joe Cocker tour called *Mad Dogs and Englishmen*. Both men felt that the earlier Elvis documentary, *Elvis—That's the Way It Is*, failed to capture the real spirit of the rock idol of millions of fans. They wanted to memorialize the young rebellious guy who frightened parents and incited teenagers to wear strange hairdos and bizarre outfits—the anti-establishment side of Elvis that had become hidden under his increasingly conservative social views and his middle-aged Vegas appeal. The film cost only $600,000 to make (in addition to the $1 million fee paid to Elvis) and recouped its cost in the first three days of its release. The film won the year's Golden Globe Award, much to Elvis's excitement. An interesting footnote to *Elvis on Tour* is that the montage supervisor on the film was Martin Scorsese, later to become one of the most successful directors in Hollywood.

Elvis Parties

A currently popular social occasion is the Elvis party, in which guests come dressed as their hero. A variant allows the women to dress as Priscilla. To give just one example, Bob Pitman, the creator of MTV, gave an Elvis party for Halloween 1988 in which Tom Brokaw was one of the Elvises and Susan Saint James one of the Priscillas.

E

Elvis the Pelvis

Noting the way Elvis Presley moved his hips while he sang, the press dubbed him "Elvis the Pelvis."

Elvis Presley

Elvis Presley was not only the first album ever issued by the star, it was also the first album in history ever to sell one million copies. The RCA album was released in March 1956, with photos of Elvis on the front and back covers. Among the songs included were "Blue Suede Shoes," "I Got a Woman," "Just Because," "Blue Moon," and "Money Honey." The album stayed on the national charts for an amazing total of forty-nine weeks, ten of them in the number one spot. A digitally recorded version was reissued in 1985 to mark Elvis's fiftieth birthday.

Elvis Presley Automobile Museum

In 1989, Graceland Enterprises opened the Elvis Presley Automobile Museum, located across Elvis Presley Boulevard from Graceland. Together under one roof fans can see the 1956 Continental Mark II, the 1973 Stutz Blackhawk, the 1975 Ferrari Dino, the pink Jeep, the Mercedes 280 SL he bought Priscilla, and the pink Cadillac Eldorado. Admission to the Museum is $4.

Elvis Presley Boulevard

On January 18, 1972, the city of Memphis officially renamed ten miles of the four-lane Highway 51 South that passes in front of Graceland Elvis Presley Boulevard. There have often been so many Elvis fans waiting to get into Graceland that the line of cars has extended all the way back to Elvis Presley Boulevard.

In 1974, a fatal accident occurred on Elvis Presley Boulevard when a fan and her young child tried to cross from the Music Gate at Graceland to the other side of the highway, where their car was parked, and were struck by a car traveling at high speed. They were killed instantly. Two years later, Elvis donated a piece of land directly in front of Graceland to be developed as a turn-out lane and parking area, to prevent a recurrence of such a tragedy.

E

Elvis Presley's Boyhood Home

When Vernon and Gladys Presley were first married in 1933, they had no home of their own but slept on the floor of the little house that belonged to Vernon's cousin Vona Mae and her husband Marshall Brown. Months later, Vernon built a house for himself and his new bride. The site was a vacant lot next door to the home of Vernon's parents, J.D. and Minnie Mae Presley, on Saltillo Road in East Tupelo, Mississippi. The land belonged to a local dairy farmer, Orville Bean; in accordance with a common custom, Bean lent Vernon the money needed to pay for the building materials and then charged the Presleys rent for occupying the house of which he was the official owner.

Elvis Presley was born in the front room of this little house his father built. Its style was called "shotgun shack," because you could fire a shotgun in the front door and it would travel straight through the house and out the back door. The house was raised off ground level on stone stilts due to the constant danger of flooding from the nearby creek. The front room served as both sitting room and bedroom for all the family; the back room was the kitchen, dining room, and usual gathering place. There was no running water, and the bathroom was an outdoor privy. The little house was wired for electricity at the time the Tennessee Valley Authority brought power to much of the South, but the Presleys could not afford to pay an electric bill and used oil lamps instead.

In 1971, the house where Elvis was born was designated a state historical monument and opened to the public. Thanks to the work of the East Heights Garden Club, the birthplace has been furnished with items typical of that type of house in that period, although not belonging to the Presleys. The road on which it stands is now officially named Elvis Presley Drive, and the area is called Presley Heights. To obtain information about the birthplace, or to make a contribution toward its upkeep, write P.O. Box 1339, Tupelo MS 38801.

Elvis Presley Day in Tupelo

On September 27, 1956, the town of Tupelo, Mississippi, celebrated Elvis Presley Day, a commemoration that was part of the Mississippi-Alabama Fair and Dairy Show. Elvis performed to a huge audience at the fair and was given a parade through the town and a key to the city. It was a sweet homecoming for the twenty-two-year-old, who remembered vividly the poverty in which he had grown up in Tupelo. He donated the fee he received for his appearance to start a youth center in his hometown for the benefit of other youngsters like himself.

The Elvis Presley Enterprisers

In the 1960s in Hollywood, Elvis Presley organized his own football team, the Elvis Presley Enterprisers, to play against other stars' teams on Sundays at DeNeve Park in Bel Air. Among those who sometimes played for the Enterprisers were Ricky Nelson, Gary Lockwood, Max Baer, Jr., and Pat Boone.

Elvis Presley Memorial Trauma Center

The Elvis Presley Trauma Center in Memphis has been established and is supported by donations from Elvis fans all over the world. It is the third busiest trauma center in the U.S., treating about 3500 people each year, with state-of-the-art technology.

A Wall of Honor at the Center pays tribute to clubs and individual fans who have contributed $1000 or more. To make a contribution, write the center at 877 Jefferson Avenue, Memphis TN 38103.

The Elvis Presley Midget Fan Club

One of Colonel Tom Parker's publicity stunts to hype his client Elvis Presley's career in the mid-1950s was obviously right out of his own carnival past. He rounded up a group of dwarfs and midgets in a hotel in Chicago patronized by carny employees and presented them to the public as the Elvis Presley Midget Fan Club.

Elvis Presley Music Company

Elvis Presley Music Company was the publishing company that handled most of Elvis's music publishing activities for the duration of his recording life. Colonel Tom Parker set up the company, which dealt with rights to songs handled through BMI, the pop music professional association, at the same time that he negotiated Elvis's contract with RCA. Elvis was one of the first pop stars to have his own publishing company, enabling him to collect the publisher's share of royalties on each record sold—a move that brought in millions over the course of his career. Of course Elvis did not actually write the music that Elvis Presley Music Company published, but

E

writers who sold their music to be recorded by the star had to agree to the arrangement that gave him an increased share of the profits. Most of them felt they still came out ahead, considering the number of records any Elvis release always sold.

Elvis Presley Plaza

After the death of Elvis Presley the city of Memphis erected a larger-than-life statue of its most famous citizen on a small area of grass on downtown Beale Street that was renamed Elvis Presley Plaza. Sculpted by Eric Parks, the statue shows Elvis with his guitar. It is presently covered with graffiti, badly corroded, and bears the marks of vandalism. Repairs have been ordered by Memphis Mayor Hackett. The plaza is located near the Lansky Brothers store, where the young Elvis used to buy the clothes that shocked a generation.

"The Elvis Presley Story"

"The Elvis Presley Story" was a twelve-hour audio documentary on the life and career of Elvis Presley. It was written by Elvis biographer Jerry Hopkins and produced by Ron Jacobs. It was first aired on the radio in 1971 and has since been rebroadcast many times.

The Elvis Presley Youth Center

The Elvis Presley Youth Center, located on fourteen acres just behind the house where Elvis was born in East Tupelo, Mississippi, was started with money donated by Elvis himself. When the star appeared in Tupelo on what was designated Elvis Presley Day in the summer of 1956, he donated his fee to start the center; he later gave additional funds as he thought they were needed. One of Elvis's conditions in founding the center was that the city would have to buy the land from Orville Bean, the Presley family's former landlord and the man who pressed the charges that sent Vernon Presley to prison. Elvis had grandiose plans for the youth center and was dismayed when the guitar-shaped swimming pool he envisioned ended up as a plain rectangle like any other public pool. He was convinced the city had wasted his money and his future support of the youth center was lukewarm.

Elvis Presley Youth Foundation

In 1958 Elvis Presley founded the Elvis Presley Youth Foundation in Memphis. The star was always its biggest contributor. The foundation provided scholarships for needy young people. Today, it still receives a portion of the income generated by the Presley estate through the sale of Elvis's image and likeness.

"Elvis Presley's Graceland"

In January 1985, the Showtime cable channel aired a program called "Elvis Presley's Graceland," which was a tour of the mansion conducted by the star's ex-wife, Priscilla. The show was produced and directed by Steve Binder, the man behind the 1968 TV special that helped revive Elvis's sagging career. Binder says he consciously modeled the program on Jacqueline Kennedy's televised tour of the White House in 1962. Priscilla walks the viewer through all the rooms of Graceland that are open to the public and adds her own running commentary on some memories of her life there with Elvis. The program is currently available on videocassette from the Graceland Gift Shop. For further information, write: Graceland Gifts, 3797 Elvis Presley Blvd., Memphis TN 38116

"Elvis Pretzel"

A derogatory nickname for Elvis Presley, invented in Hollywood, was "Elvis Pretzel." One account has it that the name was first used by Humphrey Bogart.

The Elvis Rose

In 1980, the American Rose Society registered a rose named Elvis in honor of Elvis Presley. The rose is a light red color with a touch of white at the base of the petals.

Elvis Sails

In the fall of 1958, Private First Class Elvis Presley's army unit was sent to Germany. Before he boarded the troop ship in New York, Elvis held a press conference, which was recorded and issued as an EP by RCA— already facing a shortage of new recordings by their star. The record was called *Elvis Sails*. In the interview, Elvis talked about how nice the other soldiers in his unit were, and how he was looking forward to meeting some of his German fans.

In response to a question about his mother's recent death, Elvis said somberly, "Everybody loves their mother, but I was an only child and my mother was always with me, all my life. It was like losing a friend, a companion, someone to talk to. I could wake her at any hour of the day or night if I was troubled by something." *Elvis Sails* sold briskly—even though it didn't contain a single song.

Elvis Week

Every year at Graceland, the week immediately preceding the day Elvis Presley died, August 16, is celebrated as Elvis Week. Its climax is the candlelight vigil on the night of his death, when thousands of mourning fans carry candles in a long procession from the Music Gate to the Garden of Meditation, Elvis's final resting place.

Elvis' Christmas Album

In November 1957, RCA issued *Elvis' Christmas Album*, a compilation of traditional Christmas songs added to several spiritual songs that had previously appeared on his *Peace in the Valley* LP. Packaged as a gift item, with ten pages of color photos of Elvis and a tag with spaces to write in the names of the donor and the recipient of the gift, *Elvis' Christmas Album* hit the top spot on the album charts by December and remained on the charts for a total of seven weeks. In 1985, a digitally recorded version of the album was rereleased.

Engaged to Elvis

Shortly before the Christmas season of 1966, Elvis Presley gave Priscilla Beaulieu an engagement ring. The center stone was a three-and-a-half carat diamond, which was encircled by a ring of smaller diamonds on a detachable band.

Joe Esposito

Joe Esposito was a young man from Chicago who met Elvis Presley when they were both in the army. Afterward, Joe went to work for Elvis and is generally acknowledged to have been one of the most competent and devoted of the so-called Memphis Mafia. He served as Elvis's best man at his wedding, and Joe and his wife, Joanie, were frequent companions of Elvis and Priscilla. For many years Joe acted as Elvis's accountant, and was both honest and dedicated to Elvis's interests. Elvis once got mad at Joe for telling the Colonel some of the truth about the star's increasingly drug-dependent life-style and fired him. But within six months "Diamond Joe," as he was nicknamed, was back in the entourage again and remained one of Elvis's most trusted insiders. There were continual rumors about links between Joe and the Chicago underworld, based more on the perception of Joe as businesslike and effective rather than on any reality of a criminal connection. After Elvis's death Joe became the road manager of the BeeGees. In 1988, despite his long-time friendly relationship with Priscilla, he found himself the target of a lawsuit by the Elvis Presley estate, in a dispute over rights to a video-cassette called *My Home Movies of Elvis*, film footage shot by Joe of Elvis relaxing at Graceland and the Circle G Ranch. Although the videocassette is currently being sold in Great Britain, its sale was stopped in the U.S. by the Presley estate's claim to ownership of all likenesses and images of Elvis. In the summer of 1989 a settlement was reached.

Joe has given freely of his time and energy to various Elvis fan clubs since the star's death and remains a favorite figure of many devoted Elvis fans, who are supporting his fight against the estate.

"Eternal Flame"

In 1989, the rock group The Bangles had a Number One hit with their single "Eternal Flame." According to lead singer Susanna Hoffs, who was also one of the writers of the song, it was inspired by a visit to Graceland. "When we visited Elvis's home, we went to the back where they have the grave, and it was raining. At the head of the grave there was a plexiglass box half-filled with water. We asked what it was and the tour guide said that it was the eternal flame but explained that it was actually 'semi-eternal.' "

Exploiting Elvis

From the moment Elvis Presley achieved national fame there were people who began to exploit his name, his music, his performance style, and his unusual hairstyle and clothing. Among the more blatant attempts to cash in on Elvis were the following novelty songs:

"Elvis Presley for President"
"My Boy Elvis"

"Elwood Pretzel Fan Club"
"Bye Bye Elvis"
"Dear 53310761"
"When Elvis Marches Home Again"
"Gonna Get Even with Elvis' Sergeant"
"I Wanna Be Elvis Presley's Sergeant"
"I'm Lonesome for Elvis"
"I'm Not Trying To Be Elvis"
"I Dreamed I Was Elvis"
"I Wanna Be Elvis"
"I Wanna Spend X-Mas with Elvis"
"I Want Elvis for Christmas"
"Don't Knock Elvis"
"Tupelo Mississippi Flash"
"He Ate Too Many Jelly Donuts"
"Around the World with Elwood Pretzel"
"My Baby's Crazy 'bout Elvis"
"Elvis Stole My Baby"
"The All American Boy"

The phenomenon of cashing in on Elvis continues. Stories and pictures of Elvis, dead or alive, sell magazines and supermarket tabloids. Song lyrics allude to his life and influence; for example, Mojo Nixon had a hit with his 1988 song, "Elvis Is Everywhere," about recent sightings of the star, followed by his 1989 success, "619-238-KING," the number of a hotline to report such sightings. And he is frequently invoked on TV shows, such as the 1988 episode of "Golden Girls" that had Sophia getting married before an audience of Elvis impersonators, or the episode of "Charles in Charge" in 1989 in which the family takes in a homeless Elvis impersonator. On ABC's daytime soap "Loving," leading man Todd McDurmont performed his own Elvis impersonation in 1989, singing "Blue Suede Shoes."

Ellie Ezerzer

Ellie Ezerzer was a Hollywood hair stylist with whom Priscilla Presley became involved for a time, after the breakup of her relationship with Mike Stone.

Shelley Fabares

Actress Shelley Fabares costarred in three movies with Elvis Presley—*Girl Happy* (1964), *Spinout* (1966), and *Clambake* (1967). Fabares, the niece of actress Nanette Fabray, was a child star on TV in *The Donna Reed Show* and *The Brian Keith Show*. In 1962, Shelley had a hit record that reached the number one spot on the charts, "Johnny Angel." Ironically it was knocked from the pinnacle by one of Elvis's records, "Good Luck Charm."

According to Elvis's secretary Becky Yancy, he called Shelley his favorite of all his costars and later made a point of watching all the TV episodes of "Love American Style" in which she appeared. A legendary kiss between Elvis and Shelley occurred during the filming of *Spinout*; when the director yelled "Cut" on a staged embrace, the couple continued to kiss for three full minutes. Shelley today is married to actor Mike Farrell, former star of the "M*A*S*H" TV series. In 1989 she returned to television as costar of the ABC series, "Coach."

A Fabulous Concert in Amory, Mississippi

In early 1955, there was a concert in the small town of Amory, Mississippi, that Sun Records decided to use as a showcase for its impressive roster of new talent. Lucky ticket holders that evening heard Carl Perkins, Johnny Cash, and Elvis Presley, all on the same bill.

Elvis co-starred with Shelley Fabares in three movies; this publicity still is from *Girl Happy* in 1965. They dated briefly and remained good friends thereafter. (Photo from Neal Peters Collection)

Fairgrounds Amusement Park

One of Elvis Presley's favorite activities whenever he was in Memphis was to rent the Fairgrounds Amusement Park for a night of fun with his friends. The management officially closed the park to the public during Elvis's playtime, but anyone who wanted to go on one of the fifty rides with the star could usually get invited. His favorites were the Rocket, with cars that spun around on a tilted circular base, and the Pipin, a roller coaster. He also liked to get all his buddies in the Dodgem cars, where they would spend hours happily crashing into one another with reckless abandon. When Elvis rented the park, he personally controlled all the rides, and no one could get off until he was ready to stop. He would sometimes take the roller coaster on as many as 20 circuits before he quit, and he expected everyone else to enjoy it as much as he did.

F

The Family on the Payroll

Elvis Presley felt it was his obligation to look after his entire family—both Presleys and Smiths—after he became rich and successful, and he often accomplished that goal by putting his relatives on the payroll. Employees who were also members of the family included his father Vernon, Uncle Vester Presley, Aunt Delta Mae Presley Biggs, cousins Gene, Junior, Travis, Billy, and Bobby Smith, as well as Patsy Presley and her husband Gee Gee Gambill.

Elvis signs autographs for lucky fans. His generosity toward his fans was legendary. (Photo from Neal Peters Collection)

Fan Clubs

Among the many Elvis Presley fan clubs are:

Blue Hawaiians
Elvis Crusaders
Elvis Is King
Elvisly Yours
For Ever For Elvis
Forever Faithful Elvis Presley Fan Club
House of Elvis
Hound Dog Elvis Fan Club

International Elvis Presley Fan Club
Kissin' Cousins International Fan Club
Love Me Tender Elvis Presley Fan Club
Never Ending Elvis Fan Club
Ready Teddy Elvis Presley Fan Club
Sound of Elvis Fan Club
Stuck on You Forever Elvis Presley Fan Club
Suspicious Minds
That's The Way It Is
Today Tomorrow and Forever Fan Club

F

Fans Disappointed with Lisa

Many devoted Elvis Presley fans have expressed their disappointment with his daughter Lisa Marie. They had looked to her to lead a crusade to keep her father's memory not only alive but untarnished. Her public acknowledgment of his excessive use of drugs; her support of the way the estate is running Graceland; her willingness to sign papers that defer her inheritance for a five-year period; and above all, her closeness to her mother, who will always be an object of hostility to Elvis fans, have led fans and fan club newsletters to brand Lisa a "disappointment" to their hopes.

Fans Sue Elvis

Four people who called themselves Elvis Presley fans sued the singer for $1 million apiece in 1973. Kenneth MacKenzie, Jr., Mario Martinez, Roberto MacKenzie, and Marcello Jose Filas claimed they had been attacked by the star's bodyguards at the Las Vegas Hilton on February 19, 1973. The suit, in which Elvis was defended by Los Angeles attorney Ronald Dwyer, was later dismissed in court.

Ann Farrell

Ann Farrell claims to have married Elvis Presley in 1957 in Alabama. Like other women who have claimed to be Mrs. Elvis, she is unable to produce any supporting documentation.

Fastest Guitar Alive

The movie *Fastest Guitar Alive* was a carbon copy of the first Elvis Presley movie, *Love Me Tender*, and it was originally intended by MGM to be his second feature film. But the project was put on a back burner, only to be revived ten years later as a vehicle for Roy Orbison. The 1968 movie about Confederate spies, also starring Sammy Jackson, was not a big box office success.

The Fatal Accident Outside Graceland

By the morning of the day Elvis Presley died, more than seventy-five thousand fans had already gathered outside Graceland to pay their last respects to their idol. That afternoon, about twenty thousand of them were allowed to file past his coffin as he lay in state in the mansion in a white suit and a navy shirt. Even after the Music Gate to Graceland was closed, crowds continued to gather throughout the night. In the early hours of the following morning, August 17, 1977, the day on which Elvis's funeral took place, a car driven by an eighteen-year-old Memphis youth swerved into the crowd of mourners keeping vigil on Elvis Presley Boulevard. Two young women from Monroe, Louisiana, Juanita Joan Johnson and Marie Alice Hovarter, were killed instantly, and a third, Tammy Baiter of St. Clair, Missouri, was critically injured. The driver, Trestise Wheeler, was arrested and charged with drunken driving and two counts of second-degree murder. The tragedy further darkened the sad day.

The Fate of the Fifties Idols

At the time that Elvis Presley achieved national stardom with his roll-and-rock hits, there were of course other young performers who were also making hit records and attracting fans. When you review what happened to many of the other 1950s teen favorites, you begin to appreciate the fact that rock and roll is a dangerous profession. Even though Elvis died at forty-two, he could be classified as a survivor. Look at what happened to some of the others:

- Gene Vincent was crippled in a car accident.
- Eddie Cochran was killed in the same accident.
- Jerry Lee Lewis had to drop out of public view for a time, after he admitted to marrying his thirteen-year-old cousin.
- Chuck Berry was arrested for transporting a minor across state lines. He was also charged with tax evasion.
- Buddy Holly, Richie Valens, and the Big Bopper all died in the same plane crash.

Favorite Foods

Among Elvis Presley's favorite foods were:

Meatball sandwiches
King Cotton bacon
Peanut butter and banana sandwiches
Vanilla ice cream
Pepsi, and none of that diet stuff either

Spanish omelettes
Hot dog buns—cold, dry, without a hot dog
Pork chops with sauerkraut
Mashed potatoes and gravy
Cheeseburgers, cheeseburgers, cheeseburgers

Favorite Movies

Elvis Presley loved to watch old movies on television, and many of his favorites were the sentimental ones Hollywood used to do so well. The films Elvis liked to watch over and over again included:

* *Wuthering Heights* (the Merle Oberon—Laurence Olivier version)
* *It's a Wonderful Life*
* *Monty Python and the Holy Grail*

* *Miracle on 34th Street*
* *The Godfather*
* *The Way of All Flesh*
* *A Gathering of Eagles*
* *Patton*
* *Mr. Skeffington*
* *The Great Caruso*
* *Les Miserables*
* *Letter from an Unknown Woman*
* *One Night of Love*
* *Dr. Strangelove*

Fear of Flying

For many years, Elvis Presley was afraid of flying. His fear was not completely irrational, in view of the fact that so many entertainers had been killed in crashes of small planes as they headed from one concert date to another. For example on February 3, 1959, a single plane crash killed Buddy Holly, Richie Valens, and the Big Bopper, all of whom were to appear on the same bill that evening.

Elvis told Roy Orbison that his own fear was due to a close call in a two-engine charter plane early in his career, when he was traveling with backup musicians Scotty Moore, Bill Black, and D.J. Fontana. One of the engines failed, and the pilot was lucky to be able to set the plane down safely on a tiny deserted airstrip he had spotted below. John Lennon remembered the story Elvis had told him about that experience. "I once took off from Atlanta, Georgia, in a small two-engine plane, and one of the engines failed," Lennon quotes Elvis as saying. "Boy, was I scared! I really thought my number was up. We had to take everything that was sharp out of our pockets and rest our heads on pillows between our knees. When we finally got down safely, the pilot was soaking with sweat, although there was snow on the ground outside."

Other accounts put the lion's share of

the blame for Elvis's fear of flying on his mother Gladys, who was herself terrified of planes and hated to know he was up in one. To make his early concert appearances, Elvis drove hundreds of miles across the South. Later he traveled in the comfort and luxury of a customized bus; when he was discharged from the army, he went home from New York by private train. It was not until Elvis began appearing regularly in Las Vegas that he started to fly back and forth from Graceland. Then he bought his own big jets and was very careful about seeing that they were carefully maintained.

The Federal Narcotics Officer's Badge

Elvis Presley collected badges from police departments and sheriff's offices all over the country and nothing made him happier than membership in some law-enforcement body. The star had his heart set on a badge from the Federal Narcotics Bureau, and he requested one from its head, John Finlater. Finlater said he couldn't give the badge to a civilian and offered him an F.B.I. badge instead. Elvis later brought up the subject during a meeting with President Nixon in December 1970. Nixon instantly dispatched an aide to Finlater's office to get one of the badges, which the President then formally presented to Elvis. It remained one of his most cherished possessions for the rest of his life.

Lamar Fike

Lamar Fike was a member of Elvis Presley's entourage, the so-called Memphis Mafia. An intimidating hulk weighing nearly three hundred pounds, Lamar could frighten any unruly fan simply by looming up at Elvis's side. Lamar had been near Elvis since 1957, when he left his home in Texas and simply showed up at Graceland ready to do anything he could to help his idol. Lamar, nicknamed "The Great Speckled Bird" by other members of the Presley entourage, traveled with Elvis to his live appearances and kept him company at home; he even went to live in Germany during the time Elvis was stationed there. Lamar learned to work the lighting for Elvis's Vegas shows and then became involved with the road management. In 1962, he left to work as road manager for country-and-western singer Brenda Lee and later also became the manager of the Nashville office of one of the music publishers that handled Elvis's songs, Hill & Range. He remained close to Elvis, even though he was managing other artists. Elvis arranged and paid for an intestinal bypass operation that allowed Lamar to lose weight, eventually slimming him down to about one hundred fifty pounds. After Elvis's death Lamar collaborated with author Albert Goldman in his commercially successful negative portrait of Elvis.

F

Film Grosses

In 1965 Colonel Tom Parker told the press that the seventeen films his client Elvis Presley had made to that date had already grossed more than $125 million.

The Filmography

1. *Love Me Tender* 20th Century-Fox (1956) 89 min.
   Director: Robert Webb
   Producer: David Weisbart
   Screenwriter: Robert Buckner
   Cast: Elvis Presley, Richard Egan, Debra Paget, Robert Middleton, William Campbell, Neville Brand, Mildred Dunnock

2. *Loving You* Paramount (1956) 101 min.
   Director: Hal Kanter
   Producer: Hal B. Wallis
   Screenwriters: Herbert Baker, Hal Kanter, from a story by Mary Agnes Thompson
   Cast: Elvis Presley, Lizabeth Scott, Dolores Hart, Wendell Corey, James Gleason

3. *Jailhouse Rock* MGM (1957) 97 min.
   Director: Richard Thorpe
   Producer: Pandro S. Berman
   Screenwriter: Guy Trosper, based on a story by Ned Young
   Cast: Elvis Presley, Judy Tyler, Mickey Shaughnessy, Dean Jones, Jennifer Holden, Anne Neyland

4. *King Creole* Paramount (1958) 116 min.
   Director: Michael Curtiz
   Producer: Hal. B Wallis
   Screenwriters: Herbert Baker and Michael Vincente Gazzo, based on the novel *A Stone for Danny Fisher* by Harold Robbins
   Cast: Elvis Presley, Carolyn Jones, Walter Matthau, Dolores Hart, Dean Jagger, Liliane Montevecchi, Vic Morrow

5. *G.I. Blues* Paramount (1960) 104 min.
   Director: Norman Taurog
   Producer: Hal B. Wallis
   Screenwriters: Edmund Beloin, Henry Garson
   Cast: Elvis Presley, Juliet Prowse, James Douglas, Robert Ivers

6. *Flaming Star* 20th Century-Fox (1960) 87 min.
   Director: Don Siegel
   Producer: David Weisbart
   Screenwriters: Clair Huffaker, Nunnally Johnson
   Cast: Elvis Presley, Barbara Eden, Dolores Del Rio, Steve Forrest, Rudolfo Acosta, Richard Jaeckel

7. *Wild in the Country* 20th Century-Fox (1961) 114 min.
   Director: Philip Dunne
   Producer: Jerry Wald
   Screenwriter: Clifford Odets, based on a novel by J.R. Salamanca
   Cast: Elvis Presley, Tuesday Weld, Hope Lange, Millie Perkins, Rafer Johnson, John Ireland, Gary Lockwood, Christina Crawford. Cameo by Bobby West.

8. *Blue Hawaii* Paramount (1961) 100 min.
   Director: Norman Taurog
   Producer: Hal B. Wallis
   Screenwriter: Hal Kanter, based on a story by Allan Weiss
   Cast: Elvis Presley, Angela Lansbury, Joan Blackman, Roland Winters, Nancy Walters

F

9. *Follow That Dream* United Artists (1962) 110 min.
Director: Gordon Douglas
Producer: David Weisbart
Screenwriter: Charles Lederer, based on the novel *Pioneer Go Home* by Richard Powell.
Cast: Elvis Presley, Anne Helm, Arthur O'Connell, Joanna Moore

10. *Kid Galahad* Paramount (1962) 95 min.
Director: Phil Karlson
Producer: David Weisbart
Screenwriter: William Fay, based on the 1937 Warner Brothers movie of the same name written by Francis Wallace
Cast: Elvis Presley, Lola Albright, Gig Young, Joan Blackman, Charles Bronson

11. *Girls! Girls! Girls!* Paramount (1962) 106 min.
Director: Norman Taurog
Producer: Hal B. Wallis
Screenwriters: Edward Anhalt and Allan Weiss, based on a story by Allan Weiss
Cast: Elvis Presley, Stella Stevens, Laurel Goodwin, Jeremy Slate

12. *It Happened at the World's Fair* MGM (1963) 105 min.
Director: Norman Taurog
Producer: Ted Richmond
Screenwriters: Si Rose, Seaman Jacobs
Cast: Elvis Presley, Joan O'Brien, Gary Lockwood, Vicky Tiu, Yvonne Craig

13. *Fun in Acapulco* Paramount (1963) 97 min.
Director: Richard Thorpe
Producer: Hal B. Wallis
Screenwriter: Allan Weiss
Cast: Elvis Presley, Ursula Andress, Elsa Cardenas, Paul Lukas, Alejandro Rey

14. *Kissin' Cousins* MGM (1964) 76 min.
Director: Gene Nelson
Producer: Sam Katzman
Screenwriters: Gerald Drayson Adams, Gene Nelson
Cast: Elvis Presley, Yvonne Craig, Arthur O'Connell, Glenda Farrell, Cynthia Pepper

15. *Viva Las Vegas* MGM (1964) 86 min.
Director: George Sidney
Producers: Jack Cummings, George Sidney
Screenwriter: Sally Benton
Cast: Elvis Presley, Ann-Margret, Cesare Danova, William Demarest

16. *Roustabout* Paramount (1964) 101 min.
Director: John Rich
Producer: Hal B. Wallis
Screenwriters: Anthony Lawrence, Allan Weiss, based on a story by Allan Weiss
Cast: Elvis Presley, Barbara Stanwyck, Joan Freeman, Leif Erickson, Sue Anne Langdon, Pat Buttram, Jack Albertson

17. *Girl Happy* MGM (1965) 96 min.
Director: Boris Sagal
Producer: Joe Pasternak
Screenwriters: Harvey Bullock, R.S. Allen
Cast: Elvis Presley, Shelley Fabares, Harold J. Stone, Gary Crosby, Jody Baker, Mary Ann Mobley, Jackie Coogan

18. *Tickle Me* Allied Artists (1965) 90 min.
Director: Norman Taurog
Producer: Ben Schwalb
Screenwriters: Elwood Ullman, Edward Bernds
Cast: Elvis Presley, Julie Adams, Jocelyn Lane, Jack Mullaney

19. *Harum Scarum* MGM (1965) 95 min.
Director: Gene Nelson
Producer: Sam Katzman (also produced *Rock Around the Clock*)
Screenwriter: Gerald Drayson Adams
Cast: Elvis Presley, Fran Jeffries, Mary Ann Mobley, Michael Ansara, Jay Novello

20. *Paradise, Hawaiian Style* Paramount (1966) 91 min.
Director: Michael Moore

F

Producer: Hal B. Wallis
Screenwriters: Allan Weiss, Anthony Lawrence, based on an original story by Allan Weiss
Cast: Elvis Presley, Suzanne Leigh, Donna Butterworth, James Shigeta, Irene Tsu, Grady Sutton

21. *Frankie and Johnny* United Artists (1966) 87 min.
Director: Fred de Cordova (now of the *Tonight* show)
Producer: Edward Small
Screenwriter: Alex Gottlieb
Cast: Elvis Presley, Nancy Kovack, Donna Douglas, Sue Anne Langdon, Harry Morgan

22. *Spinout* MGM (1966) 90 min.
Director: Norman Taurog
Producer: Joe Pasternak
Screenwriters: Theodore J. Flicker, George Kirgo
Cast: Elvis Presley, Shelley Fabares, Diane McBain, Deborah Walley, Dodie Marshall, Carl Betz, Cecil Kellaway, Una Merkel

23. *Easy Come, Easy Go* Paramount (1967) 97 min.
Director: John Rich
Producer: Hal B. Wallis
Screenwriters: Allan Weiss, Anthony Lawrence
Cast: Elvis Presley, Dodie Marshall, Pat Priest, Pat Harrington, Skip Ward, Sandy Kenyon, Elsa Lanchester

24. *Double Trouble* MGM (1967) 92 min.
Director: Norman Taurog
Producer: Judd Bernard, Irwin Winkler
Screenwriter: Jo Heims, based on a story by Marc Brandel
Cast: Elvis Presley, Annette Day, John Williams, Yvonne Romain, Norman Rossington, Chips Rafferty

25. *Clambake* United Artists (1967) 98 min.
Director: Arthur H. Nadel
Producers: Arnold Laven, Arthur Gardner, Jules Levy
Screenwriter: Arthur Browne, Jr.

Cast: Elvis Presley, Shelley Fabares, Will Hutchins, Bill Bixby, Gary Merrill, James Gregory

26. *Stay Away Joe* MGM (1968) 102 min.
Director: Peter Tewksbury
Producer: Douglas Laurence
Screenwriter: Michael Hoey, based on the novel by Dan Cushman
Cast: Elvis Presley, Burgess Meredith, Joan Blondell, Katy Jurado, Thomas Gomez, L.Q. Jones, Quentin Dean. Cameo by Sonny West.

27. *Speedway* MGM (1968) 94 min.
Director: Norman Taurog
Producer: Douglas Laurence
Screenwriter: Philip Shuken
Cast: Elvis Presley, Nancy Sinatra, Bill Bixby, Gale Gordon, William Schallert

28. *Live a Little, Love a Little* MGM (1968) 90 min.
Director: Norman Taurog
Producer: Douglas Lawrence
Screenwriters: Michael A. Hoey, Dan Greenburg, based on Greenburg's novel, *My Firm but Pliant Lips*
Cast: Elvis Presley, Michele Cary, Don Porter, Rudy Vallee, Dick Sargent, Sterling Holloway

29. *Charro!* National General (1969) 98 min.
Director: Charles Marquis Warren
Producer: Charles Marquis Warren
Screenwriters: Charles Marquis Warren
Cast: Elvis Presley, Ina Balin, Victor French, Barbara Werle, James Sikking

30. *The Trouble with Girls* MGM (1969) 104 min.
Director: Peter Tewksbury
Producer: Lester Welch
Screenwriters: Arnold and Lois Peyser, based on the novel *The Chattaqua Man* by Day Keene and Dwight Babcock
Cast: Elvis Presley, Marilyn Mason, Nicole Jaffe, Sheree North, Edward Andrews, John Carradine, Dabney Coleman

F

31. *Change of Habit* Universal International (1969) 93 min.
    Director: William Graham
    Producer: Joe Connelly
    Screenwriters: James Lee, S.S. Schweitzer, Eric Bercovici, based on a story by John Joseph and Richard Morris
    Cast: Elvis Presley, Mary Tyler Moore, Barbara McNair, Jane Elliot, Edward Asner, Regis Toomey
32. *Elvis—That's the Way It Is* MGM (1970) 107 min.
    Director: Denis Sanders
    Producer: Herbert F. Solow
    Screenwriter: No credit
    Cast: Elvis Presley, appearances by the Sweet Inspirations, cameos of Cary Grant, Sammy Davis, Jr. and Xavier Cugat
33. *Elvis on Tour* MGM (1972) 93 min.
    Directors: Pierre Adidge, Robert Abel
    Producers: Pierre Adidge, Robert Abel
    Screenwriters: Pierre Adidge, Robert Abel
    Cast: Elvis Presley. Appearances by the Sweet Inspirations and comedian Jackie Kahane

Finishing School

Priscilla Beaulieu Presley took modeling courses at the Patricia Stevens Finishing School in Memphis; she occasionally modeled dresses at lunchtime at a local restaurant. She used a fictitious name so patrons were unaware of her identity.

Fire Eyes

"Fire Eyes" was the nickname Priscilla Presley used for her husband Elvis when he was in an angry mood.

The First Assembly of God Church

When Elvis Presley was growing up in East Tupelo, Mississippi, in the 1930s and 1940s, the Presley family attended services every Sunday morning at 11 A.M. at the First Assembly of God church near their home. Vernon Presley eventually became a deacon of the church in East Tupelo. The First Assembly of God church was housed in a one-story frame building, really quite similar to the houses nearby, such as the Presleys'. It was built by a distant relative of Gladys Presley on her mother's side, the Reverend Gains Mansell, who was also for a time the preacher there. When Elvis was a boy, the preacher was the Reverend Frank Smith, who often played the guitar during his sermons.

The First Assembly of God was a fundamentalist Christian sect, founded in the nineteenth century in Anderson, Indiana.

The church emphasized the reality of the supernatural and focused on the power of the Holy Spirit. It had strict views on the evils of such activities as singing and dancing, smoking and drinking. Music was permitted only to praise the Lord and as long as the purpose was pure any and all gyrations stimulated by the Holy Spirit were acceptable; that's how the church got its nickname of "the Holy Rollers."

The First Christmas at Graceland

The first Christmas Elvis Presley spent at Graceland was in 1957; it was also the last Christmas his mother Gladys was alive. According to the recollections of Gladys's nephew Billy Smith, the Christmas tree at Graceland that year was obviously chosen by Elvis—white with red ornaments, sitting in the middle of a white-carpeted room, and covered with hundreds of lights that made it look like fairyland. Elvis had bought nearly $2,000 worth of holiday fireworks, which he used on Christmas Eve to play a game he made up and called War, in which each side hurled the lighted fireworks at the other until they were all gone. Each of Elvis's employees received a $1,000 bill and the children in the Presley family were given $100 apiece. He used other $1,000 bills in a strange test of the honesty and loyalty of his family and friends, laying the big bills out on his bed and then arranging to leave each person alone in the room for a brief period with the money. Perhaps some of Elvis's manic behavior during the holiday season was due to the fact that he had a few days earlier received his own Christmas present from Uncle Sam—his notice that he would be called up for induction into the army in January.

The First Concert Appearance

Elvis Presley's first live concert performance came a few weeks after the release of his first Sun recording, "That's All Right." The singer was booked to appear at the Overton Park Shell in Memphis as an opener for country star Slim Whitman on July 30, 1954. Elvis later recalled that he was confused by the screams and shouts he heard as he was singing on the open-air stage, unable to comprehend that the noise had been generated by his own performance. He later explained, "I came out on stage and I was scared stiff. It was my first big appearance in front of an audience. I was doing a fast-type tune, one of my first records, and everybody was hollerin' and I didn't know what they were hollerin' at. Everybody was screaming and everything. When I came offstage, my manager told me they were hollerin' because I was wigglin' my legs. I was unaware. I went back out for an encore and I did a little more, and the more I did the louder it went."

F

The First Contract

On July 12, 1954, Elvis Presley signed his first management contract. It was with Winfield Scott "Scotty" Moore, the guitar player who was then backing up Elvis in the Sun recording studio and in live performances. The contract described Scotty as "a band leader and booking agent," but in fact he was simply an older, somewhat more experienced musician who saw that Elvis might have a real future as a performer and thought he could help the young singer out with contracts and bookings while making a little extra money for himself.

Elvis was only nineteen at the time the contract was drawn up, so his parents, Vernon and Gladys Presley, also had to sign the document. The one-page agreement stipulated that Moore "will take over the management of the professional affairs of the said Elvis Presley, book him professionally for all appearances that can be secured for him, and to promote him, generally, in his professional endeavors." In return, Scotty was to receive 10 percent of all Presley's earnings.

This arrangement lasted only a few months. When it became obvious that Elvis had the potential to be a big star, Scotty Moore was the first to acknowledge that the young man should have a truly professional manager. So when Memphis deejay and promoter Bob Neal revealed an interest in managing Elvis, Scotty bowed out gracefully. The first contract was simply allowed to lapse.

The First Fan Club

The first Elvis Presley Fan Club was organized in September 1954, about six weeks after the release of his first record on the Sun label. The secretary at Sun, Marion Keisker, who had pushed Elvis from the moment she heard him make his own $4 record a year earlier, was the organizer of the club, in response to the young singer's rapidly growing popularity.

The First Gold Record

Elvis Presley received his first gold record on August 11, 1958, to mark the fact that his single "Hard Headed Woman" had sold one million copies. The first-ever gold disc had been presented earlier that year to Perry Como for his smooth rendition of "Catch a Falling Star."

The First Interview

The first interview Elvis Presley gave was on radio station WHBQ in Memphis. One of the station's deejays, Dewey Phillips, had just premiered Elvis's first Sun record,

"That's All Right," and the listener response was so great that Phillips thought he ought to get Elvis on the show that same evening. When he called the Presley household, he reached Gladys, who promptly went to the movie theater where her son was hiding while his first record was being played.

"What's happened, Mama?" Elvis asked anxiously.

"Nothing but good, son. They want you at the station."

On the air, Elvis nervously told Dewey Phillips that he didn't know anything about being interviewed, and Phillips told him simply to avoid saying anything dirty. One of Phillips's first questions was where Elvis had gone to school; he knew that the audience would recognize L.C. Humes High as all-white and be surprised to learn that the performer was not black.

Legend has it that Phillips relaxed the nervous young performer by telling him the interview was just a practice. At the end, Elvis asked the deejay when they would do the real thing, and Phillips answered that they had just finished.

The First Meeting with Priscilla

Elvis Presley's first meeting with the girl who would later become his wife took place in early October 1959. Priscilla Beaulieu, whose father was a career military officer then stationed in Germany, often went after school to a gathering place for army families called the Eagles Club. One day she was approached there by a man in his early twenties who asked her if she was a fan of Elvis Presley. When she said yes, he asked if she'd like to meet her hero. The man was Airman Currie Grant, and he and his wife were part of Elvis's circle during the star's military duty in Germany. Elvis, who always hated being alone, had a group of people over for a party nearly every evening, and the Grants often invited carefully selected teenage fans to join the gang.

Priscilla, wearing a rather childish white sailor dress with white socks and shoes, was driven by Grant to the house in Bad Nauheim, where Elvis lived off base with his father and grandmother. She later recalled, "I walked in the door and there— sitting across the room in a red sweater —was Elvis. I went over in my little sailor dress and said hello. I felt so . . . *young*." Elvis got up and shook her hand, seemed instantly taken with the fourteen-year-old, and obviously tried to stay near her all evening. The entertainment that night, Priscilla later remembered, included listening to Elvis sing and do his Jerry Lee Lewis imitation and watching him eat five bacon sandwiches smothered in mustard. Elvis enjoyed Priscilla's company so much that Currie didn't get her home until 2 A.M., which made her parents none too happy about the situation.

Several days later, Currie called Priscilla and told her Elvis wanted to see her again. Her parents decreed that she could go only if Elvis came to pick her up in person and guaranteed he would have her home on time. The star agreed to their conditions.

The First RCA Recording Session

On January 10, 1956, Elvis Presley drove to the Nashville studio of RCA at 1525 McGavock Street (in a building RCA shared with a Methodist church) to make his first recordings for the label, with which he had signed a contract several months earlier. Manager Colonel Tom Parker went with him and the session was supervised by Parker's friend at RCA, Steve Sholes. Guitar great Chet Atkins, hired by RCA to manage the Nashville office and act as producer for many of the artists who would record there, was in charge of the session and played guitar for it as well. The rest of the backup team consisted of Scotty Moore on guitar, Bill Black on bass, D.J. Fontana on drums, Floyd Cramer on piano, and the male gospel group, the Jordanaires, on vocals. This was the first time Elvis had worked with the singers who would for years to come be his regular backup group.

The result of that recording session was a sound that instantly appealed to record buyers all over the country. "Heartbreak Hotel," recorded at that time, became the number one single all over the world and made Elvis an international star. As many critics have pointed out, the RCA records lack some of the raw energy that characterized the earlier Sun releases of Elvis Presley, but that was precisely what made them hit records. In a time when the top pop songs were innocuous ballads like "Cherry Pink and Apple Blossom White," Elvis's wild sound had to be made a little smoother to reach a broad national audience.

The First Sun Recording Session

On July 6, 1954, Sam Phillips decided that he was ready to record singer Elvis Presley, along with backup musicians Scotty Moore and Bill Black, with whom Phillips had paired Elvis for a short period of rehearsal, in order to find a style that was right for the young man. The song the trio tried to record was a slow ballad called "I Love You Because," written by Leon Payne, but Sam Phillips felt from the beginning that the session was not going well and the group couldn't get anything on tape that satisfied him.

At one point in the session, the musicians were taking a break while a discouraged Sam Phillips fiddled with something in the next-door control booth. To break the tension, Elvis picked up his guitar and started fooling around. Suddenly he was playing a song called "That's All Right (Mama)," which had been written and recorded in 1947 by blues singer Big Boy Crudup. As he sang the infectious music, he was jumping around all over the studio. First Bill and then Scotty joined in the impromptu jam session.

As the music was going full tilt, Sam stuck his head out of the control booth and shouted, "What in the devil are you doing?" Elvis started to apologize for wast-

F

ing time, but Sam told him to "try to find a place to start and do it again." He had finally heard what he wanted. The result of the jam session was one side of Elvis's first record; the *B* side was recorded in a second studio date. Elvis's own version of the Crudup blues song, which mixed classic delta blues with a hillbilly sound, was an immediate hit in the Memphis area, just as Sam had predicted.

An interesting footnote to the session is the fact that the tapes of the beginning of that session were sold to RCA along with all other Elvis material in 1956. Sam Phillips may not have considered Elvis's version of "I Love You Because" worth releasing, but RCA did. It can be heard on the album *Elvis Presley*, and all five versions recorded by Sam in that first session are available on the huge multirecord album, *The Complete Sun Sessions*.

The First Riot at an Elvis Presley Concert

The first time that Elvis Presley fans got so excited the police were unable to control them was at a concert at the Gator Bowl in Jacksonville, Florida, on May 13, 1955. After his performance, the singer was mobbed in his dressing room and his clothes were torn to shreds by adoring souvenir hunters. Although it was undoubtedly a dangerous moment, Elvis laughed it off and insisted that his fans didn't mean him any harm.

First Words of a Father

After Elvis Presley's daughter Lisa Marie was born on February 1, 1968, the proud father told reporters, "Oh, man, she's just great. I'm still a little shaky. She's a doll. She's great. I felt all along that she'd be a girl."

Flaming Star

In 1960, Elvis Presley starred in his sixth film, *Flaming Star.* In it he played an Indian half-breed named Pacer Burton, son of a white farmer and his Kiowa wife, who broods continually over the injustices of a situation in which whites and Indians hate and kill one another. The role of Pacer Burton, intended as a good dramatic opportunity, had originally been offered to Marlon Brando, who turned it down and left the field clear for Elvis. (Frank Sinatra had been slated originally to costar with Brando.) Elvis's Indian mother was played by the beauteous Dolores Del Rio and other supporting cast members were Steve Forrest as Elvis's brother and Barbara Eden as the brother's girlfriend. The producer of the Paramount picture was David Weisbart and the director was Don Siegel, who would later produce Clint Eastwood's early Westerns.

Flaming Star was a halfhearted attempt by Paramount to try featuring Elvis as a serious actor, in a screenplay that credited veteran Hollywood writer Nunally Johnson of *The Grapes of Wrath* and *How to Marry a Millionaire*. It featured only one musical number and included scenes that make clear Elvis's real acting potential.

However, the movie itself turned out to be a poor one, especially because of its uneasy mix of action scenes with overly long brooding closeups of the star. Unfortunately, *Flaming Star* was about the last time anyone attempted to consider Elvis an actor rather than a singing, fighting, girl-chasing star. Elvis's performance did bring him one honor of which he was very proud: He was made a blood brother of the Los Angeles Tribal Indian Community.

Fluff

Fluff was the name of Lisa Marie's pet cat when she was a little girl at Graceland. Fluff was white and long haired.

D.J. Fontana

D.J. Fontana was a drummer who became part of Elvis's backup group after he met the singer on the set of the radio show "Louisiana Hayride." Fontana toured with Elvis in the early days and stayed with him when he became a success, recording with him at RCA and for the early film soundtracks. Today Fontana is a session musician in Nashville. In the summer of 1988, he toured in a group called The Sun Rhythm Section, made up of musicians who had backed up Sun recording artists.

"A Fool Such As I"

One of the songs Elvis Presley recorded when he went into the studio in early 1958, before he entered the army, was "A Fool Such As I," Hank Snow's big 1952 country hit (written by Bill Trader). RCA, trying to make its limited amount of new Presley material go a long way, didn't release the single until the fall of that year. It was an immediate hit, rising to the number two position on the charts.

For LP Fans Only

In February 1959, while Elvis Presley was still in the army and stationed in Germany, RCA issued a new Presley LP, called *For LP Fans Only*, with a picture of Elvis in uniform on the back cover. (A few albums, now collector's items, have the same photo on the front cover as well.) Although the singer had not been in the recording studio since entering the army, RCA stretched out the scant new product by adding some of Elvis's early Sun recordings, to which they had purchased the rights along with his recording contract in 1955. The album reached the number nineteen spot on the album charts.

The Force of Jesus

The Force of Jesus, written by Frank Adams, was the book Elvis Presley was reading in the bathroom of Graceland in the last moments of his life.

Forever Elvis

Forever Elvis is a British rock musical, first seen on the stage in 1981, that has run for seven years. Produced by Elvis fan Barry White, the show sent a touring version to the Soviet Union, the first rock musical to be seen by Russian citizens. The musical features White's daughter, Elvisa Lisa Marie White, in the dual roles of the very young Elvis and of Lisa Marie Presley.

Lillian Smith Mann Fortenberry

Lillian Smith, born in 1906, was an older sister of Gladys Smith Presley, and she was close to Gladys, Elvis, and Vernon in the 1950s. Lillian married Charlie Mann, who died in June 1957; after his death, she worked at Graceland for a time as a secretary. She subsequently remarried and became Mrs. Fortenberry.

Fort Hood, Texas

After Elvis Presley entered the army in March 1958, he was sent to Ford Hood, near Killeen, Texas, for his basic training. For eight weeks he lived in the barracks with the other new recruits. Then he took advantage of an army regulation that allowed any soldier who had relatives nearby to live with his family. Elvis bought a three-bedroom trailer and sent for his parents to join him. He remained at Fort Hood until September, when his unit, the Second Medium Tank Battalion, was sent to Germany.

Alan Fortas

Alan Fortas was a member of the so-called Memphis Mafia, the group of close buddies that constantly surrounded Elvis Presley and kept him company, acting as gofers, bodyguards, playmates, and confidants for the King. Alan was an All-Memphis football player during his high school years, playing for a team that rivaled Humes High, Elvis's alma mater, and he went on to make the team at Vanderbilt University. Introduced to Elvis by George Klein, Alan joined the Elvis entourage in 1958, first serving as a bodyguard during the filming of *King Creole.* He was still with Elvis in the early 1960s, and was the employee who took Priscilla Beaulieu shopping the first time she came to visit Elvis. She remembered that Elvis's favorite nickname for Alan was "Hog Ears." In the late 1960s, Alan managed Elvis's Circle G Ranch in Mississippi; he left the payroll when the ranch was sold, although he remained close to Elvis until the star's death. The nephew of former Supreme Court Justice Abe Fortas, Alan is now a successful Memphis businessman who treasures his memories of Elvis.

Founders Award

One of the awards of which Elvis Presley seemed proudest was the Founders Award given him in 1971 by Memphis Music Inc. in its First Annual Memphis Award Show, at which "Suspicious Minds" also won the award for Record of the Year. The Founders Award was given in recognition of the creation of the "Memphis Sound" and the winners were blues composer and performer W.C. Handy, Sun Records head Sam Phillips, record producer Chips Moman, Stax Records head Jim Stewart, Hi Records founder Joe Cought, and Elvis Presley. For many years Elvis kept that award in his bathroom at Graceland rather than in the showcase of the Trophy Room, where most of his other awards were located.

Foxhugh

Foxhugh was the name of a pet Maltese terrier given by Elvis Presley to his girlfriend Linda Thompson in the mid-1970s. Linda often teased Elvis that Foxhugh would bite him if he treated her badly.

Joe Frank

Joe Frank was a manager who handled country-and-western singers in the 1930s and 1940s. Among his clients were Gene Autry, Roy Acuff, and Ernest Tubb. He was also managing Eddy Arnold when Tom Parker moved in and stole him away. Most observers agree that as a manager Tom Parker to a great extent tried to model his public demeanor after Joe Frank, a true "good ole boy" from the South.

Freud's Views on Spoiled Sons

Sigmund Freud had some thoughts on sons who were spoiled by their mothers, the way Elvis Presley had undoubtedly been: "If a man has been his mother's undisputed darling, he retains throughout life the triumphant feeling, the confidence in success, which not seldom brings actual success along with it."

Candy Jo Fuller

Candy Jo Fuller is a country-and-western singer best known for claiming to be the illegitimate daughter of Elvis Presley. Her mother, Terri Taylor, says she and Elvis were lovers back in the 1950s, at the correct time in relation to Candy Jo's birth. According to Terri's account, Elvis subsequently sent her money from time to time and stayed in touch with her over the years. Since he did the same for many people who had at one time or another touched his life, most Elvis biographers don't accept his generosity as proof she was the mother of his child.

Fun in Acapulco

Fun in Acapulco was a movie starring Elvis Presley that was made and released in 1963. It was produced by Hal B. Wallis for Paramount, and costarred Ursula Andress as a hotel social director with whom Elvis, playing a singing trapeze artist with a fear of heights, falls in love. Of course there are complications: Elvis is also involved with a lady matador (played by Elsa Cardenas) and Ursula is being pursued by rival lifeguard and diver Alejandro Rey. But the story ends happily, with Elvis overcoming his fear of heights and proposing to Ursula.

Shot in part on location in Mexico (although all of Elvis's scenes were filmed on a Hollywood set), the movie is notable for its backdrops of gorgeous scenery, a welcome change from the low-budget studio productions to which Elvis fans were already growing sadly accustomed. The movie is also of interest to Elvis fans because it continues a familiar motif in Elvis vehicles (all, of course, selected and approved by manager Colonel Tom Parker)—that of the greedy or selfish manager. In this version, Elvis's manager is a nine-year-old Mexican boy who gets the star a job singing at the hotel in exchange for 50 percent of his earnings—just as the Colonel would later do in Vegas. Life *does* imitate art.

RCA released a soundtrack album for *Fun in Acapulco*, containing eleven songs, some of which, such as "El Toro," "Bossa Nova Baby," and "Marguerita," showed a definite Latin influence. RCA claimed sales of more than $1 million for the album but that figure was never officially certified. Even Elvis fans would be hard put to recognize most of the songs.

The Funeral of Elvis Presley

Elvis Presley's funeral was held privately on August 17, 1977, at Graceland. Throughout the previous day, Elvis, dressed in a white suit and navy shirt and wearing his eleven-carat diamond "TCB" ring, had lain in the Graceland hall in an immense copper coffin as thousands of distraught fans filed by for a final farewell to their idol. The funeral took place in the morning. The officiating minister was an old friend, C.W. Bradley of the Woodland Church of Christ in Memphis. The Reverend Rex Humbard, of the Cathedral of Tomorrow with its television ministry, also spoke briefly. The eulogy was delivered by comedian Jackie Kahane, who had often appeared with Elvis in live performances. Music included several of Elvis's favorite gospel songs, performed by Kathy Westmoreland ("My Heavenly Father"), Jake Hess, James Blackwood, and the Stamps. Mourners included Priscilla Presley and daughter Lisa Marie, Vernon Presley, Elvis's grandmother Minnie Mae Presley, and girlfriends Linda Thompson and Ginger Alden. Among the celebrity guests were Ann-Margret and her husband Roger Smith,

Tennessee governor Ray Blanton, and soul singer James Brown. The pallbearers were all long-time associates of Elvis: Charlie Hodge, Joe Esposito, Lamar Fike, George Klein, Felton Jarvis, and Dr. George Nichopoulos. A funeral cortege of sixteen cream-colored Cadillacs accompanied Elvis as he left Graceland for the last time for the trip to nearby Forest Hills Cemetery. The heavy coffin was gently pushed into place in a mausoleum located near the grave of Elvis's beloved mother, Gladys Presley. More than three thousand floral tributes from his fans all but concealed Elvis's resting place. The total cost of the funeral was $23,789.73

Within only days of the funeral, Elvis's father Vernon became concerned about security at the cemetery. After three men were arrested on August 28 on suspicion of plotting to kidnap Elvis's body and hold it for $10 million ransom, Vernon applied for permission to remove the body from Forest Hills. Elvis and his mother were moved during the night of October 2, 1977, to the grounds of Graceland, in an area that Elvis had called the Meditation Garden.

The Funeral of Gladys Presley

Elvis Presley's mother Gladys died at Methodist Hospital in Memphis on August 14, 1958, of a heart attack while she was being treated for severe liver damage. Elvis was home on leave from the army, although he was not actually with her when she died.

Gladys Presley lay in state for a day at Graceland, in an ornate silver casket, wearing a baby blue dress. Originally her funeral was to be held at Graceland, but at the last minute Colonel Tom Parker, Elvis's manager, insisted that "for security reasons" the funeral should take place in a Memphis funeral home (some suspected his real motive was to obtain as much publicity for his client as possible). The Rev. James Hamill of the First Assembly of God church conducted the service. The music consisted of Gladys's favorite gospel songs and hymns—"Precious Memories" was the one she always liked the best—sung by her favorite gospel group, the Blackwoods. She was buried at nearby Forest Hills Cemetery. Her son placed a marker on her grave that read, "Not Mine, But Thy Will Be Done." Later he put a monument over her burial place, a life-sized statue of Jesus with welcoming arms. He also added an inscription on her tombstone:

Gladys Smith Presley
April 25, 1912—August 14, 1958
Beloved wife of Vernon Presley and mother
of Elvis Presley
She was the sunshine of our house

After Elvis died in 1977, he was initially buried beside Gladys at Forest Hills. Within a few weeks, Vernon Presley had reason to worry about security at the cemetery, so he moved both Elvis and Gladys to Graceland, where they rest side by side in the Meditation Garden.

G. I. Blues

In 1960, as soon as Elvis Presley was discharged from the army, he went to Hollywood to star in the movie *G. I. Blues.* It was his fifth film and his third under his original contract with Paramount. Elvis played a soldier stationed in Germany (surprise!) who just happened to be able to sing (surprise, surprise). But the star was quick to deny that the plot of this movie was in any way based on his own experiences. "It's not about my actual experiences in the army—they couldn't film that!" he joked. On the other hand, producer Hal Wallis emphasized, "I decided to take advantage of the situation and do a picture based on his real-life experiences in the army." To make the movie more authentic Wallis traveled to the base where Elvis was stationed in Germany even before the army's most famous soldier was discharged, and hired one hundred men from the Third Armored Division to work as extras in the movie. Wallis shot background footage of these soldiers doing maneuvers on location in Frankfurt, Wiesbaden, Friedberg, and Idstein-on-the-Rhine.

Elvis's leading lady was dancer Juliet Prowse, at that time engaged to Frank Sinatra, whose daughter Nancy was rumored to be having a romance with Elvis. Elvis had embarked on this movie with high hopes that producer Hal Wallis and veteran director Norman Taurog would depart from what was already becoming something of a formula, but he ended by feeling very disillusioned about his movie career. He told Priscilla Presley, "I hate it. They have about twelve songs in it that aren't worth a cat's ass. I just had a meeting with Colonel Parker about it. I want half of them out. I feel like a goddamn idiot breaking into a song while I'm talking to some chick on a train." The Colonel calmed Elvis down and the film was released just as Paramount had made it.

G. I. Blues, like all of Elvis's movies, made money for the studio but did little or nothing for Elvis's reputation. The soundtrack album, backed by the Jordanaires and featuring a photo of Elvis in army uniform, also sold well, occupying a position at the top of the album charts for six weeks, despite the fact that none of the songs—"Wooden Heart," "Big Boots," to name just a few—was particularly memorable. This movie also gave audiences their first clue that the post-army Elvis was going to be toned down. *New York Times* film critic Bosley Crowther commented approvingly, "Gone is the wiggle, the lecherous leer, the swagger, the unruly hair, the droopy eyelids, and the hillbilly manner of speech." Alas.

G.I. Blues was the first movie Elvis made after he came out of the army, and no doubt it was intended to capitalize on all the publicity surrounding his own tour of duty. His co-star was Juliet Prowse, with whom he was briefly involved in an off-camera romance. (Photo from Neal Peters Collection)

G

Patsy Presley Gambill

Patsy Presley was Elvis Presley's double first cousin. Her father Vester was the brother of Elvis's father Vernon; her mother, Clettes Smith, was the younger sister of Elvis's mother Gladys. People often commented on how much the cousins looked alike. They grew up together in East Tupelo, Mississippi, and when Elvis achieved his initial success, the Vester Presley family moved to Memphis too. Patsy's father was a gate guard at Graceland; Patsy herself started working as Elvis's secretary in 1963. Her husband, Marvin "Gee Gee" Gambill, Jr., acted as Elvis's valet and chauffeur.

"Brother" Dave Gardner

"Brother" Dave Gardner was a friend of Elvis Presley's and a comedian who often appeared as a warm-up act for Elvis before concerts.

Marco Garibaldi

Marco Garibaldi is the father of Priscilla Presley's second child, her son Navaronne Garibaldi. Marco, of Italian parentage, was raised in Brazil but became a U.S. resident in the 1970s. He is about ten years younger than Priscilla, with whom he lives. Although the couple has embarked on parenthood, they have not yet undertaken marriage. Garibaldi is a writer, director, and producer.

Navaronne Garibaldi

Navaronne Garibaldi is the name Priscilla Presley chose for her second child, a son born on March 1, 1987. The baby is the child of producer-writer-director Marco Garibaldi, with whom Priscilla currently lives.

Pat Geiger

Pat Geiger is the grandmother of seven who has led the fight to get a postal stamp commemorating Elvis Presley. Geiger, born in 1920, dates her strong interest in Elvis from the time she saw his 1968 TV comeback special. "I sat in my living room and said to myself, 'No one is *that* good looking.' But he was that good-looking! Being sixteen years older than he was, I kept my feelings to myself. I told only one person at work that Elvis could put his shoes under my bed anytime." Pat started to collect

Presley memorabilia and after his death she began to think about a commemorative stamp. She has herself written to the Postmaster's Citizen's Stamp Advisory Committee more than sixty times, and she has also urged Elvis fan clubs around the world to write more than fifty thousand letters in support of the stamp.

When warned that the Post Office will issue stamps only in honor of people who have been dead for at least ten years, Pat responds that she is sure Elvis is dead but adds jokingly, "If I get this stamp for him and he turns out to be alive, I'll kill him."

Larry Geller

Larry Geller became Elvis Presley's personal hairstylist in 1964. He encouraged Elvis's interest in spiritual matters and introduced him to writers on the subject of metaphysics. It was Larry who first took Elvis to visit the Self-Realization Fellowship Center on Mount Washington in the Hollywood Hills. According to reports from various Presley insiders, Colonel Tom Parker and Vernon Presley both became worried by the extent of Geller's influence over the star and eventually managed to separate them. Larry Geller styled Elvis Presley's hair one last time—for his funeral. In 1989, he published a book called *Elvis Speaks*, a vigorous defense of Elvis and an attack on other members of his entourage, calling it the book Elvis himself wanted to write.

Getlo

Getlo was one of Elvis Presley's favorite dogs, a chow of which he was especially fond. In 1975, before she was a year old, Getlo developed serious kidney problems and Elvis spent thousands of dollars in an effort to save her life. She was flown to a Boston animal hospital for treatment, which improved her health for a short time. However, she died several months after her return to Graceland.

Getwell Street

In mid-1955, Elvis Presley's earnings from his records and concert dates were slowly increasing and he felt able to move his family from a four-room rented house on Lamar Avenue to a bigger one on Getwell Street. The house at 1414 Getwell was a three-story brick dwelling in a lower-middle-class neighborhood, with a lawn in front and back. It was the nicest house the Presleys had lived in to date.

The current owner of the house is moving it to make way for an auto parts store. He hopes to find another site and open the house to fans. Meanwhile, he is selling souvenir bricks from the structure for $10 a piece.

Dr. Elias Ghanem

Dr. Elias Ghanem was a physician practicing in Las Vegas who treated many show-biz patients. Allegedly, one of them was Elvis Presley, for whom Ghanem wrote prescriptions for narcotics.

Khalil Gibran

Elvis Presley was greatly impressed by the writings of Khalil Gibran, particularly his book *The Prophet.*

Gifts To Charity

For most of his career, Elvis Presley wrote more than $100,000 in checks every year to various charities he supported. Among the regular recipients were the March of Dimes, the YMCA and YWCA, Muscular Dystrophy Association, Cerebral Palsy Association, Boys' Town, Father Tom's Indian School, the Salvation Army, and the Motion Picture Relief Fund. He gave a $35,000 Rolls-Royce to SHARE, to be auctioned at a fund-raiser, and he gave a $55,000 yacht, formerly the presidential yacht *Potomac*, to St. Jude's Children's Hospital. He gave money to the town where he was born, East Tupelo, Mississippi, for a youth center, and he established a scholarship fund. All these gifts to organized charities, of course, were in addition to his renowned willingness to help nearly anyone who really needed it. He gave people cars, jobs, checks, jewelry, and cash when he perceived a need. Total strangers were sometimes the recipients of his generosity.

Homer "Gil" Gilliland

Homer "Gil" Gilliland was Elvis Presley's personal hairdresser from 1967 to 1977, charged with the responsibility of keeping the famous pompadour coal black and perpetually curling over the star's forehead. According to secretary Becky Yancy, Gil was given an American Airlines credit card so he could fly out to wherever Elvis was working to tend to his hairstyle. One reason that Elvis decided to use a personal hairdresser was that barbers frequently saved the shorn locks and then sold them later to fans. Gil was the lucky recipient of the $10,000 gold suit Elvis had worn several times but found too hot and bothersome to appear in again.

Girls! Girls! Girls!

The eleventh film in which Elvis Presley starred was *Girls! Girls! Girls!* (1962), in which he played a Gulf shrimp fisherman. Elvis particularly disliked the stupidity of the production numbers in this tired vehicle and complained bitterly about having to sing a song to some shrimp. But the album went gold and reached number three on the charts, which was Colonel Parker's justification for all of Elvis's formula films.

Gladys and Elvis Go to the Hospital

After the burial of Jesse Garon Presley, Elvis Presley's stillborn twin, mother Gladys Presley began to hemorrhage badly. At the same time, the doctor became concerned about baby Elvis, who seemed precariously small and weak. Both mother and child were therefore sent to the charity ward of the Tupelo hospital, where they stayed for three weeks until they were both strong enough to return to the little house where Elvis had been born.

Gladys and the Colonel

According to all reports, Gladys Smith Presley never liked her son's manager, Colonel Tom Parker. One reason may have been jealousy over the important role Parker played in Elvis's life and the way Elvis depended on him rather than, as before, on his family. Another reason was that Parker didn't really fit in with the attitudes and values of the Presley-Smith clan. As Gladys's sister Lillian explained, "He didn't look like our kind of people . . . he didn't act like our kind of people either."

Gladys and Vernon Get Married

Gladys Smith was a young woman in Mississippi recently turned twenty-one, working at the Tupelo Garment Center to earn money to support her invalid mother and her younger siblings, when she decided to move the family from a farm outside town to a little house on Kelly Street in East Tupelo. Shortly thereafter, she met the handsome young son of a neighbor family, Vernon Presley, seventeen. Their courtship was rapid and on June 17, 1933, they ran away to get married. Vernon had to borrow the $3 for the license from Marshall Brown, his cousin Vona Mae's husband. The wedding was performed by the circuit clerk of nearby Pontotoc County, where the couple went so that Vernon, still a minor, could lie about his age and marry without his parents' consent. He told the clerk he was twenty-two and Gladys took the opportunity to shave a few years off her own age, putting herself down as nineteen. According to Vona Mae, who, along with her husband, acted as a witness for the ceremony, "Vernon was very nervous and Gladys smiled right through the whole thing. In fact, she smiled right through the rest of the day."

Gladys Music Company

Gladys Music Company, named after Elvis Presley's mother, was one of the corporations manager Colonel Tom Parker set up to handle the rights to the star's recordings. Gladys was the corporation that controlled publishing rights handled through ASCAP, the professional association that primarily specializes in classical music. Most of Elvis's recorded music was handled through the other association, BMI, and his Elvis Presley Music Corporation.

Gladys's Last Words

According to the book written by nurse Marian J. Cocke, Elvis Presley told her that his mother's last words to him when he left the hospital on the night she died, were, "Son, when you get here tomorrow I want you to see that all these flowers are given to other patients."

Glasses from the Dennis Roberts Optical Boutique

The nearsighted Elvis Presley never appeared in a pair of regular glasses but he habitually wore prescription sunglasses, which he purchased from the Dennis Roberts Optical Boutique in Los Angeles. Each pair cost several hundred dollars, and had his motto, TCB, stamped in gold on the earpiece. Members of his entourage also sported the expensive sunglasses.

Godfrey Says No

In March 1955, Elvis Presley, accompanied by backup musicians Scotty Moore and Bill Black, went to New York to audition for an appearance on Arthur Godfrey's television variety show, *Arthur Godfrey's Talent Scouts.* Presley was rejected.

G

Going to Germany

In September 1958 Elvis Presley's army unit, the Second Medium Tank Battalion, was sent to Germany. His mother Gladys had died only weeks earlier, and Elvis didn't want to be separated from friends and family at the time of his deepest grief. He solved the problem by arranging for them to go to Germany too. His father, Vernon, grandmother Minnie Mae, and friends Red West and Lamar Fike all joined him after the arrival of his troop ship, the *USS General Randall*. Elvis explained to reporters, "One of the last things Mom said was that Dad and I should always be together . . . Wherever they send me, Dad will go too." Elvis rented a house near the base and lived there with his family for the duration of his service in Germany.

Elvis's gold Cadillac was a 1960 limousine customized by George Barris. The paint contained diamond dust and gold flakes. (Photo courtesy of the Country Music Foundation, Inc.)

The Gold Cadillac

In the mid-1960s, Elvis Presley ordered a custom Cadillac from Barris Kustom City of North Hollywood. It was almost a "solid gold Cadillac," with gold-plated bumpers and hubcaps and an interior furnished with electric razor, record player and television, shoe buffer, and telephones covered in solid gold. The exterior was finished with forty coats of hand-rubbed glitter paint that included crushed diamonds and Oriental fish scales to enhance the sparkle. The passengers were screened from view by gold lamé curtains.

Elvis soon realized that the car was impractical, since it always drew a crowd and had to be guarded every second. He relegated it to a garage at Graceland, where it sat for a few years until Colonel Tom Parker had the bright idea of sending it out on tour as a sort of Elvis substitute. Today Elvis's gold Cadillac can be seen in the Country Music Hall of Fame in Nashville.

G

The Gold Suit

Not long before Elvis Presley went into the army, he appeared in one of his most famous outfits, a $10,000 gold lamé suit. It can be seen on the cover of his 1959 compilation album *50,000,000 Elvis Fans Can't Be Wrong.* Worn with a ruffled and tucked white shirt and gold shoes, it was made by famous Hollywood costumers Nudie's in the tuxedo style and featured jewel-encrusted lapels and cuffs. Elvis wore the suit, basically a publicity gimmick, only a few times—one of them at a 1957 concert in St. Louis when an adoring fan stole the gold shoelaces right out of his gold shoes—because it was too hot and bothersome. He finally gave it to one of his hairdressers, Gil Gilliland.

Elvis in the famed gold lamé suit. Although it was custom-made for him, it never seemed to fit very well. It's easy to understand why he soon gave it away! (Photo from Neal Peters Collection)

G

The Golden Pyramid

In 1989, a consortium of investors announced plans to construct a 32-story pyramid in Memphis, as a tribute to Elvis Presley and the music he made famous. The pyramid, sheathed in steel that will gleam golden in the sun, will house a performance arena, a museum, and the American Music Awards Hall of Fame, which will include not only Elvis, but also such greats as Chuck Berry, Buddy Holly, Jerry Lee Lewis, and Michael Jackson. One of the investors is Jack Soden, the head of Graceland Enterprises.

Albert Goldman

Albert Goldman was the biographer whose 598-page book, *Elvis*, published in 1981, caused the most outrage to the most fans. One reason is that Goldman is a better writer than most of those who have attacked Elvis; another is that he seemed to be genuinely outraged by his subject's behavior. Fan reaction notwithstanding, the book was on the best-seller list for weeks, and the paperback rights sold for more than $1 million. Goldman went on to administer much the same treatment to John Lennon in 1988.

"Good Career Move"

When Elvis Presley died, one show-business cynic joked, "Good career move!" And so it turned out to be. Since Elvis's death, his estate has made more than $70 million and his popularity is even greater than it was in the last few years of his life.

"Good Luck Charm"

In the fall of 1961 Elvis Presley recorded "Good Luck Charm," written by Aaron Schroeder and Wally Gold. It was released that winter and rose to the number one position on the pop charts, producing another gold record for Elvis.

"Good Rockin' Tonight" B/W "I Don't Care If the Sun Don't Shine"

The *A* side of Elvis Presley's second single for Sun was a recording of Roy Brown's "Good Rockin' Tonight," a hit for blues artist Wynonie Harris that Elvis was already performing in the Memphis area. Like most of the Sun recordings, the blues tune was backed with a country number. This one was written by Mack David, called "I Don't Care If the Sun Don't Shine," and originally intended for use in Walt Disney's movie version of *Cinderella.* The tune had been a hit for Georgia Gibbs in 1951. Both sides of the second single were recorded on September 23, 1954, and the record was released at the beginning of 1955. It quickly zoomed to number three on the Memphis charts, although the record never sold more than five thousand copies.

Diana Goodman

Diana Goodman, a 1975 Miss Georgia, dated Elvis Presley at the time of her reign. She told reporters that Elvis's steady girlfriend, Linda Thompson, often went along on their dates—acting, she said, more as a "buddy" to Elvis than a rival to her.

Robert Goulet

Elvis Presley used to say that he hated singers who were "all technique and no emotional feeling." One star he put in that category was Robert Goulet. On at least one occasion, Elvis shot out the screen of a television set when he saw Goulet's face on it. Supposedly he felt much the same way about Mel Tormé.

Graceland

In 1957, Elvis Presley bought the mansion called Graceland for $100,000, trading in a smaller ranch-style house on Audubon Drive in Memphis and paying the balance in cash. According to one report, the mansion had already been sold for $35,000 to the YMCA when Elvis spotted it, so he had to bid up the price to get the property he wanted for its style and its seclusion.

Graceland had been built in the late 1930s by a Dr. Thomas Moore, who named the estate after his wife's Aunt Grace Toof, from whom the Moores had inherited the land. Elvis bought Graceland from Mrs. Moore after her husband died. The mansion was situated on thirteen and a half acres on the southern outskirts of Memphis, Tennessee, in what was then the unincorporated town of Whitehaven; it was later annexed by the city of Memphis. The stretch of road passing in front of the mansion, Highway 51 South, was renamed by the city Elvis Presley Boulevard, and thereafter Graceland had the street address of 3764 Elvis Presley Boulevard.

Graceland was a bit run down when Elvis bought it and he promptly began to remodel the house, adding the touches he deemed appropriate to his stardom. Among the first changes were a kidney-shaped swimming pool and big white pillars on the front. He also added the huge wrought-

Elvis proudly posed in front of Graceland soon after he bought the stone mansion on the edge of Memphis. (Photo from Neal Peters Collection)

G

115

iron double gate at the entry, ornamented with guitars and musical notes, called the Music Gate. While Elvis worked on improving the facade, his parents added their own touches in the backyard: a vegetable garden and a chicken coop.

The house itself was built of reddish-tan Tennessee limestone and white-painted wood trimmed with dark green shutters. The number of rooms in Graceland varied over the years, since Elvis often remodeled and changed the layout, but there were at least seventeen rooms and sometimes as many as twenty-three.

Although the exterior of Graceland is similar to many southern houses built in the antebellum style, the interior was pure Presley. Color schemes included lots of red,

pink, and a pinky-purple color Elvis loved and called heliotrope. There was always an abundance of velvet, mirrors, and deep shag carpeting. Gold trim was *de rigueur* throughout.

In 1982, on the anniversary of Elvis's death, Graceland was officially opened to the public. As journalist Bob Greene ruminated, "Before Elvis died, Graceland had been shrouded in total secrecy. Virtually no one outside Presley's inner circle was allowed on the property." Graceland had been his private refuge, off limits to all but a chosen few. Now hundreds of thousands of people visit the mansion every year; according to one report, Graceland is second only to the White House in the number of tourists it draws, about 650,000 annually.

"Graceland Express"

Graceland Enterprises publishes a quarterly newsletter called "Graceland Express" for Elvis Presley fans to keep them up to date on activities at the mansion and else-

where involving the memory of Elvis. For information or subscriptions, write P.O. Box 16508, Memphis TN 38186-0508.

Billy Graham Reacts to Elvis Presley

When Elvis Presley first gained national stardom in 1956, religious leader Billy Graham said he was appalled. "Elvis isn't the

kind of boy I'd like my children to see," Graham opined.

Sheilah Graham on Elvis Presley's Film Career

In her book *Hollywood Revisited*, Hollywood columnist Sheilah Graham takes the position, also that of the official propa-

ganda from manager Colonel Tom Parker, that Elvis Presley was "grateful to the Colonel for advising him to make those nine successful films with Hal Wallis." She further concludes that "his film career diminished only when he wanted a change from the rock-and-roll singing that his fans demanded."

The Grammy Awards

Elvis Presley won only three Grammy awards during his recording career. In 1967, he won the award for Best Sacred Performance for the album *How Great Thou Art*. In 1972, he won Best Inspirational Performance for *He Touched Me*. And in 1974 he won Best Inspirational Performance for a rerelease of *How Great Thou Art*.

The "Grand Old Opry" Appearance

On September 25, 1954, after the release of Elvis Presley's second single on the Sun label, the singer was invited—mostly at the urging of Sam Phillips, the head of Sun—to appear on "Grand Old Opry," the live country music show broadcast on radio from Nashville. Apparently, the wild young man with greasy hair, flashy clothes, and long sideburns was not very well received by the conservative country-music Opry audience. In fact, after his number was over, the Opry's manager and booking agent, Jim Denny, told Elvis he ought to go back to driving a truck. The failure in Nashville must have been a blow to the young man who was just at the beginning of his professional performing career. According to one friend, "Elvis cried all the way home. It took him weeks to get over it." He himself later once commented simply that Jim Denny had broken his heart.

A Grandchild for Elvis

Eight days after Lisa Marie Presley married Danny Keough in October 1988, her mother made an official announcement that Lisa Marie was expecting a baby the following spring. Her baby Danielle, born on May 29, 1989, was Elvis's first grandchild.

Currie Grant

Currie Grant was the U.S. serviceman who earned a footnote in history because he was the one who introduced Priscilla Beaulieu to Elvis Presley. Afterward Grant spoke of his recollections of the event, which occurred when he escorted Priscilla to a party at Elvis's house; a Presley insider, he often invited young people he thought would enjoy meeting their idol. Knowing Elvis's fondness for keeping a party going until the wee hours of the morning, Grant was rightly worried that he would be unable to return the fourteen-year-old girl back to her home by the midnight curfew decreed by her parents. He remembered that Elvis noticed Priscilla right away and seemed especially enchanted by the prim little sailor dress she had chosen to wear. Grant and his wife continued their friendship with young Priscilla even after Elvis had returned to the States.

Great Balls of Fire

In the spring of 1989, a movie about the life of rocker Jerry Lee Lewis was released, with Dennis Quaid playing the lead. *Great Balls of Fire* included a scene of Elvis, played by Michael St. Gerard, watching Jerry Lee on TV whacking the life out of a piano. Elvis's lip was curled in a sneer, which presumably was meant to indicate his opinion of the performance.

Dick Grob

Dick Grob was a former fighter-pilot and ex-policeman who was the head of Elvis Presley's security force at Graceland in the last years of the star's life. After Elvis's death, Grob for a time put out a newsletter for fans.

A Guitar for His Birthday

In January 1946, in honor of his tenth birthday, Elvis Presley received his first guitar. Apparently what he had really wanted was a .22 rifle, but Gladys Presley, always the protective mother, vetoed that idea as both too expensive and too dangerous. According to the recollections of Forest Bobo, the owner of the hardware store in Tupelo at that time, Elvis threw a temper tantrum when he learned he wasn't getting the rifle he wanted, but Gladys stood firm and bought her son a guitar instead. Bobo carried three models: one for $3.50, one for $6.25, and one for $12.50, and he says Gladys opted for the most expensive model. Elvis was shown a few basic chords on the instrument by his uncle Vester Presley and thereafter he taught himself to sing and play by listening to the radio.

A "Guitar-Playing Marlon Brando": The Tommy and Jimmy Dorsey Show

Renowned big band leaders of the 1940s swing era, the brothers Tommy and Jimmy Dorsey had a television variety show in the 1950s that was broadcast live from the CBS-TV studios in New York City. Called "Stage Show," it was produced by comedian Jackie Gleason and served as a lead-in for his own hit series, "The Honeymooners." "Stage Show" was basically a review, starring the Dorsey Brothers, the June Taylor Dancers, and special guests every week. Typical guests were jazz greats such as Sarah Vaughan and Ella Fitzgerald, and such comedians as Henny Youngman, Joe E. Brown, and Jack E. Leonard.

In an attempt to attract a more youthful audience, the variety show booked young singer Elvis Presley in early 1956. As one of the producers put it, "This kid is a guitar-playing Marlon Brando." In the first of his six appearances on the show, on January 28, Elvis sang "Shake, Rattle and Roll" and "I Got a Woman." He sang his just-released single, "Heartbreak Hotel," on three separate shows, and performed a cover of the Carl Perkins song, "Blue Suede Shoes," which he would record on his next trip to the RCA studios a few weeks later. The impact of Elvis on the audience of the usually sedate variety show was apparent the day after his first appearance, when calls and letters began to pour in to the station. Some of the viewers were startled, some were outraged, and some fell in love at first sight—but it seemed that no one could be indifferent to the young man with the pompadour and sideburns who wore wild clothes, sneered and snarled at the camera, and gyrated wildly to the beat of his energetic music.

The Hamburger Connection

Elvis Presley's appetite for hamburgers and cheeseburgers was well known. The first recording session the star had after he came out of the army was to be kept secret, to prevent adoring fans from mobbing the RCA Nashville studio. Session producer Chet Atkins recalled that RCA's efforts to hide Elvis's presence were successful until the early hours of the following morning. Then somebody called the Crystal Hamburger stand down the road and ordered one hundred hamburgers to go. The young women who worked at the hamburger stand were quick to make the connection: A hundred hamburgers plus RCA equals Elvis! Suddenly the news that Elvis was recording was all over town.

The Handsomest Man Ever

Part of Elvis Presley's appeal to his fans was certainly his looks. The star stood just a hair over 6 feet tall and his normal weight was around 180 pounds (although in his later years he ballooned up as high as 260). Elvis's hair was naturally a dark blonde color, which he began dyeing black about the time he became a big star. His eyes were blue, framed with long lashes and made more interesting by a small scar over his left eye. Many considered that his most arresting feature was his mouth, formed to display a perpetual pout, a key ingredient of his sexiness.

"Hard Headed Woman"

"Hard Headed Woman" was a song that Elvis Presley recorded in Hollywood in early 1958, before he entered the army, for the soundtrack album of *King Creole.* In the movie, the song, by Claude De Meterius, is barely audible, heard offstage. It was released as a single later that year and made it onto the charts immediately. It was the first of Elvis's singles to be certified by the Recording Industry Association of America as a gold record; shortly thereafter RCA submitted many of Elvis's earlier hits for certification.

Zelda Harris

Zelda Harris claims that she met Elvis Presley at a concert in Alabama in 1960 and married him only twenty-four hours later. She shares with several other claimants to the title of Mrs. Elvis the awkward inability to produce any proof of the fact—that old "lost document" syndrome.

The Hawaiian Concert

In April 1961, Elvis Presley made an appearance at a concert in Hawaii to help raise money for a navy war memorial. After the concert he stayed on to film *Blue Hawaii.* According to reports, he gave a sensational performance at the concert. It was the longest of his life and included an electrifying moment when, according to one observer, he "dropped to his knees and slid twenty feet to the front of the stage with the microphone in his hands, never missing a note." Sadly for his fans, it was his last live performance for seven years.

Heartbreak Hotel: The Movie

In 1988, the movie *Heartbreak Hotel* was released. Called a rock-and-roll fantasy, the movie, set in 1972, tells the story of a boy who is worried about his mother and decides to cheer her up by kidnapping and bringing home her idol, Elvis Presley. In an ironic piece of casting, the mom is played by Tuesday Weld, once Elvis's leading lady in *Wild in the Country* and reportedly also involved with him personally. Elvis, played by David Keith, solves all the family's problems before returning to his own life (which, as the audience knows, isn't all that great either). A feature of the

H

movie of interest to Elvis fans, besides the recreations of his performance at that time, is the deliberate imitation of some of the fight scenes from Elvis's own movies. And look for the name of the motel owned by Mom—the Flaming Star!

"Heartbreak Hotel": The Song

The song that made Elvis Presley a national idol was "Heartbreak Hotel," recorded in the first RCA session in Nashville in early January 1956. Backing Elvis were Floyd Cramer on piano, Scotty Moore and Chet Atkins on guitar, D.J. Fontana on drums, and Bill Black on bass. To get the echo effect that made the record so unusual, Elvis left the recording studio and sang part of the song standing in a stairwell of the old building that housed the RCA offices. Sam Phillips, head of the first record label to issue Elvis Presley recordings, later told a reporter that the record was so bad that Colonel Tom Parker was thinking of withdrawing it and called it a "morbid mess."

The morbid mess was released a month after it was recorded, in February 1956. "Heartbreak Hotel" made it onto the national charts on March 24 and by the first week of April it was not only the number one pop song in America, but also number one on the country-and-western and the rhythm-and-blues charts—the first triple crown for any recording artist. The first check the song's publisher, Hill & Range, received for rights to "Heartbreak Hotel" was for nearly a quarter of a million dollars —so large a sum the managers initially thought it must be a mistake. Elvis's finger-snapping, hip-swiveling performance of the song on the Tommy and Jimmy Dorsey television show had a significant influence on the record's sales.

To date, more than eighteen million copies of "Heartbreak Hotel" have been sold. It was the first song Elvis had recorded that wasn't a cover of an old hit by another performer. It was written by the songwriting team of Tommy Durden and Mae Boren Axton, a singer-composer who is the mother of singer-actor Hoyt Axton. Mae later said she got the idea for the song from a newspaper story about a well-dressed suicide the police were unable to identify, who was found clutching a slip of paper on which he had written the words, "I walk a lonely street." Originally conceived as a slow ballad, the song was switched to an up-tempo number in a demo for Elvis, and that's the way he recorded it. Elvis was given cowriting credit for the song; according to Mae Axton, that was a generous gesture toward the young singer whose early popularity had not yet brought in much hard cash. According to some other songwriters, that was standard procedure, initiated by the Colonel, for anyone who hoped to sell a tune for Elvis Presley to record.

Dave Hebler

Dave Hebler, born in Pittsfield, Massachusetts, in 1937, was a fifth-degree black belt karate champion and teacher who met Elvis Presley in California in 1972 through their shared interest in the martial arts.

Hebler later joined the Presley payroll as part of the security force. Dave, fired by Vernon Presley in 1975, collaborated with Red and Sonny West to write the Elvis exposé, *Elvis: What Happened?*

"Hell on Wheels": The Second Armored Division

When the army's new recruit, Private Elvis Presley, was sent to Fort Hood, Texas, he was first assigned to the Second Armored Division, A Company. The motto of the Division is "Hell on Wheels."

Jake Hess

Jake Hess was the lead singer of a white male gospel group called the Statesmen that often performed in the Memphis area when Elvis Presley was a teenager. Jake Hess was acknowledged by Elvis to have been a significant influence on his own performing style, although Hess's deep bass voice was out of Elvis's range. Hess was one of the gospel vocalists to sing a hymn at Elvis's funeral.

Hi-Lo

Hi-Lo, established by Sam Phillips to handle rights for Sun artists, was the first music publishing company to own rights to the songs of Elvis Presley. Hi-Lo sold its rights to all the music Elvis had recorded on the Sun label to Hill & Range in 1955 as part of the deal that sent Elvis to RCA.

Hill & Range

Hill & Range was a music publishing company, dealing primarily with country-and-western music, that in 1956 signed a contract with the Elvis Presley Publishing Company for the publishing rights to Elvis's songs. Hill & Range had been founded by two refugees from Hitler's Germany, brothers Jean and Julian Aberbach, in the late 1930s. Later Hill & Range was managed by Freddie Bienstock (nicknamed "Fast Freddie"), and then for a time by Lamar Fike, one of the members of the "Memphis Mafia." When RCA bought Elvis's recording contract from Sun Records, Hill & Range was a party to the complicated deal and put up $10,000 of the money paid to Sun.

The Hillbilly Cat

When Elvis Presley began to perform in the Memphis area after the release of his first record on the Sun label in August 1954, he sometimes called himself the Hillbilly Cat. It wasn't long before his own name was better known.

His Hand in Mine: The Album

The LP album *His Hand in Mine* was recorded in 1960 by Elvis Presley, backed by the gospel group, the Jordanaires, who had sung backup on his rock and pop recordings. This album was devoted to religious music and the title cut is one of Elvis's most moving performances. Other songs included such favorites as "Joshua Fit the Battle" and "In My Father's House." *His Hand in Mine* was a certified gold album and according to RCA figures it eventually sold more than five hundred thousands copies.

"His Hand in Mine": The Song

"His Hand in Mine" is a classic gospel tune recorded by Elvis Presley as the title song for the album of the same name in 1960, after his discharge from the army. Oddly this gospel tune never made the charts.

His Master's Voice (HMV)

His Master's Voice, or HMV, was the subsidiary of British Decca, which released the early Elvis records—up until 1958.

H

A Hit in Vegas

In the summer of 1969, Elvis Presley was booked to perform in the two thousand-seat theater of the International Hotel in Las Vegas. His contract called for him to be paid $150,000 a week, top money in those days. It also called for him to fill, night after night, a huge auditorium—a feat that had been too much for many singers booked there, including the very popular and talented Barbra Streisand. The booking was Colonel Tom Parker's idea and Elvis was extremely nervous about it. He had appeared in Vegas only once before, back in 1956, when his brand of youthful raw energy failed miserably in front of the middle-aged Vegas audience.

To insure his success Elvis spent lavishly on costumes, backup singers, and musicians, and insisted on three dress rehearsals. He hired many of the musicians from Memphis with whom he had played and recorded in the early days of his career, because they made him feel comfortable and confident. As it turned out, Elvis was an enormous hit from the moment he first walked on the stage on the night of July 31, 1969. He was greeted by a deafening roar from the audience and fans never stopped demonstrating their satisfaction with his performance. He gave two shows a day for a solid month, for a total of more than one hundred thousand spectators, and received a standing ovation every time he walked out on the stage. That was the start of the regular Vegas appearances he made for the rest of his life.

Hits in 1955

In 1955, Elvis Presley had three hit songs that made it to the country charts. "You're Right, I'm Left, She's Gone" and "Mystery Train" climbed onto the charts in the first half of the year; "I Forgot to Remember to Forget" made it all the way to the number one spot on the country charts in the second half of the year.

Charlie Hodge

Charlie Hodge was a long-time member of Elvis Presley's entourage. The two men's acquaintance dated back to Elvis's days in the army; according to one report, Charlie was the soldier assigned to keep his fellow Southerner company on the troop ship over to Germany at a time when Elvis was still deeply grieved over the death of his mother. They hit it off well and after Charlie got out of the service, the five-foot, three-inch ball of energy was put on Elvis's payroll. Charlie was so close to the star that he was sometimes described as Elvis's shadow and for many years he lived in an apartment above the garage at Graceland. He is best known for his special job of handing Elvis the scarves that he threw to the audience during performances. Charlie also helped Elvis arrange his hair before he went on stage, played touch football and went riding with him when he wanted to relax, did his errands and listened to his complaints, and served as one of the witnesses to his will. Charlie, a musician himself, had played backup with Roy Rogers and Gene Autry and had sung with a gospel group called the Foggy River Boys. He can be heard singing a duet with Elvis on the recording of "Could I Fall in Love." After Elvis's death, Charlie continued to serve the memory of his friend and boss.

Dr. Lester Hoffman

Dr. Lester Hoffman was Elvis Presley's dentist in Memphis. Elvis, accompanied by Ginger Alden, visited Dr. Hoffman on the last night of his life.

Buddy Holly Pays Tribute to Elvis

The great rock-and-roll star Buddy Holly, who died in a plane crash in 1959, said of Elvis Presley's trailblazing importance to the field of popular music, "Without Elvis, none of us could have made it."

Honey

Honey was the name of the puppy Elvis Presley gave Priscilla Beaulieu for Christmas in 1962. Honey was an adorable poodle who was good company for young Priscilla.

The Hospitalizations

Starting in late 1974, Elvis Presley underwent a series of extended hospitalizations. Most of these took place in Memphis's Baptist Hospital and they were blamed on a wide variety of health problems—intestinal blockage, enlarged colon, pneumonia, glaucoma, eye strain, gastric flu, and plain old obesity. Elvis usually took a suite of rooms, so his entourage could be near him, and brought his own bodyguards to limit access to the ailing superstar. The hospital was asked to prepare for his arrival by blacking out the windows with aluminum foil, Elvis's standard procedure in hotels. The frequent hospital stays gave rise to rumors of serious illness, and there was speculation that Elvis had cancer, cirrhosis of the liver, or was undergoing plastic surgery.

One of the nurses who attended Elvis during some of those hospital stays, Marian J. Cocke, wrote a book about her famous patient. Among the procedures she mentions that Elvis underwent were a liver biopsy and an examination of the colon to ascertain whether surgery was indicated. Her report indicates that Elvis was generally a cheerful and cooperative patient.

Hound Dawg One

The radio call sign of Elvis Presley's Convair, the *Lisa Marie*, was "Hound Dawg One."

"Hound Dog"

"Hound Dog" was perhaps the most famous of all the early Elvis Presley songs. It was written by the team of Jerry Leiber and Mike Stoller for blues singer Willie Mae Thornton, whose recording of the song reached the top spot on the rhythm-and-blues charts in 1953. Elvis, who had heard a version of the song performed by Freddie Bell and the Bellboys, recorded it on July 2, 1956. Elvis demanded thirty-one takes before he was satisfied. The recording features Scotty Moore on guitar, D.J. Fontana on drums, Bill Black on bass, and vocal backup from the Jordanaires. It's classic Elvis all the way. Of course the single went gold, with sales in the year of the record's release topping six million copies.

The House in Palm Springs

Elvis Presley built a fifteen-room house in Palm Springs, on Chino Canyon Road, as a retreat from the pressures of Hollywood and, later, from his performing career in Las Vegas. Although the Palm Springs house was the scene of Elvis and Priscilla Presley's honeymoon night, Elvis later used it as a bachelor pad and an escape from domesticity. Colonel Parker also had a home in Palm Springs. Today, Elvis's single-story Spanish-style house in Palm Springs is owned by singer Frankie Valli.

How Great Thou Art

In May 1966, Elvis Presley recorded an album of religious songs, *How Great Thou Art*, with a cover that showed him wearing a suit and standing in front of a New England-style country church. To make sure the album was heard in the proper way, Colonel Parker offered money to stations that would play it without commercial interruption. The best song on the album, and the first to go gold as a single when it was released in 1967, is surely the title cut, a classic piece of sacred music recorded by many other singers. Elvis's rendition is pure, simple, and incredibly moving. He is backed up by Floyd Cramer on the piano and both the Jordanaires and the Imperials on vocals. The album, which contained another gold single, "Crying in the Chapel," also went gold as an LP, reaching as high as number eighteen, an exceptionally strong showing for a gospel album. The recording of *How Great Thou Art* won Elvis Presley his first Grammy, for best sacred performance of the year.

How Much Does Elvis Make Today?

The Elvis Presley estate continues to earn money at an amazing rate—more than Elvis himself made in any one year of his life. Some of the money comes from the ongoing sale of his recordings, which RCA is presently reissuing on compact disc. Most of the income, however, is derived from so-called "intellectual property," meaning the image of Elvis as it is seen on various items, from T-shirts to charge cards, that are licensed by the estate. According to *Forbes*, the Presley estate earned more than $15 million in 1987 and expected to top that figure in 1988. Elvis earns more dead than most pop music stars do alive; for example, his 1988 earnings were greater than those of Sting or U2.

L.C. Humes High School

When the Presley family moved to Memphis, Elvis was just old enough to start high school. He went to a technical and vocational school, L.C. Humes High School on Manassas Avenue, which housed more than seventeen thousand students in a huge and aging three-story brick building, under the watchful eye of principal T.C. Brindley. According to legend, Elvis ran away on his first day because he was frightened by the crowds and the confusion. Thereafter, his mother walked the teenager to school every day.

Few of his fellow students noticed the shy boy from the country during his first two years at school. They remembered him as a junior and senior only because he wore outrageously flashy clothes and a greasy pompadour hairstyle that made him a laughingstock at school. Yet Elvis did participate in the normal high school activities. The Humes High Yearbook for 1953 lists Elvis's major subjects as history, English, and shop. He was a member of the Biology Club, English Club, History Club, Speech Club, and Reserve Officers' Training Corps. He was a student assistant in the library, and he went out for the football team in 1951, although coach Rube Boyce remembered that he "wasn't thrilled" with the young man's appearance and Elvis didn't make the cut.

In high school in Memphis, Elvis Presley was one of the library workers. That's our hero on the far right of the back row. (Photo from Neal Peters Collection)

LIBRARY WORKERS

Back Row, left to right: Richard Flaniken, Billy Barber, George Makrus, Joe Coyle, Geraldine Barber, Herbert Blooming, Larry Holmes, Ralph Shinbaum, Charles Catros, Val Crotts, Elvis Presley.

Middle Row, left to right: Charlotte Young, Doris Varnavas, Ruth Mandelman, Joyce Beard, Billie May Chiles,

Louise Carson, Lillian Davis, Joan Liberts, Rachel Maddox, Joe Collins, Flois Gwaltney.

Front Row, left to right: Maureen Kapell, Nina Faverty, Jane Garey, Peggy Simmons, Norma Banks, Annie Varnavas, Billie Banks, Evelyn Hicks.

Hymns Sung at Elvis's Funeral

The hymns sung at Elvis Presley's funeral were:
- "My Heavenly Father Watches Over Me," sung by Kathy Westmoreland
- "Known Only to Him," sung by Jake Hess and the Statesmen
- "How Great Thou Art," sung by James Blackwood and the Stamps
- "When It's My Turn," sung by Bill Baize of the Stamps
- "His Hand in Mine," sung by the Stamps
- "Sweet, Sweet Spirit," sung by the Stamps

H

Hypnotism

In 1976, Elvis Presley worked for a while with hypnotist William Foote to try to learn to relax and to block out pain. It was an effort to lessen his dependence on the drugs he used to achieve those same goals, but it seems not to have solved the problem.

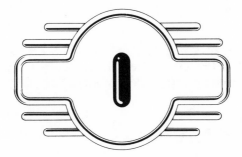

I.C. Costume Company

Many of the gaudy jumpsuits that Elvis Presley made his stage trademark were custom made for him by the I.C. Costume Company. Most of them cost about $800, but occasional specialty suits could run as high as $2,500.

"If I Can Dream"

"If I Can Dream" was a song written for Elvis Presley by Earl Brown, which Elvis introduced during his 1968 television special, using it to close the show. It was released as a single in November, a few weeks before the special was aired, and after Elvis fans heard him sing it on TV, the song quickly became a million-seller—his first in a number of years. It was also included on the LP *Elvis TV Special*, which was released at the end of the year and became another gold album for Elvis.

Immaculate Conception High School

When Priscilla Beaulieu moved to Graceland to be with Elvis, she still had a year and a half of high school to complete. She enrolled at Immaculate Conception High School in Memphis in the spring of 1963, and graduated from the Catholic school in June 1964. Elvis's graduation present to Priscilla was a bright red Corvair. He wanted to attend her graduation but she asked him to wait outside, because she knew his presence would overshadow the ceremony for herself and her classmates.

The Imperials

The Imperials were a gospel group that sometimes backed up Elvis Presley in the recording studio. The members were Jake Hess (who also sang with the Statesmen), Jim Murray, Gary McSpadden, and Arnold Morales.

Impersonating Elvis

Ever since Elvis Presley first attracted national attention back in 1954, there have been scores of Elvis imitators and Elvis impersonators. Among those who have turned impersonating Elvis into a profession are:

Morris Bates
Larry Blong
Jim E. Curtin
Terry Dene
El-Ray-Vis
Jim Gutierrez
Bill Haney
Johnny Harra
Ron Hutchison
Kiyoshi Ito
Storey Jones (the only female Elvis impersonator)
Rich Locknane
Alan Meyer
Nick Paulichenko

Richard Presley
Terry and Jerry Presley
Tony Presley
Johnny Risk
Bud Sanders
Rick Saucedo
Freddie Starr
Robert Stefanon
El Vez
Elvis Wade
Denis Wise

Elvis impersonators continue to enliven many public gatherings. On July 4, 1986, more than two hundred Elvis look-alikes made an appearance at the big birthday party for the Statue of Liberty in New York. At the 1988 Olympics in Seoul there was a "delegation" of Elvises from the States, as well as a number of Asian Elvis impersonators, some of whom made dogged attempts to capture the King's down-home accent.

"In the Ghetto"

"In the Ghetto" was a song written by Mac Davis that Elvis Presley recorded in January 1969. It was released as a single in the spring of that year and immediately went gold, reaching the number three spot on the pop charts. It is a ballad about the despair of the black ghetto, sung powerfully and touchingly.

Induction into the Army

In early March 1958, after Elvis Presley finished shooting the Paramount movie, *King Creole*, he returned to Graceland for a few weeks of rest and privacy before entering the army. The star told avid reporters how he planned to report for induction, as ordered by the U.S. Army: "My induction notice says for me to leave my car at home. Transportation will be provided. They tell me just to bring a razor, a toothbrush, a comb, and enough money to hold me for two weeks." After an all-night party with his buddies and girlfriend Anita Wood, the star told his parents goodbye and reported to the Memphis draft board at 6:30 on the morning of March 24, like any other new recruit. At the instigation of Colonel Tom Parker, Elvis's manager, photographers thronged the induction center to snap the moment America's superstar became one of its soldiers. Then the army's most famous recruit was sworn in. Along with the other young men from Memphis, Elvis Presley boarded a bus for Fort Chaffee, Arkansas. His new salary as a soldier would be $78 a month.

The Influence of Preachers

When Elvis Presley was a boy he attended services at a Pentecostal church near the Presley family home. Elvis later explained that the behavior of the preachers was an influence on his own stage performance. "During the singing the preachers used to cut up all over the place—that's how I was introduced to the onstage wiggle. The preachers did it. And the congregation loved it—why, I even remember one day a preacher jumping on a piano. I liked them, and I guess I learned a lot from them."

The Ink Spots

A major influence on Elvis Presley's singing style was his admiration for the Ink Spots, a black male quartet popular in the 1930s and 1940s. The first record Elvis made, as a present for his mother, was of two songs made popular by the Ink Spots. He especially admired leader Bill Kenny and the way he sang the high notes. The other Ink Spots were Orville "Hoppy" Jones, Ivory "Deek" Watson, and Charlie Fuqua. Their biggest hit was their soulful rendition of "If I Didn't Care."

Insider Books About Elvis

Even before Elvis Presley died the people close to him began to write about some of the intimate details of his life, and his death loosened more lips. If you want to know what the insiders say about the star, here are the books to read:

- Charlie Hodge, *Me 'N Elvis*
- Marty Lacker, Patsy Lacker, and Leslie S. Smith, *Elvis: Portrait of a Friend*
- Ed Parker, *Inside Elvis*
- Dee Presley and Billy, Rick, and David Stanley, *Elvis: We Love You Tender*
- Priscilla Beaulieu Presley, *Elvis and Me*
- Vester Presley, *A Presley Speaks*
- Billy Stanley, *Elvis, My Brother*
- David Stanley, with David Wimbish, *Life with Elvis*
- Red West, Sonny West, and Dave Hebler, *Elvis: What Happened?*

Some books were written by people who knew Elvis as an employer. These include:

- D. J. Fontana, *D.J. Fontana Remembers Elvis*

- Marian J. Cocke, *I Called Him Babe: Elvis Presley's Nurse Remembers*
- Harold Loyd, with George Baugh, *The Gates of Graceland*
- Neal Mathews, *Elvis: A Golden Tribute*
- Nancy Rooks, with Mae Gutter, *The Maid, The Man and the Fans: Elvis Is the Man*
- Jess Stern with Larry Geller, *The Truth About Elvis*
- Kathy Westmoreland, *Elvis and Kathy*
- Becky Yancy and Cliff Linedecker, *My Life with Elvis*

A third category of insider books were written by people who claim to have known Elvis, in one life or another. These include:

- Lucy de Barbin, *Are You Lonesome Tonight?*
- Hans Holzer, *Elvis Presley Speaks*

Into the Night

The 1985 movie *Into the Night* featured a plotline about an Elvis Presley impersonator who drives a 1959 Cadillac. Carl Perkins had a small part in the movie, as did Don Siegel, the director of the 1960 Elvis movie *Flaming Star*. *Into the Night* was directed by John Landis of *Animal House* fame.

Investigating the Drug Sources

In 1975, Vernon Presley and Colonel Parker became alarmed by the quantity and variety of drugs used by Elvis Presley, as they observed that his drug use more and more often affected his performances. In an effort to cut off the drugs at their source,

I

the pair hired Hollywood private detective John O'Grady to find out where the drugs were coming from. His report concluded that the drugs were obtained legally from physicians treating Elvis for various medical problems.

Later, Elvis insiders concluded that the only way to tackle the drug problem was to try to get Elvis to quit. The star's ex-wife Priscilla approached him about the matter directly and tried to induce him to agree to enter a treatment center in California. His unwillingness to consider the matter put an end to that notion.

Is Elvis Alive?

In 1988, Gail Brewer-Giorgio's book *Is Elvis Alive?* examined the body of evidence that convinced many fans that Elvis Presley had faked his own death in order to live the rest of his life out of the glare of publicity and off the stage. The book, which concluded that there *was* reason to believe that Elvis still lives, became an immediate best-seller, spending six weeks on the national list. *Is Elvis Alive?* was packaged with an audiotape that purported to be a recent recording of the voice of Elvis—its voice print identical to an authentic recording of the King. The publishers, Tudor Books, licensed the rights to the tape to a firm that set up a telephone-for-pay number for callers who wanted to listen to a portion of it. More than half a million people called the number.

"Is it a Sausage?"

When Elvis Presley made his film debut in *Love Me Tender*, critics were scathing. The film critic for *Time* was one of the most hostile. He wrote:

> Is it a sausage? It certainly is smooth and damp-looking, but whoever heard of a 172-lb. sausage, six feet tall? Is it a Walt Disney Goldfish? It has the same sort of big, soft beautiful eyes and long curly lashes, but whoever heard of a goldfish with sideburns? Is it a corpse? The face just hangs there limp and white with its little drop-seat mouth, rather like Lord Byron in the wax museum. A Voice? Or merely a noise produced, like the voice of a cricket, by the violent stridulations of the legs?

The Isolation of Elvis

It is widely agreed that for most of his professional life, Elvis Presley was isolated—not from his fans but from the professionals who might have positively influenced his work and his growth as a musician and an actor. For example, although Elvis always sang songs that were written for him by other people, he himself never actually met the songwriters. After his first few movies, he also didn't spend time with screenwriters or directors to talk about the movies he was in or his performance on the screen. The musicians he loved to jam with, most of them guys from Memphis that he had known before he was famous, such as Bill Black and Scotty Moore, only had access to him in the recording studio.

This creative isolation diminished Elvis Presley's career accomplishments, if not his earning power. Like most people, he did his best work when he was stimulated and challenged by his professional peers. His early recordings at Sun, his first few movies, the recording session at American Studios in Memphis, the 1968 TV special—these were the artistic highlights of his career, and, not coincidentally, the times he was able to work closely with other professionals. The more isolated the star was, the less interesting his work became, both to the public at large and to himself.

What caused Elvis Presley's professional isolation? One frequent answer is the careful planning of Colonel Tom Parker, who wanted to keep Elvis totally dependent on him and unable to form other professional relationships. Another answer is that Gladys Presley wanted to isolate her son from his colleagues—not understanding his professional world and unable to enter into it, she jealously tried to shut it out of the Presley household. Once the family settled in Graceland, her attempts were largely successful, setting a pattern that continued even after her death.

It must also be considered that Elvis himself contributed to the problem of his isolation. Sensitive and thin skinned in regard to criticism, he was the victim of a career that moved so fast he never really caught up with it until he was locked into a routine that was hard to break. He was afraid to attempt the more difficult challenges because he was afraid to fail. Much of what was written about him in the early days of his career suggested he had no talent and was simply an inexplicable flash in the pan, making it even harder for him to consider exposing himself by trying to be taken seriously as an actor or musician. Thus he was willing to remain isolated even though the isolation bored him and stifled his creativity.

"It's Now or Never"

One of Elvis Presley's biggest hit singles was "It's Now or Never," which was written by Aaron Schroeder and Wally Gold and based on the Italian classic, "O Sole Mio," previously recorded by Enrico Caruso and Mario Lanza. Elvis recorded "It's Now or Never" in April 1960 and the song marked the beginning of his movement away from rock and into pop music. The single remained in the number one spot on the charts for five weeks and sold nearly ten million copies when it was first released. To date it has sold more than twenty-two million copies worldwide, making it the most successful single Elvis ever created.

I

"It's a Wonder People Are Still Buying It"

According to Priscilla Presley, in one of her last conversations with Elvis, he commented nostalgically about his manager, Colonel Tom Parker. "Good old Colonel," he said. "We've come a long way. He's still puttin' out that same old stuff. It's a wonder people are still buying it."

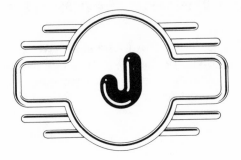

Jailhouse Rock: The Movie

The third movie that Elvis Presley made was *Jailhouse Rock.* It was his first for MGM, under a nonexclusive contract that would pay Elvis $250,000 plus 50 percent of the profits. The movie was based on an original story by Ned Young, a writer who was blacklisted at the time of the McCarthy Communist hunts, and produced by Hollywood veteran Pandro S. Berman. Critic Steven H. Scheuer, author of *Movies on TV*, calls this movie the best Presley musical.

The none-too-believable plot has Elvis going to prison at the beginning of the movie for accidentally killing a man. During his incarceration he makes a record that brings him fame and fortune when he is released. In the performance of the title song, Elvis is backed up by his musical collaborators from his recording days at Sun, Scotty Moore on guitar and Bill Black on bass. Elvis also dances in this number, around a set built to look like a prison. He surprised his critics—but not his fans—by displaying the grace and style of a professional dancer.

The movie co-starred comedian Mickey Shaughnessy as Elvis's cellmate who signs him to a contract that makes him a partner in Elvis's profits; Judy Tyler as his manager, with whom he falls in love; and Anne Neyland, whom Elvis was dating in real life at the time, as an ingenue. The script features a number of inside references to Elvis's own life. For example when Elvis, as the character named Vince Everett, starts to play the guitar, his cellmate cautions, "Don't break the strings." Later Elvis comments, "I had an uncle who had one of these things," which fans picked up as a reference to Vester Presley, the uncle who taught Elvis his first few chords on the guitar. Vince owns a pair (the twin motif) of basset hounds, just like the one Elvis sang to on the *Steve Allen Show.* And there are frequent references to Vince/Elvis's obsession with cars.

Jailhouse Rock had its world premiere in Memphis in October 1957, although Elvis did not attend—and neither did costar Judy Tyler, who was killed in an automobile crash on her honeymoon after the shooting was finished. The movie recouped its costs quickly and by the end of the year was number fourteen on the box office list. The soundtrack album, with songs written by Jerry Leiber and Mike Stoller (who appears briefly on screen), included the title cut, as well as "Baby I Don't Care," "Don't Leave Me Now," and "Young and Beautiful." The EP was number one on the album charts for an amazing twenty-eight weeks and was named *Billboard's* EP of the Year.

According to the accounts of several members of Elvis's inner circle, the star was very unhappy throughout the filming of *Jailhouse Rock* and avoided seeing it or talking about it thereafter. One possible explanation advanced by several Elvis biographers is that the spectacle of a Presley in jail hit a little too close to home for comfort. At that time, Vernon's prison term at Parchman Farm was still unknown to Elvis fans.

In 1956 Elvis signed on to play Clint in a move called *The Reno Brothers* (note the call board). When he sang "Love Me Tender" the producers changed the film title accordingly. (Photo from Neal Peters Collection)

J

"Jailhouse Rock": The Song

"Jailhouse Rock" was the title song from the movie of the same name and the one big production number of the picture. The song was released as a single in mid-1957 and rose to the number one position on the charts, where it stayed for seven weeks.

"Jailhouse Rock" was written by Jerry Leiber and Mike Stoller, who were responsible for the movie's soundtrack; the master was recorded within six takes. It remains quintessential Elvis.

The Jamboree Attractions Tour

In 1955, Elvis Presley's then manager, Bob Neal, booked the singer to appear with a touring country-and-western show. It was organized and headlined by Hank Snow; also featured were Slim Whitman, Mother Maybelle Carter and her daughters June and Anita, the Davis Sisters, Skeeter and Georgie, and Faron Young. Elvis was billed as "Elvis Presley with Bill and Scotty" (backup musicians Bill Black and Scotty Moore). The first time Elvis went onstage, the management decided that he would be the last to perform before the intermission. His effect on the audience was so electrifying that none of the other artists wanted to follow him.

The tour was the catalyst that put Elvis on the road to becoming a superstar. There were two reasons. One was his demonstrated effect on audiences, who screamed his name, tore his clothes, mobbed his dressing room, and even wrote their names in nail polish all over his car. Another was that on the tour he met Hank Snow's manager, Colonel Tom Parker, who knew just how to turn the talented performer into an international superstar.

Felton Jarvis

Felton Jarvis started his career in the record business in 1959 by making a novelty record called "Don't Knock Elvis." He was the RCA record producer who in 1966 replaced Chet Atkins as the producer of Elvis Presley's records. Four years later, Jarvis left RCA to work full time for Elvis, helping him not only with recording sessions but also with his Vegas shows and his concerts. Most insiders agree that Jarvis was devoted to Elvis's career and did his best to find Elvis good quality material to showcase the star's vocal talents. After Elvis's death Jarvis produced the shows for the 1979 TV movie *Elvis* and then made a limited album for RCA entitled *Felton Jarvis Talks About Elvis*. Jarvis died in 1981.

Jesse

According to *Jesse*, a book reportedly being written by Laurel King, Elvis Presley's twin brother was not really stillborn but instead was both retarded and hidden from public view throughout his childhood at the home of an aunt. (How the family could keep the secret so successfully is not clear.) King contends that after Elvis became a star, Jesse lived with him at Graceland, where she claims to have met him. She believes that Jesse left the mansion when Elvis died and has been living in seclusion for years. She explains that Jesse's recent re-emergence is the reason for all the so-called sightings of Elvis.

Elton John

Elton John, always a big fan of Elvis Presley, was an idol of Lisa Marie Presley, Elvis's daughter. In 1975, Elvis invited Elton to Graceland, primarily so Lisa Marie would have the chance to meet him.

Johnny J. Jones Exposition

In 1932, Tom Parker left the army and took a job with the Johnny J. Jones Exposition. Once one of the biggest and most profitable of the traveling carnivals, the Johnny J. Jones Exposition had fallen on hard times with the onset of the Depression and the death of its founder. In 1933, the show was purchased by E. Lawrence Phillips and somewhat revitalized. Parker first worked as an assistant to the advance man, Peazy Hoffman. He stayed with the Jones Exposition more or less full time until the summer of 1935, when he went to work for the American Royal Show, a bigger and better carnival. But for several years thereafter, he occasionally turned up to help Peazy Hoffman for a few days or weeks at a time.

Don Johnson

Miami Vice star Don Johnson had the starring role of Elvis Presley in the 1981 TV movie, *Elvis and the Beauty Queen*, about the liaison between Elvis and Linda Thompson. In his hit TV show, Johnson played a character named Sonny Crockett who, in his first season, lived on a boat with an alligator named Elvis.

President Lyndon B. Johnson

The first president to meet Elvis Presley was Lyndon B. Johnson. LBJ stopped by the location shooting of *Spinout* in 1966.

"Holly Jones"

In the 1961 movie *Follow That Dream* the hero, played by Elvis Presley, falls in love with a sexy young woman named Holly Jones, played by Anne Helm, who is adopted by his family and grows up in his home. The year after the movie was released Elvis attempted to make life imitate art when he brought Priscilla Beaulieu to Graceland, ostensibly to be under the care of his family while she grew up. We know how the story ends.

Tom Jones: Friendly Rival

Elvis Presley had obvious respect for the vocal talents of Welsh singer and Vegas performer Tom Jones. The first Tom Jones record Elvis ever heard was his rendition of "The Green, Green Grass of Home," and Elvis found the sound of Tom's singing so soulful he was convinced the singer was black—just as people had thought he himself was black when his records were first broadcast. He met Jones a few months later when Elvis and Priscilla were vacationing at the Ilikai Hotel in Hawaii and Tom was headlining there. A friendship between the two singers developed, although it always contained a certain element of rivalry. Elvis recorded not only "Green, Green Grass of Home" (1975) but also two other Tom Jones hits, "Without Love" and "I'll Never Fall in Love Again."

The Jordanaires

One of Elvis Presley's favorite backup groups was the Jordanaires, a group of white gospel singers. The Jordanaires started out in Springfield, Missouri and moved to Nashville in the early 1950s. At that time the group consisted of Gordon Stoker, Hoyt Hawkins, Neal Matthews, and Hugh Jarrett. Elvis met them when they were appearing with Eddy Arnold and he selected them for his backup group at the first RCA recording session in January 1956. Thereafter the Jordanaires sang with Elvis in live performances, at recording sessions, and in a number of his movies, including *Loving You, King Creole, G.I. Blues,* and *Blue Hawaii.*

The Jordanaires stopped performing live with Elvis in 1968 because they didn't want to play Vegas with him and go on his ex-hausting road tours. They worked in the studio with other pop musicians, backing up Marty Robbins and Rick Nelson. They also continued to record with Elvis right up until the end of his career. Their smooth harmonies are a characteristic element of the Presley sound.

Elvis once told his vocal backup group, The Jordanaires, "If it hadn't been for you guys, there might not have been a me." (Photo courtesy of the Country Music Foundation, Inc.)

The Jumpsuits

Elvis Presley's most elaborate jumpsuits were created by Hollywood costume designer Bill Belew, who also designed his karate coats and the black leather outfit he wore in the 1968 TV special. It was Priscilla Presley who first suggested the idea of the jumpsuits to Elvis, and they became his performing trademark. Many of the jump-suits were given names, such as Inca Gold Leaf, Sundial, Burning Flame, Blue Aztec, Mad Tiger, American Eagle, Red Lion, King of Spades, and Blue Rainbow. The fabulous gem-encrusted jumpsuit that Elvis wore in his 1973 TV special "Aloha from Hawaii" is now on view at the Las Vegas Hilton.

J

Elvis in 1970, filming his first concert in 13 years in Las Vegas. His relatively simple jump suit would soon give way to more elaborate, bejeweled styles. (Photo from Neal Peters Collection)

Junk-Food Junkie

Those close to Elvis Presley in his last years were appalled at the amount of junk food he habitually consumed. His karate instructor, Ed Parker, wrote, "He would consume cheeseburgers, French fries, ice cream, Popsicles by the box, banana and peanut butter sandwiches, Pepsi-Cola, and a stomach-wrenching assortment of junk foods." One member of the Memphis Mafia joked that Elvis held the world record for number of cheeseburgers eaten at a single sitting. Elvis's physician Dr. George Nichopoulos, actually labeled Elvis a junk-food junkie. He added, "Instead of helping him to break his bad eating habits, the cooks at Graceland prepared whatever he ordered. They had diet sheets in the kitchen, but it was hopeless . . . He'd say, 'Fix a hamburger and fries,' and they'd send up enough for six people." Of course, as Elvis's employees, they were in no position to dictate what their boss should eat.

Pauline Kael Talks About Elvis the Actor

Film critic Pauline Kael wrote about her opinion of Elvis Presley as an actor in her review of the film made about him after his death, *This Is Elvis.* Kael commented, "He walks through his starring roles with his face somnolent and masked; you don't have a clue to what he's thinking." She concluded, "He was a terrible actor. He must have understood that he would never amount to diddly in these crum-bum movies, and been resentful and bored."

Jackie Kahane

Jackie Kahane was a comedian who often opened Elvis Presley's shows, both in Las Vegas and on tour. Kahane, who had worked with Sophie Tucker and Wayne Newton, was unusual among Vegas comics in that he didn't do blue material. He was the one who always closed Elvis's shows with the line, "Ladies and gentlemen, Elvis has left the building." Kahane delivered the eulogy at Elvis's funeral.

Karate

For more than twenty years, Elvis Presley practiced karate almost every day. He took the sport up when he was in the army, and continued to perfect his technique afterward in private lessons at his home and at the Tennessee Karate Institute in Memphis, owned by Red West. Red and his cousin, Sonny West, often sparred with Elvis to help the star keep his competitive edge. Elvis did his own karate stunt scene in the movie *G. I. Blues,* which resulted in his breaking a bone in his hand. Nevertheless he continued to work out regularly as a way to relieve the stress of his existence. In the early 1970s, he got his wife Priscilla interested in the sport as well; unfortunately she turned to karate instructor Mike Stone for the emotional support and intimacy she found lacking in her marriage.

Even afterward, karate remained an important part of the Presley regimen. He studied with a master in Memphis, Kang Rhee, and with expert Ed Parker in Los Angeles. It was the opinion of many who saw Elvis work out that he might have been a great master himself but he didn't put the time required into the sport. Still he respected the discipline, even if he didn't always follow it. "It's a way of life," he said once. "It's so much more than a sport. It teaches discipline, patience, and makes you more spiritual."

The *Karate*

In the 1960s Elvis Presley owned a speedboat that he used to run up and down the California coast. He called the boat the *Karate*, because of the way it chopped through the water.

Milton Katselas

Milton Katselas is the Los Angeles acting teacher with whom Priscilla Presley studied for a time. His former students include Tom Selleck and Cheryl Ladd. His class combines an emphasis on the discipline needed to be a good actor with the upbeat philosophy of Scientology that encourages students to believe they can accomplish any goals they set for themselves.

Senator Estes Kefauver

Estes Kefauver, a senator from Tennessee and the Democratic vice presidential candidate in the 1956 election, read a glowing tribute to Elvis Presley into the Congressional Record in March 1960, when Elvis was discharged from the army.

Marion Keisker

Marion Keisker was Sam Phillips's secretary, helping him with both Sun Records and the Memphis Recording Studio. She had previously had a radio talk show herself on the all-woman Memphis station WHER, and had been named "Miss Radio of Memphis." Marion was at work the day in 1953 that young Elvis Presley came to the recording studio to pay his $4 to cut a record. She listened to him sing and thought her boss ought to know about the "kid with the long hair and sideburns" who imitated the style of black vocalists such as the Ink Spots. She played some of the tape for Sam and he commented that Elvis sounded promising but needed work.

Marion kept Elvis's name on file, writing beside it "good ballad singer," and she mentioned the young man's name from time to time to Sam. According to Elvis's buddy Red West, the star always said that Marion was really the one who got him started in his career. "If it wasn't for that lady, I would never have got a start. That woman, she was the one who had faith, she was the one who pushed me. Sure, Sam had the studio but it was Marion who did it for me."

Aaron Kennedy

Aaron Kennedy was a friend of Vernon Presley, whom Vernon admired greatly. At the time Vernon's son was born, Kennedy, a Sunday school superintendent, and his wife were living in East Tupelo at the home of J.D. Presley, Vernon's father. Vernon chose his son's middle name as a tribute to the friendship. According to one report, Vernon simply misspelled the middle name on Elvis's birth certificate, writing it as "Aron"; other reports suggest the alternate spelling was intentional, so the name would match the middle name given Elvis's still-born twin, Jesse Garon. Elvis later had the spelling of his middle name officially changed to match that of Aaron Kennedy. Kennedy, confined to a wheelchair after an injury while working on the railroad, still lives in Tupelo.

Caroline Kennedy

Caroline Kennedy, at the behest of Kennedy family friend Pete Hamill, was given an assignment by *Rolling Stone* to cover the funeral of Elvis Presley. There was some controversy about her presence because it was at first assumed she was there privately as a representative of the Kennedy family. The fact that she was there as a member of the press came as an unpleasant surprise to some of the Presley circle.

Danielle Riley Keough

Danielle Riley Keough is the daughter of Lisa Marie Presley and her husband Danny Keough. Elvis Presley's first grandchild was born at 8:15 p.m. on May 29, 1989. She weighed 7 lbs., 2 oz., and had a head of dark hair. The momentous event took place, under a cloak of secrecy, at St. John's Hospital in Santa Monica. Lisa Marie had attended Lamaze classes to prepare for the birth, and her husband was with her in the delivery room.

K

Danny Keough

Danny Keough is the musician who married Lisa Marie Presley in October 1988. Keough was born in Chicago on November 6, 1964, the son of Francis and Janet Keough. After his parents were divorced, his mother married Alan Hollander, a Scientologist who was a local church director and later founded a private school under the Scientology banner. Danny and his younger brother both attended the school, the Delphian school in Portland, Oregon. Danny moved to Los Angeles in 1984 and began dating fellow church member Lisa Marie, with whom he shared an interest in music and an aversion to drink and drugs. Keough, a bass player who has worked in clubs in the L.A. area, is said to hope for a successful career as a rock musician. Lisa says proudly of her new husband, "Danny is his own man—not trying to be Elvis . . . He's got a lot of integrity, and he's really out to make it on his own."

Danny is the father of Elvis Presley's grandchild Danielle, born May 29, 1989.

Kid Creole

The 1980s pop star Kid Creole grew up listening to both his West Indian father's calypso records and his own Elvis Presley collection. Born August Darnell, the young man changed his name to Kid Creole to pay homage to Elvis, the star of *King Creole.*

Kidnapped by "Elvis"

In November 1988, a Tampa teenager was kidnapped by a man who looked like Elvis Presley. The Elvis impersonator forced the girl at gunpoint to drive with him to Birmingham, Alabama, where she was able to make her escape. The kidnapper sang along with the radio the whole way, provoking the victim to comment, "He looked like Elvis, but he sure didn't sing like him."

King Creole: The Movie

The fourth movie that Elvis Presley made was *King Creole*, released in 1958. The plot, adapted from Harold Robbins's best-selling novel *A Stone for Danny Fisher*, revolved around a high school student working as a busboy in a New Orleans nightclub. Thanks to his talent, he becomes the club's singing star, and then gets involved with the "criminal element" hanging around the club. Hal Wallis of Paramount had originally bought the property as a vehicle for James Dean, who was

ccident shortly
Michael Curtiz,
blanca, to di-
ded to be the
g role.
arolyn Jones,
heart of gold
ntually killed
cast included
o spent his
ney at poker
Tom Parker)
. Dean Jag-
Dolores Hart
s returns at
was shot in
e was some
where fans
een sched-
d-January
ern at Par-
to report

for induction into the army on January 20. The Memphis draft board granted Elvis a delay to allow him to finish the movie.

King Creole was released in the summer of 1958 and was a big success at the box office. It was also treated respectfully by critics; The *New York Times*, for example, called *King Creole* "a surprisingly colorful and lively drama, with Elvis Presley doing some surprisingly credible acting."

The EP soundtrack album went gold and stayed at the top of the album charts for the longest time of any Elvis album, a total of twenty-nine weeks. An LP version, released simultaneously, contained eleven songs, five of them written by the team of Jerry Leiber and Mike Stoller. Backed up by the Jordanaires, Elvis sang not only the title cut but also "As Long As I Have You," "Hard Headed Woman," and "Steadfast, Loyal and True."

he Song

...g Creole" was the title song from the movie Elvis Presley made in early 1958, just before he went into the army. The movie was released in the summer of that year, and at the same time RCA released "King Creole," written by Jerry Leiber and Mike Stoller, as a single. It quickly climbed onto the charts.

James Kingsley

James Kingsley, a friend of Elvis Presley who had grown up in the same North Memphis neighborhood as the star, was a reporter for the *Memphis Commercial Appeal.* Kingsley wrote about Elvis frequently and broke many news stories concerning his activities. On February 22, 1989, Kingsley died of a self-inflicted gunshot wound.

Kissin' Cousins

Kissin' Cousins was a movie starring Elvis Presley that was produced by MGM in 1964. By this time the Elvis vehicle was down to a formula, so the movie—produced by Sam "King of the Quickies" Katzman—was shot in just eighteen days and cost no more than $1 million to make. Of special interest to Elvis fans is the experience of seeing him play a dual role, the two cousins referred to in the title. As hillbilly Jodie Tatum, Elvis wears a blonde wig and plays a down-home country boy who tries to stop the government from building a missile site near his family's home. As Josh Morgan, Elvis looks like his usual self, with dark hair that keeps falling over his forehead, as he plays the air force lieutenant who is assigned to persuade his cousins to sell. As usual, there are two attractive female costars, one a member of the hillbilly family and the other a WAC. Thanks to Elvis's dual role this movie ends with his getting *both* the girls. RCA issued a soundtrack album for the movie, which reached the number six spot on the album charts and achieved sales of more than $1 million.

A footnote of interest to trivia buffs: Maureen Reagan, the daughter of Ronald Reagan and Jane Wyman, appears in the movie as one of the hillbilly girls who tries to capture the soldiers.

In *Kissin' Cousins,* Elvis played a dual role as the hillbilly Jodie Tatum (left) and clean-cut Air Force officer Josh Morgan (right). Fans loved the chance to see two Elvises for the price of one. (Photo from Neal Peters Collection)

George Klein

George Klein was for some years a member of the Elvis Presley entourage that was nicknamed the Memphis Mafia. George and Elvis went to high school together; George was the popular president of their class at Humes High School in Memphis and the student voted "Most Likely To Succeed" in his senior year. He often traveled with Elvis in the early days of his career, and Elvis was George's best man at his wedding.

About the time Elvis went into the army, George Klein embarked on a successful career as a disc jockey, becoming one of the best-known radio voices in the Memphis market. In 1977, Klein was convicted of mail fraud and served a short term in the county jail. He remained close to Elvis until the star's death and Elvis once commented, "George will be my friend forever, I'll never forget how friendly and kind he was to me at Humes." After Elvis's death, Klein lectured on the subject of the star at a Memphis university and wrote a screenplay for a movie about Elvis, never completed, called *The King of Rock and Roll.* Currently George Klein hosts a daily radio show devoted to the subject of Elvis on Memphis station WEZI-AM.

Kriya Yoga

In 1964, Elvis Presley became interested in a yoga discipline called Kriya Yoga. He said he was attracted to it because he wanted to be freed from the conditions of cause and effect that govern human existence.

"Kung-Fu"

One of Elvis Presley's favorite television shows was "Kung-Fu," starring David Carradine as the cryptic master of that ancient martial art. While watching the show Elvis routinely made the comment that the discipline of kung-fu was decidedly inferior to his own sport of karate.

The LSD Experiment

According to Priscilla Presley, Elvis Presley only once experimented with LSD, the hallucinogenic drug so popular in the 1960s. He did so with great caution, making sure his entourage was nearby in case things got out of hand. He and Priscilla had a generally positive experience but agreed that the drug was too potent to experiment with any further.

Marty Lacker

Marty Lacker, born in New York City, moved to Memphis in 1952 and attended L.C. Humes High School, where he played on the football team with Red West and became friends with fellow students George Klein and Elvis Presley. After serving his army hitch, Marty returned to Memphis and renewed his friendship with his classmate, by then a famous star. Marty worked for Elvis from 1961 until 1968 and remained a part of the Presley inner circle even after he was no longer on the full-time payroll as secretary and sometimes bookkeeper. Marty, nicknamed "Moon" by Elvis and his friends, was one of two best men at Elvis's wedding in 1967, and he and his wife Patsy and their two daughters lived for a time in an apartment over what had once been the garage at Graceland. After Elvis's death, Marty and Patsy Lacker, along with professional writer Leslie S. Smith, authored a book called *Elvis: Portrait of a Friend*.

Lamar Avenue: Moving on up in Memphis

In the spring of 1955, the Presley family was living in a cramped two-room apartment on Alabama Avenue in Memphis, near the Lauderdale Courts housing project where they had previously lived for several years. Then Elvis's second record was released, quickly hitting the charts in the Memphis area. His manager Bob Neal was booking him into a number of one-night stands through the South. Elvis decided he could afford to move his parents and grandmother into a better place and rented a trim little four-room brick house on Lamar Avenue. The Presleys were there for only about six months before Elvis felt prosperous enough to move the family on to a bigger house on Getwell Street.

Lansky Brothers

Lansky Brothers was a store on Beale Street in Memphis that sold costumes to the black entertainers who performed in nearby clubs. When Elvis Presley was a Memphis high school student he used to shop at Lansky Brothers, buying outrageous outfits which he then wore to school. One of his favorite combinations in those days was pink and black—definitely not yet the style for red-blooded American boys. Many of the clothes in Lansky's at that time featured a popular 1950s motif, the lightning bolt, which was later adopted by Elvis as a kind of personal logo. After Elvis became famous he swapped proprietor Bernard Lansky a strange three-wheeled German car called a Messerschmidt in return for free clothes from the store thereafter.

In late 1988, Lansky Brothers changed its name to Hercules Big and Tall Men's Shop, a division of Lansky's. A small portion of the store is being made into a small museum and gift shop dedicated to Elvis. Right across the street from the store is the Elvis Presley Plaza, where the city of Memphis has erected a statue in honor of its most famous citizen.

The Last Car

The last car that Elvis Presley bought for his personal use was a 1976 Cadillac Eldorado with a sun roof and all the luxury gadgets available—bar, TV, telephone, and CB radio.

The Last Concert

The last concert Elvis Presley gave was at the Market Square Arena in Indianapolis on June 26, 1977. The evening was opened by a selection of songs by J.D. Sumner and the Stamps, followed by an appearance by the Sweet Inspirations. Then comedian Jackie Kahane told jokes for twenty minutes. As the strains of "Also Sprach Zarathustra" filled the air, Elvis appeared, dressed in a jumpsuit and carrying his guitar, singing the old blues classic, "See See Rider." He sang a mix of old and new hits and sat down at the piano to play "Unchained Melody." After about half an hour he was visibly tired, sweating heavily, and his face had become puffy and swollen. Fifteen minutes later he signaled road manager Charlie Hodge and the closing number, "Can't Help Falling in Love Again," brought the evening to a close.

The Last Photograph

Elvis Presley drove through the gates of Graceland just after midnight on the morning of August 16, 1977, a few short hours before his death. A fan, Robert Call, who was standing at the Music Gate, snapped his idol's picture with a Kodak Instamatic. The picture was later published by the *National Enquirer* as the last photo that was ever taken of the star.

The Last Prescription

A document reproduced in the 1988 book *Elvis: His Life from A to Z*, by Fred L. Worth and Steve D. Tamerius, is the last prescription Dr. George Nichopoulos wrote for Elvis Presley. Dated August 15, 1977, the prescription includes fifty Dilaudid tablets plus additional Dilaudid solution for injection, one hundred and fifty Quaaludes, one hundred Dexedrine tablets, one hundred Percodan, Amytal in capsules and ampules, and one hundred Biphetamine spansules.

The Last Television Show

In the spring of 1977, Elvis Presley made his last television show. It was a CBS-TV special that was filmed live at a concert in Rapid City, South Dakota. Worried fans and mean-spirited critics noted that Elvis was extremely overweight and sweating uncontrollably. Wearing a skin-tight white jumpsuit with a Mayan calendar design that was not kind to his bulging figure, Elvis was unable to do his usual moves around the stage; instead, he just held on to the microphone and sang. He forgot some of the words to "Are You Lonesome Tonight" and seemed bored with many of the other songs. Yet his voice was still strong and beautiful, and fans at the concert still screamed with delight. The show was broadcast after Elvis's death, with a special appearance by his father, Vernon Presley, saying a few words at the end.

L

The Last Words

According to the report of Elvis Presley's last hours given by Ginger Alden, who was with him in his Graceland bedroom on the night of August 16, 1977, she said to him as he was going into his bathroom with a book, "Don't fall asleep." His answer presumably can be set down as the last words of Elvis Presley: "Okay, I won't."

Abe Lastvogel

Abe Lastvogel was Elvis Presley's personal agent, the man who drew up the contracts and collected the fees for the star's recordings and appearances. When Lastvogel first met the singer, he was the head of the William Morris Agency, which handles many show business talents. Lastvogel was also a pal of Colonel Parker, Elvis's personal manager.

Lauderdale Court

After the Presley family had been in Memphis about a year, their low income qualified them for a 433-unit low-income housing project called Lauderdale Court, located at 185 Winchester Avenue. Compared to the single room in which Vernon, Gladys, Elvis, and Minnie Mae (Vernon's mother) had been living on Poplar Avenue, the small two-bedroom apartment on the ground floor of Lauderdale Court was practically a paradise, and for the same rent of $35 a month. The Presleys stayed in the Lauderdale project until about the time Elvis graduated from high school. Then Vernon hurt his back and Gladys took sick, and neither was able to work steadily, making them unable to keep up with the rent. They were forced to move to a smaller, much less comfortable place on Cypress Street.

Learning to Drive

Elvis Presley, like many boys who grew up in rural America, learned to drive when he was very young—only ten, according to some accounts. He loved to drive and soon became the official chauffeur of the family car. That may have been one of the reasons that his mother never bothered to learn to drive; Gladys could always count on Elvis to drive her anywhere she wanted to go.

Learning to Play the Guitar

Elvis Presley explained to one interviewer how he learned to play the guitar: "I'd play along with the radio or phonograph, and taught myself the chord positions." He was also helped along by his uncle, Vester Presley, who taught him a few chords, and later by a country-and-western singer in Tupelo named Mississippi Slim, who helped the youngster expand his repertoire.

Leaving the Army

Sergeant Elvis Presley was officially discharged from the army on March 6, 1960, at Fort Dix, New Jersey. Afterward manager Colonel Tom Parker arranged for Elvis to return to Memphis on a private train. At every town along the train's route crowds of fans were waiting to catch a glimpse of their idol.

Kui Lee

Kuiokalani "Kui" Lee was a Hawaiian singer and composer who penned the song "I'll Remember You," which Elvis Presley sang first in *Spinout* in 1966. That was the same year that Lee died of cancer, and a fund for cancer research was set up in his name. A portion of the proceeds from Elvis's 1973 TV special *Aloha from Hawaii* went to the Kui Lee Cancer Fund. "I'll Remember You" was a frequent staple of Elvis's concert performances in the 1970s.

Legends in Concert

In May, 1989, a revue opened on Broadway called *Legends in Concert*. The concept of the show was a performance by entertainers who died before audiences were ready to say goodbye. The "cast" included Marilyn Monroe, Judy Garland, Buddy Holly, Liberace, and John Lennon. Initially, it was also to have included Elvis Presley, but the Presley estate refused permission to use the name and likeness of the star. Thus the Elvis imitator was billed under his own name, Tony Roi. According to the program notes, Tony Roi was playing himself, and it wasn't his fault that he just happened to look and sound so much like . . . someone else, while singing such standards as "My Way," "See See Rider," and "An American Trilogy." As one reviewer put it, "He was darned good, the best not-Elvis I've seen."

Leiber and Stoller

Jerry Leiber and Mike Stoller were a songwriting team who wrote many of Elvis Presley's hits in the 1950s. Among their songs were the title cut and most of the other tunes from Elvis's 1957 movie *Jailhouse Rock*, in which Mike Stoller made a brief onscreen appearance at the piano. Presley legend has it that Leiber and Stoller were called on by Jean Aberbach of Elvis's music publishing company, Hill & Range,

L

to provide the music for the film. A few days went by during which the project was discussed but no music had emerged. Finally, according to Mike Stoller, "Jean Aberbach . . . barged in. He moved a big chair in front of the door, parked himself in the chair, closed his eyes and said, 'I'm not leaving and you're not leaving, until the score's finished.' We started writing at about two in the afternoon, and by six we were out on the street again."

Leiber and Stoller, both just two years older than Elvis, composed many other songs for him. Among their hits were "Fools Fall in Love," "Hound Dog," "King Creole," and "Loving You." After Elvis's death, a British album called *Elvis Presley Sings Leiber and Stoller* appeared on the market.

John Lennon Comments on Elvis

In the 1960s, the media tried to build up a rivalry between Elvis Presley and the decade's new teen idols, the Beatles. But the Beatles remained most respectful of Elvis's stature. John Lennon once commented to the press, "Nothing really affected me until I heard Elvis. If there hadn't been an Elvis, there wouldn't have been the Beatles."

Levitch's Jewelry Store

One of the premier jewelry stores in Memphis is Levitch's, owned by jeweler Harry Levitch. The store was one of Elvis's favorite shopping spots and he often bought dozens of rings and necklaces at a time. He carried boxes with him wherever he went and gave the diamond-studded gold jewelry to the people he encountered who made his day a little more pleasant, such as traffic cops, nurses, and secretaries.

The owner of the store, Harry Levitch, became a personal friend and often traveled with Elvis, bringing along some of his merchandise in case the shopping urge struck. Harry and his wife Francis were among the very few guests at Elvis's 1967 wedding to Priscilla Beaulieu. Elvis once introduced Harry to a group of celebrities in Las Vegas by saying, "Nobody's diamonds shine like Mr. Levitch's."

Barbara Jean Lewis

In 1988, a woman who claimed to be the daughter of Elvis Presley and Barbara Jean Lewis filed suit in Shelby County (Tennessee) probate court to claim her fair share of the Presley estate. According to the papers that were filed, Barbara Jean Lewis met Elvis Presley in Charlotte, North Caro-lina, in June 1954 when he was in town to record commercial jingles. The result was a year-long romance that culminated in the conception of their daughter, Deborah Delaine Presley, some time in June 1955, in Jackson, Mississippi. Deborah, an aspiring actress who has sold her story to

L

the tabloids, denounces Lucy de Barbin's daughter Desiree as a fake and contends that she is the only genuine illegitimate Presley offspring. Deborah, a movie extra and law clerk, and her mother have not yet provided incontrovertible proof of her claim and the probate court has declined to hear the case.

Jerry Lee Lewis Visits Graceland

In the late fall of 1976, the great rocker Jerry Lee Lewis turned up at the Music Gate of Graceland around 4 A.M. in his brand new Lincoln Continental and politely asked if Elvis was in. Told that Elvis was probably sleeping, Lewis immediately left—only to return the following evening at midnight. This time he demanded to see Elvis and was only persuaded to leave with great difficulty. "The Killer" returned three hours later, waving a pistol and threatening the guard at the gate. The guard called the police, who arrested Lewis and charged him with drunkenness and carrying a weapon. At a hearing six months later Lewis was found not guilty of both charges.

Jerry Lee Lewis later alleged that he had been the victim of a "setup" by Elvis, claiming that he had received an invitation to visit Graceland and had been purposely humiliated. Elvis never made a public comment on the situation but he had always maintained that he admired Jerry Lee Lewis as a musician and performer, and cited Lewis's 1957 hit record "Whole Lotta Shakin' Goin' On" as one of the most original and influential songs of the 1950s (Elvis himself covered it in 1970). Lewis, of course, had been one of the Sun recording artists at the same time Elvis was signed to that label and the two had occasionally appeared on the same stage together. Insiders say that Jerry Lee envied Elvis's phenomenal success, for many years so much greater than his own, despite his similar early promise.

In a 1989 interview, Jerry Lee Lewis created an uproar by calling Elvis a dummy whose backbone was made of jelly. He subsequently embellished his charges in the pages of the *National Enquirer*. "Elvis Presley was a yellow-bellied mama's boy," he asserted.

Liberace

If ever there was a show business duo made for one another, it was Liberace and Elvis Presley. The two men met before Elvis went into the army and a photo recording that fateful day shows Liberace with a guitar, obviously imitating Elvis. Later, it was Elvis who would imitate Liberace on the stages of Vegas hotels with the same brand of glitz and schmaltz.

One of the highlights of the 1988 TV movie *Liberace: Behind the Music* was a dramatization of that meeting between Elvis and Liberace.

L

Two performers who taught us the meaning of the word "glitz." Liberace pretends to play the guitar while Elvis sits at the piano bench when the two meet in Vegas. (Photo from Neal Peters Collection)

The Lifetime Film Grosses

According to informed estimates the grosses from the first release of the thirty-three films starring Elvis Presley were nearly half a billion dollars. The profits, of which Elvis got 50 percent (which he then had to share with Colonel Parker and his agents, William Morris), were at least $200 million. All this for vehicles that even his fan club magazine, *Elvis Monthly*, called "puppet shows for not overbright children." Today the sales continue, as videocassettes of Elvis's old movies, released by Warner Bros., still sell to his loyal fans.

Yvonne Lime

Yvonne Lime was a starlet, featured in a few of Roger Corman's low-budget thrillers, who had a small part in Elvis Presley's second movie, *Loving You.* Elvis and Yvonne dated at the time they worked together and she visited him in Memphis. He told one reporter he was "crazy about her." But when that movie was finished and the next one begun, Yvonne faded from Elvis's life.

The *Lisa Marie*

After the birth of his daughter Elvis Presley named his biggest private plane after her, calling it the *Lisa Marie*. The plane was a Convair 880, which he had bought from Delta Airlines for $1 million. He then spent almost a million dollars more to have it refurbished to his taste. With a range of three thousand miles, the *Lisa Marie* could take Elvis anywhere in the continental United States. The plane required a crew of four, including a stewardess to look after the passengers. The private bedroom featured a queen-sized bed and had its own bathroom with gold-plated fixtures and a shower. At the dining room table, surrounded by eight chairs, full meals were served that were cooked in the galley, where the coffeemaker was always kept running. The conference room had four television sets and there were seven telephones aboard the plane. Elvis liked to call the plane his "penthouse in the sky." It is now on display at Graceland, somewhat in need of refurbishing.

Lisa Marie Gets Married

On October 3, 1988, Lisa Marie Presley was married to musician Danny Keough in a very private ceremony held before a quarters of the Church of Scientology, a place that could have held thousands of people, and was conducted by the Reverend Sarah Gualtieri. In attendance were the mother of the bride, Priscilla Presley; the bride's maternal grandparents, Ann and Paul Beaulieu; her aunt, Michelle Beaulieu Hovey; and three unidentified close friends of the family. The bride, twenty, wore a knee-length pink silk dress, the groom, twenty-three, a plain dark suit. It was the first marriage for both. After the ceremony total of only nine people—five fewer than attended the wedding of her parents. The ceremony took place in the Hollywood headthere was a privately catered reception at the same location.

The entire event took place in the greatest secrecy to avoid media attention. Under California law cohabiting couples do not have to take a health test and they can wait ninety-six hours before filing notice of the wedding. So details were not released until several days after the event, by which time the couple had left for their honeymoon, giving Lisa Marie and Danny the privacy they had wanted.

Lisa Marie's Honeymoon

After Lisa Marie Presley's wedding to Danny Keough on October 11, 1988, Elvis's daughter and her new husband embarked on their honeymoon. The couple jetted to the Caribbean island of Aruba, where they According to others on the cruise the honeymooners kept to themselves, didn't leave the ship at its other ports of call, and occupied their time taking courses in Scientology and studying the teachings of boarded the cruise ship *Freewinds*, which is owned and operated by the Church of Scientology, to which they both belong. its founder, L. Ron Hubbard. Lisa Marie and Danny cut the projected cruise short because she was suffering from morning sickness.

Littlebit

Littlebit was a toy poodle given to Anita Wood by Elvis Presley.

"Little Elvis"

According to Elvis biographer Albert Goldman, Elvis Presley referred to his penis as "Little Elvis" and frequently spoke of it in the third person.

"Little One"

When Elvis Presley first met young Priscilla Beaulieu, his favorite nickname for her was "Little One."

Little Richard

Little Richard (Richard Penniman) is the early rock-and-roll star much admired by Elvis Presley. Elvis covered several of Little Richard's hits, including "Tutti-Frutti," "Good Golly Miss Molly," "Long Tall Sally," and "Ready Teddy."

"Lives"

The name Elvis is an anagram of the word "lives," an appropriate label for the twin who survived. Of course, "evils" is also an anagram of Elvis, as is "veils."

"A Living Doll"

Elvis Presley often treated young Priscilla Beaulieu like the "living doll" he called her, dressing her up to suit his own tastes. He insisted that she wear her hair long and teased, her make-up heavy, her collars high. He disliked prints and preferred strong clear colors, such as red or blue, black or white. He asked her to dye her hair from light brown to black, to make a greater contrast with her blue eyes. Years later Priscilla realized that most of the changes Elvis dictated had the effect of making her look more like him.

The Living Legend

In 1978, a short-lived show based on the life of Elvis Presley appeared on Broadway. Called *The Living Legend*, it starred Elvis imitator Rick Saucedo and featured gospel singer Kathy Westmoreland as well as Elvis's long-time backup vocal group, the Jordanaires.

The same title was used two years later for a movie loosely based on the romance between Elvis Presley and Ginger Alden. The lead character was played by producer Earl Owensby, lip-synching to a soundtrack by Roy Orbison. Ginger Alden played the central character's girlfriend.

Dixie Locke

Dixie Locke was a high school student in Memphis in the early 1950s who had the distinction of being the first serious girl-friend of Elvis Presley. The two young people met at the Assembly of God church and began dating the summer after Elvis graduated from high school. Dixie was only fifteen at the time, a petite brunette who attended Southside High. A frequently published photograph shows Elvis, in a rented white tux, escorting Dixie to her junior prom in 1954. Elvis later recalled his first love: "She was kind of small with long, dark hair that came down to her shoulders and the biggest smile I've ever seen anywhere. She was always laughing, always enjoying herself . . . We were a big thing. I gave her my high school ring. She loved me to pour letters of sand down her back. For two years we had a ball." After Elvis made his first records and began to tour extensively, Dixie could see him only infrequently so their romance was carried on primarily by means of his loving phone calls from the road. In the summer of 1955, after Dixie graduated from high school, she became engaged to someone else. This event came as a real blow to Elvis, who had assumed Dixie would always be there waiting for him when he was back in Memphis and able to see her.

Loew's Palace

Loew's Palace was a movie theater on Union Street in Memphis where Elvis Presley worked evenings as an usher during high school. The teenager was fired after a only a few weeks on the job because he was always watching the movie instead of showing people to their seats.

The Long Autopsy

The official results of the autopsy on the body of Elvis Presley were not released until nearly two months after the star's death in August 1977. It has been suggested that the long delay was related to some coverup. But Dr. Jerry Francisco, the chief medical examiner of Shelby County, Tennessee, has explained that the delay was merely the result of his decisions about how to handle a case that he realized would be the subject of so much publicity and speculation. At the suggestion of Los Angeles coroner Dr. Thomas Noguchi, himself a veteran of cases that attracted enormous public attention, Francisco appointed a distinguished panel of pathologists to help him with the autopsy. He also sent many tissue samples to top pathology laboratories all over the country for a wide variety of tests. According to Dr. Francisco it was the scrupulous care with which the whole procedure was conducted that created the delay. The coroner didn't want to release any results until he was sure he had a complete, final, and unassailable report.

"Louisiana Hayride"

A popular country radio show of the 1950s in southern states was called "Louisiana Hayride." It originated in Shreveport, Louisiana and was broadcast on Saturday nights throughout the South on station KWKH. Elvis first appeared on the show in October 1954 and was thereafter signed to perform regularly for a year. He sang live and also read some of the commercials for such items as biscuits and feed. For each appearance Elvis was paid only union scale: $18 for himself and $12 each for backup musicians Scotty Moore on guitar and Bill Black on bass. In March 1955, one "Louisiana Hayride" show was televised and Elvis was one of the featured performers. It was the success of his "Louisiana Hayride" appearances that finally convinced Elvis it was safe to quit his truck-driving job at Crown Electric in Memphis and rely on music for a living.

Love Me Tender: **The Movie**

The first film to star Elvis Presley was *Love Me Tender*. Elvis had just signed a three-picture contract with Paramount but the moving force behind that contract, producer Hal B. Wallis, was still looking for the right property for the young singer. So he agreed to lend Elvis to 20th Century-Fox for a film they were preparing for production. Some sources have suggested that Wallis wanted to let someone else take the risk of making the first Elvis film, but the loan proved to be no risk for Fox, which recouped the $1.5 million it spent to make *Love Me Tender* in the first three days of the movie's release.

Elvis went to Hollywood to begin shooting in August 1956, accompanied by Memphis buddies Red West and Lamar Fike. Elvis's manager, Colonel Tom Parker, was on the set too and received credit as a technical adviser on the film (a credit which he was to be awarded on most of the subsequent Elvis vehicles as well). *Love Me Tender* was a period piece set at the end of the Civil War; Elvis played Clint Reno, the youngest of four brothers and the only one who doesn't go off to fight for the Confederacy. In the belief that his brother Vance (Richard Egan) was killed in the war, Elvis marries his brother's sweetheart, played by Debra Paget. Naturally, the brother turns up later to complicate matters. As far as Elvis fans were convinced the only thing that marred their hero's film debut was the fact that Elvis gets killed in the end—although not before he gives his wife and his brother his blessing for their future happiness. To soften the blow to the audience of seeing Elvis cut down in his prime the film faded out with Elvis in the upper right hand corner singing "Love Me Tender." Incidentally the producer, David Weisbart, had also produced James Dean's biggest film, *Rebel Without a Cause.* He characterized his new star as immature, open, and impulsive and predicted future stardom as an actor. An opposing point of view was registered by the editorial staff of Harvard's *Lampoon*, which gave Elvis their Worst Supporting Actor Award.

The movie originally had another title—*The Reno Brothers*—but before it was re-leased Elvis's recording of a song from the movie, "Love Me Tender," written by Otis Blackwell and based on the Civil War song "Aura Lee," was climbing to the number one spot on the charts. Fox seized the opportunity to capitalize on the success of their star's single and changed the name of the movie.

Love Me Tender had its opening gala in New York on November 15, 1956. Throngs of teenagers gathered outside the theater just to see a thirty-foot cardboard image of their hero; Elvis did not attend in person. Although critics were not particularly impressed by Elvis's screen debut, his fans made the movie one of the most successful of the year.

"Love Me Tender": The Song

"Love Me Tender" was a song based on the nineteenth-century ballad "Aura Lee." Although Elvis Presley received songwriting credit for it, that was the result of the deal he struck with composer Ken Darby and his wife, Vera Matson, and represented financial rather than musical realities. Elvis recorded the song in the late summer of 1956 for use in the soundtrack of his first film. When advance sales of the single topped one million copies, the title of the movie was changed from *The Reno Brothers* to *Love Me Tender*, to take advantage of the record's enormous success. "Love Me Tender" was the number one pop song in the country for four weeks.

Love Is Forever

In 1983, Priscilla Presley appeared in a made-for-TV movie called *Love Is Forever*. The star of the movie was Michael Landon, who reportedly gave Priscilla a rough time throughout the on-location shooting in Thailand. She played the role of a scuba instructor who teaches an Australian journalist (Landon) how to swim underwater to help him make a daring attempt to rescue his Laotian fiancée (played by "Moira Chen," a former porno film star). Priscilla's sequences called for swimming in shark-infested waters and diving from the three-meter board, and she achieved her personal goal of shooting the scenes without the help of a stunt double.

Loving You

Loving You was the second movie Elvis Presley made and the first of his films produced by Hal B. Wallis of Paramount, the man who had signed him to a movie contract in the summer of 1956. *Loving You* scream," biographer Elaine Dundy quotes Gladys as saying to her sister, Lillian Mann. "There's always someone around especially to comb his hair, and someone else to help him get dressed, and there was one man with nothing else to do except knock on his door and ask him if he was *ready* to work."

The script for *Loving You* was written by Hal Kanter, who also directed the pic-

started shooting in January 1957, and this time Elvis took his parents, Gladys and Vernon, out to Hollywood to be with him. His mother was amused by life on the set. "The way they kowtowed to him was a unlike the glossy Hollywood production numbers mounted in most of his movies, were a close imitation of the early stage performances that made him a national idol. Among the featured songs were the title cut, "Teddy Bear," "Gotta Lotta Livin' To Do," and "Mean Women Blues." Backing Elvis up on some of the numbers were the Jordanaires, as well as musicians Scotty Moore, Bill Black, and D.J. Fonture and who later achieved fame as the producer of TV's "All in the Family." At Hal Wallis's suggestion, Kanter spent a few days with Elvis and came to admire the star, a feeling that comes across on the screen. Although the screenplay was supposedly developed from a short story in *Good Housekeeping*, Kanter's plot was loosely based on Elvis Presley's own life, telling the story of a truck driver who becomes a nationally popular rock-and-roll star. The singer, Deke Rivers, is manipulated by his scheming manager, played by the glamorous Lizabeth Scott, in her last screen appearance; there are clear parallels to Elvis's real-life relationship with his own manager, Colonel Tom Parker, which seem almost to be a warning to Elvis from Kanter.

Loving You is unique among Elvis films for the realism of its concert scenes, which,

tana. *Loving You* was premiered in Elvis's hometown of Memphis on July 9, 1957, for thousands of screaming fans. The soundtrack album, which had to be padded out with unrelated songs, including a cover of Fats Domino's hit, "Blueberry Hill," was released at the same time and quickly rose to the number one spot on the album charts, where it remained for ten straight weeks.

A special moment for Elvis fans when they watch *Loving You* comes in the musical number "Gotta Lotta Livin' To Do." Elvis walks off the stage and into the audience as he sings, and for a moment he pauses by a woman in the audience and sings straight to her as she claps her hands and taps her foot in response while exchanging a brief smile with the star—the woman is his mother, Gladys Presley.

Low-Budget Productions

After the first five or six movies Elvis Presley starred in, the quality of his film vehicles began to slide noticeably until they reached the level of the absolutely ludicrous. The scripts were a hackneyed formula of fight scenes and tepid romances, the songs uninspired, costumes pointless, and locations film budgets—the less they cost, he reasoned, the more money would be left over. Eventually this disregard for the audience killed the Elvis movies; not even his fans

inauthentic. Why were most of the Elvis pictures so bad? The answer lies in the contracts manager Colonel Tom Parker had negotiated on behalf of his star. Elvis was to get 50 percent of the *profits* from the film. The Colonel figured that one way to insure big profits was to hold down the wanted to see the last ones. Only the two documentary films of the 1970s brought the Elvis audience back into the theaters.

Ronnie McDowell

Ronnie McDowell is a country singer whose voice bears an uncanny resemblance to Elvis Presley's. The similarity has been the making of McDowell's career. He has dubbed the voice of Elvis in a number of productions, including *Elvis; Elvis and the Beauty Queen;* and the TV miniseries, *Elvis and Me.* In 1977, "The King Is Gone," his trib-ute to the star he had idolized ever since he was a boy of eight watching *King Creole* at the movie theater, was a hit single. In 1988, he released an album called "I'm Still Missing You," on which he is backed by vocals from the Jordanaires and sings one of Elvis's old hits, "Suspicion."

Bonya McGarrity

Bonya McGarrity was one of Elvis Presley's secretaries. She left his employ in 1961 when her husband finished school and joined the Air Force.

Madame Tussaud's

Madame Tussaud's in London is the most famous museum of wax figures in the world. The museum unveiled a wax figure of Elvis on the first anniversary of his death, but the representation met with heavy criticism from Elvis fans. A second figure was thus created, which is the one on view in the museum today. Most fans agree that it is only marginally better than the first effort.

John Mansell

John Mansell was Elvis Presley's maternal great-great grandfather. John was born on a farm in western Alabama in 1828, the oldest child of William Mansell and his Cherokee wife, Morning Dove. Sometime before 1850, John married Elizabeth Gilmore, with whom he had at least nine children; he also fathered children with his wife's sister Rebecca. In 1880 John lost the family farm. He thereupon dumped his wife, his sister-in-law, and all his minor children at the home of his grown son White Mansell and departed for Oxford, Mississippi, with an attractive young woman. No more is known of his life.

White Mansell

White Mansell was Elvis Presley's great-grandfather on the maternal side. He was the third child of John Mansell and his wife Elizabeth, born in 1850 on the family farm in western Alabama. White left home when he was eighteen and headed into northeast Mississippi, where he met neighbor Martha Tackett, whom he married in 1870. They had five or six children; White also took in his mother and her two minor children and his mother's sister and her two children by White's father, after his father abandoned them all on his doorstep.

William Mansell

William Mansell was Elvis Presley's great-great-great-grandfather on his maternal side. A descendant of Scots-Irish immigrants, William Mansell was born in western Tennessee in 1795. In his teens, he farmed, and then for a time he turned soldier, fighting under General Andrew Jackson in the wars throughout the South against the native Indians. In 1818, he was back in Tennessee, where he married a full-blooded Cherokee Indian, Morning Dove. Shortly thereafter the couple moved to western Alabama and Mansell staked claim on fertile farmland there. William and Morning Dove had three children—John (1828), Morning Dizenie (1832), and James (1835). Morning Dove died from complications of the last birth. By the time William himself died in 1842, he owned a sizable farm and a comfortable house.

Mare Ingram

Mare Ingram was the name of one of Elvis Presley's horses during the time he owned the Circle G Ranch. Mare Ingram was named after *Mayor* William Ingram of Memphis.

Martian Statue of Elvis

One of the more farfetched stories about Elvis Presley in the tabloids was run in *The Sun* in mid-1988. According to that report the Russians have found and photographed an eight-foot statue of Elvis on Mars.

Dean Martin

One of the idols of the teenage Elvis Presley was singer-actor Dean Martin. In the early 1950s, when Elvis was still in high school, Martin was costarring in classic comedies with Jerry Lewis and releasing hit records such as "That's Amore" (1953). His movie persona was to some extent a model for the one that Elvis would later assume—a ladies' man with a bit of a macho swagger who is given to bursting into song. In 1954, at the Sun studio, Elvis recorded "I Don't Care If The Sun Don't Shine," a song Martin had performed the year before in the movie *Scared Stiff*. It was not released until after RCA bought Elvis's contract and the rights to all the unreleased recordings in 1955. Years later Elvis sang another Martin hit, "Everybody Loves Somebody," during a 1970 engagement in Las Vegas, when Martin was in the audience.

The Master Bedroom at Graceland

Elvis Presley's own bedroom at Graceland was decorated to his taste in red and black with a pseudo-Spanish motif. The crimson curtains were heavily lined, so he could sleep during the sunny part of the day; the doors were padded black leather. His huge bed was custom made; it was so large (nine feet by nine feet) that it necessitated custom-made sheets as well. Two television sets were mounted in the ceiling so he could watch his favorite programs without sitting up. There were also television sets at the foot of the bed, standing atop a mound that rose up out of the red carpeting. A full-sized refrigerator stood in the large closet, stocked with Pepsi, yogurt, and ice cream treats.

In the later years of his life Elvis sometimes spent days in his Graceland bedroom without emerging. His meals were brought up to him on a tray, friends and lovers visited him there when he felt like inviting them, and he would doze, read, and watch television without regard to the clock or any demands from the outside world.

Sri Daya Mata

Sri Daya Mata (born Fay Wright) was the head of the Self-Realization Fellowship, with which Elvis Presley became involved in 1964. He frequently visited her at the organization's headquarters on Mount Washington, in the Hollywood Hills, hoping that she would help him achieve the highest form of meditation and self-control. Interestingly, according to Priscilla Presley, Daya Mata strongly resembled Gladys Presley.

Mealtime at Graceland

During the years that Priscilla and Elvis Presley lived together at Graceland they generally ate all their meals in the master bedroom. The cook would bring up a tray loaded with the "comfort" foods Elvis loved, such as pork chops, crisp bacon, cornbread, and mashed potatoes, and leave it discreetly outside their door. Priscilla later carried the tray in and the couple would eat while they watched TV. As soon as they finished, Priscilla would clear up the dishes, because Elvis objected to seeing any remnants of his meal afterward.

The Meditation Garden

Within a few weeks of Elvis Presley's death, three men were arrested on the suspicion of planning to steal Elvis's body from its resting place in a mausoleum at Forest Hill Cemetery and hold it for ransom. Elvis's father Vernon was worried about inadequate security at the cemetery, so he sought and received permission to move both Elvis and Elvis's mother Gladys to Graceland, to an area called the Meditation Garden.

The Meditation Garden had been created for Elvis in 1963 by Bernie Granadier and his wife Anne, sister of Marty Lacker, when the star expressed a wish for a quiet place to be with his own thoughts at Graceland. Elvis's grave in the Meditation Garden is now covered with a huge bronze plaque. At the foot, Vernon added an eternal flame, mounted on a plinth carved with the motto TCB and the lightning flash that Elvis used as an emblem. Later a small stone was erected nearby in memory of Elvis's stillborn twin brother, Jesse Garon Presley. After Vernon's own death in 1979, he too was buried in the Meditation Garden at Graceland. The last to join the group was Vernon's mother, Minnie Mae, who died in 1980.

Meeting Bill Haley

In October 1955, Elvis Presley was booked to perform at a high school in Cleveland. Other performers that evening were the Four Lads, Pat Boone, and headliner Bill Haley and the Comets. Afterward Elvis asked to meet Bill Haley, whose single, "Rock Around the Clock," was a national best-seller and who was about to release his next big record, "Shake, Rattle and Roll." As the two men who changed the face of popular music in the 1950s shook hands, the moment was immortalized in a photograph.

Two rock-and-roll legends meet: Elvis Presley and Bill Haley. The year is 1955. (Photo from Neal Peters Collection)

Memphis Bank of Commerce

Elvis Presley maintained his checking account at the Memphis Bank of Commerce, signing all checks as "E.A. Presley." Characteristic of the amateurish way his money was managed was the fact that he usually kept more than $1 million in the account, which paid no interest. After the death of Vernon Presley the Memphis Bank of Commerce became one of the trustees of the Presley estate.

The Memphis Mafia

When Elvis Presley required his entourage to wear dark mohair suits so they would look more respectable, reporters dubbed them the "Memphis Mafia." The group included boyhood friends Red and Sonny West and Lamar Fike, army pals Charlie Hodge and Joe Esposito, his cousin Patsy's husband Gee Gee Gambill, and other changing faces. Most of the members of the Memphis Mafia were on Elvis's payroll and their function was to protect him, to help him, to keep him company, and to agree with him.

Elvis himself did not like the nickname "Memphis Mafia." He told a reporter jokingly, "I prefer to think of them as members of a little country club I run." In a more serious vein, he added, "Most of them are my friends from back home. They are not bodyguards. One is my accountant, another my travel consultant. I need a valet, a security officer, and a wardrobe man with me nearly all the time." To Elvis, they were just "the guys."

"Memphis Flash"

An early nickname given Elvis Presley was "Memphis Flash," in reference to his eye-catching attire.

Memphis Recording Service

In 1950, a young Memphis disc jockey named Sam Phillips thought he could make a little money on the side by opening a recording studio for black musicians in the area. "It seemed to me," he later commented, "that the Negroes were the only ones who had any freshness left in their music, and there was no place in the south where they could go to record. The nearest place where they made so-called race records [which were soon to be called rhythm and blues] was Chicago, and most of them didn't have the money or time to make the trip to Chicago."

Sam Phillips opened the Memphis Recording Service at 706 Union Avenue while he still worked as a recording engineer at Memphis radio station WREC. The new company's motto was "We Record Anything—Anywhere—Anytime." The studio itself consisted of one big room with about eight mikes. The control booth was at the back of the long narrow room and featured two tape recorders and one master console. Most of the recordings were made by simply taping the performers in one continuous take. In addition to making recordings of such events as weddings and public speeches, the studio was open to anyone who wanted to come in and pay $4 to make a short 78-rpm record. One such drop-in was young Elvis Presley.

"Memphis, Tennessee"

"Memphis, Tennessee" was one of Chuck Berry's big hits in 1959, which he himself composed. Elvis, who had covered other Berry hits, recorded the ode to his hometown in 1964 but it wasn't released for nearly eighteen months.

Messerschmidt

In 1956, Elvis Presley purchased an unusual three-wheeled German car called a Messerschmidt. After a short period of ownership he traded the rare vehicle to Bernard Lansky in exchange for free run of the Lansky Brothers clothing store in Memphis.

Metro-Goldwyn-Mayer

In 1963, Colonel Tom Parker negotiated a new contract for his client Elvis Presley with Metro-Goldwyn-Mayer. The contract, which ran for five years, made Elvis the highest-paid actor under contract in Hollywood. It also virtually guaranteed the mediocrity of Elvis's film career. The MGM movies were cheaply made, with a plot formula that rarely varied. The studio agreed with the Colonel that quality was an unnecessary ingredient of movies starring Elvis Presley; as one studio employee remarked, "They could be numbered [instead of titled] and they'd still sell."

Dr. David Meyer

Dr. David Meyer was Elvis Presley's ophthalmologist in Memphis. In the last years of his life, the star was troubled by glaucoma, and he credited Dr. Meyer with saving his sight.

Milam School

In sixth grade Elvis Presley transferred from the grade school in East Tupelo, Mississippi, when his family moved to a different house. His new school was Milam School in Tupelo, and it seems to have been the place that made Elvis self-conscious about his family's poverty and their country ways. A frequently reproduced photograph from his days at Milam shows Elvis in a back row, wearing the overalls that proclaimed his status as a poor farm boy.

"Milk Cow Blues"

One of Elvis Presley's early records on the Sun label was "Milk Cow Blues." A blues standard written by Kokomo Arnold, it had also been recorded by Joe Williams, who made the tune sly and soulful. Elvis's version starts out with a good imitation of Williams. Then he says to his band (Scotty Moore and Bill Black). "Hold it, fellas. That don't move me. Let's get real, real gone for a change." The band picks up the tempo and suddenly the song belongs to Elvis. Scotty Moore has singled this record out as one of his favorites of all Elvis's work.

The Million-Dollar Offer

In late 1988 the tabloid newspaper *Globe* offered a check for $1 million to anyone who could prove Elvis Presley was still alive. To collect the money, the claimant must not only produce Elvis in person but get him to agree to submit to a battery of tests and questions to prove his identity.

The Million-Dollar Photos of Elvis's Grandchild

When Elvis Presley's first grandchild, Danielle Keough, was born, nearly twelve years after his death, the world was eager to get a look at the new baby. Although the family had managed to keep the birth itself private, they felt the responsibility of sharing the happy event with Elvis's fans. So when Danielle was one day old, photographer Cesare Bonazza was invited to the hospital in Santa Monica to take pictures of Lisa Marie, Danny, and the new baby. The pictures were sold to *Star* and *People* in the United States, and many other publications all over the world. According to one estimate, Bonazza made about $1 million from that single ten-minute photographic session.

The Million-Dollar Quartet

Sun Records often referred to its "Million-Dollar Quartet"—Elvis Presley, Carl Perkins, Johnny Cash, and Jerry Lee Lewis.

The Million-Dollar Quartet Recording Session

On December 4, 1956, a historic gathering of talent occurred at the Sun recording studio in Memphis. The occasion was a session to record a new song by Carl Perkins. Jerry Lee Lewis—not yet a star—was sitting in on piano. Johnny Cash was hanging out in the control booth, chatting with the engineer. Then Elvis Presley dropped in to say hello. After a bit of idle chatter Elvis went to the piano and started to play the Fats Domino hit "Blueberry Hill." He was quickly joined by Perkins, Lewis, and Cash. The group that was later to be called Sun's "Million-Dollar Quartet" was making music together.

The engineer had the presence of mind to keep the tape running, capturing two to three hours of vintage rock and roll.

Sam Phillips put out a press release describing the moment but he somehow failed to see the commercial potential of the taped session. The historic tape sat in the Sun archives until it was sold along with thousands of other tapes in 1969. It was not until after Elvis's death that it resurfaced, and then it was the subject of lawsuits by RCA as well as Perkins and Cash. In 1980, a bootleg version of the tape appeared on the market, followed by a longer version, including thirty-nine songs, in 1987. The sound is rough and raw, the atmosphere impromptu, but it is must listening for anyone who loves early rock and roll. It's wonderful to hear Elvis in the company of his musical peers.

M

Ronnie Milsap

Country-and-western singer Ronnie Milsap sang backup on several of Elvis Presley's recording sessions in Memphis in 1968 and 1969. Milsap, who was born in Robbinsville, North Carolina, in 1946, didn't achieve his own success until several years later, with "Let's Fall Apart" and "I Hate You." In the late 1960s, he also sang frequently at T.J.'s, a Memphis club where Elvis liked to hold large parties.

Mississippi Slim

Mississippi Slim was a respected country-and-western star in the small town of Tupelo, Mississippi, in the days when Elvis Presley was growing up there. Born Carvel Lee Ausborn, Mississippi Slim was Elvis's first musical mentor. Slim performed live on the local radio station WELO for an hour every day. By the time Elvis was eight years old, he had started hanging around the station and had scraped up an acquaintance with his hero. He followed Slim around town, and after Elvis got his first guitar, Slim taught him some more complicated chords than the ones he had taught himself or learned from his Uncle Vester.

Slim later recalled that he had invited his young fan to sing on his program at least once. He thought the kid had a good voice but a shaky sense of rhythm.

A Mistake by Mitch Miller

Early in 1955, band leader Mitch Miller happened to hear one of the Sun Records made by young Elvis Presley. Intrigued, Miller called Sam Phillips, the owner of the record label, to ask if Elvis's recording contract was for sale. Phillips, who needed money to promote the other singers under contract to Sun, said yes, and named a figure of $20,000. Miller responded by slamming down the phone in disgust. Before the year was over, RCA had paid $35,000, plus a personal bonus of $5,000 to Elvis, for the contract from which they were eventually to make countless millions.

"Mister, That's Me Singing"

After Elvis Presley's first record, "That's All Right," was released in the summer of 1954, the nineteen-year-old continued to work as usual driving a truck for Crown Electric in Memphis. It was not for another six or seven months that he had acquired enough faith in his career as a performer to quit his steady job. One story has it that while Elvis was driving around Memphis in the battered old Ford truck, he stopped at a light next to a car that had the radio turned on full blast. The station happened to be playing Elvis's record. Proudly, Elvis leaned out of his window and shouted at the driver of the car, "Mister, that's me singing.' "

Mary Ann Mobley

Mary Ann Mobley, the former Miss Mississippi who became Miss America, costarred with Elvis Presley in two movies, both released in 1965: *Girl Happy* and *Harum Scarum*. There were rumors at the time that the two were involved off the screen as well as on. Mary Ann later married actor and talk-show host Gary Collins.

Monovale Road

After Lisa Marie Presley was born, her parents Elvis and Priscilla found that their house in the Trousdale Estates in Los Angeles was too small for them and the usual entourage that collected around them. In 1970, they sold that four-bedroom house and bought a bigger one at 144 Monovale Road in the fashionable Holmby Hills section, located between Bel Air and Beverly Hills. The purchase price was $335,000 and the couple spent about the same amount in redecorating and purchasing new furnishings. According to a realtor who tried to sell the house for Elvis in 1975, the decor was so tacky it was practically impossible to find a buyer for the place. The bedroom, for example, featured a platform bed on a marble slab, surrounded by mirrors. The luxurious house had a den, a game room, and a small private movie theater. Elvis's house in Holmby Hills was finally purchased by actor Telly Savalas.

Moody Blue

Moody Blue was the album released by RCA just a few weeks before the death of Elvis Presley. Originally just two hundred thousand copies of the record were pressed on blue vinyl. But after August 16 grieving fans thronged record stores to buy their idol's last recording and it quickly sold more than one million copies, thus certifying it as a platinum album. It reached as high as number three on the album charts. Among the songs included were "Unchained Melody," "He'll Have to Go," "Pledging My Love," and the title cut, "Moody Blue."

Mary Tyler Moore

Mary Tyler Moore costarred with Elvis Presley in the 1970 movie *Change of Habit*, in which she played Sister Michelle, a nun who was also Elvis's love interest. Although there were the inevitable rumors of romance, the two were *really* just good friends. Elvis always said he especially enjoyed working with her and she called him gentlemanly and kind—and gorgeous. Mary Tyler Moore, of course, went on to become the star of one of the most successful and creative TV sitcoms and to win praise for her acting ability both on Broadway, in *Whose Life Is It Anyway?* and on the screen, in *Ordinary People*.

Change of Habit had Elvis falling in love with Mary Tyler Moore. . . . Of course, he didn't know she was a nun! (Photo from Neal Peters Collection)

Scotty Moore

Winfield Scott "Scotty" Moore was the Tennessee-born guitar player who for many years backed up Elvis Presley on recordings and in live performances, and who helped the singer evolve his characteristic musical style. Scotty began playing guitar when he was about eight years old and was, like Elvis, largely a self-taught musician. He moved to Memphis in 1950 to work at his brother's dry-cleaning plant as the hat specialist. At nights Scotty was performing regularly with a group that called itself the Starlight Wranglers, which he described as "just straight Hank Williams-type country."

In 1954, the Starlight Wranglers were in the Sun recording studio to make a record and Sam Phillips asked Scotty, along with bass player Bill Black, to rehearse with unknown singer Elvis Presley, whom Phillips was also planning to record. Thus Scotty and Bill became Elvis's backup group and were credited (without benefit of last names) on his debut recording, "That's All Right (Mama)." For the first few months of Elvis's career as a performer, Scotty acted as the singer's manager, under a contract signed by Elvis, then a minor, and both his parents. When it became obvious that Elvis was on the brink of stardom Scotty gracefully exited in favor of someone with better contacts and a more professional approach—deejay Bob Neal, to whom Scotty sold his manager's contract.

Scotty Moore played on a number of Elvis's recordings for Sun and his style of solo guitar thus became influential for several generations of musicians who tried to imitate the Elvis sound. One of the characteristics was a full, echoing sound produced by a tape slap built specially for him. Scotty says his personal sound developed as he rolled several different guitar styles into one. "I was a big fan of Merle Travis, of Chet Atkins with his thumb and finger styles, and a lot of the blues players."

Moore can be seen performing with Elvis in the movie *Jailhouse Rock*, as well as on the 1968 TV special. Scotty was paid only $200 a week for backing up one of the most successful stars in the entertainment business; he was even responsible for his own touring expenses. He quit working regularly with Elvis after Colonel Tom Parker took over as Elvis's manager, although he continued off and on to play behind him for recording dates. Moore still works today as a studio musician in Nashville and occasionally produces country-music records.

Rita Moreno

In 1957, Elvis Presley's name was romantically linked with that of Latin singer-dancer-actress Rita Moreno.

Morning Dove

During Elvis Presley's lifetime people often commented that his dark good looks made it seem likely that the star had an Indian ancestor. Author Elaine Dundy was able to confirm this suspicion. Through extensive and meticulous genealogical research she learned that Elvis's maternal great-great-great-grandmother was a full-blooded Cherokee Indian named Morning Dove. She was born around 1800 and married William Mansell, a Tennessee farmer, in 1818; at that time, liaisons between white settlers and Indians were not uncommon and many culminated in official marriages. The couple moved to Alabama a few years later, where they claimed land and built a house. They had three children—John (1828), Morning Dizenie (1832), and James (1835). Morning Dove died the same year her last child was born, presumably of complications from the birth.

Most Popular Jukebox Record of All Time

A 1988 poll of owners and operators of jukeboxes revealed that the most popular jukebox record of all time is Elvis Presley's "Hound Dog," backed with "Don't Be Cruel."

Most Promising Newcomer of 1955

In the fall of 1955, Elvis Presley's new manager, Colonel Tom Parker, arranged for his client to perform in Nashville at the Country-and-Western Disc Jockey Convention. At that time Elvis had three hit songs on the country charts—"Baby, Let's Play House," "Mystery Train," and "I Forgot to Remember to Forget," which eventually reached the number one spot. Impressed by the young man's talent and performance energy, the assembled deejays voted Elvis Presley the "Most Promising Newcomer of the Year." It was an accurate prediction.

A Mother Loses Her Son

From the moment of Elvis Presley's birth, his mother had never been separated from him for more than a few days at most. Gladys Presley became increasingly upset as Elvis's success began to take him away from home more and more frequently, and when he had to go into the army in early 1958, Gladys was utterly distraught. She feared that he would be hurt or killed, but even more she feared that she would be separated from him for long periods. Elvis did his best to keep that from happening. He arranged for his parents to live near Fort Hood, Texas, where he was first stationed. They shared a house with him there and he planned to do the same thing when he was sent to Germany. But Gladys could not bear the separation his military service had already brought, and she could not conceive that the Presley family could be together as usual in a foreign country. Many Presley family insiders agree that it was grief and worry that really killed Gladys Presley just weeks before Elvis was scheduled to be sent overseas.

Elisha Matthew "Bitsy" Mott

Elisha Matthew "Bitsy" Mott was the younger brother of Marie Parker, Colonel Tom Parker's wife. Bitsy went to work for his brother-in-law and helped the Colonel promote Elvis Presley's career during the 1950s and 1960s. Bitsy traveled with Elvis in the 1950s and had bit parts in several of his early movies.

Mountain Valley Water

Elvis Presley drank only bottled water once he became rich enough to afford it. His preferred brand was Mountain Valley and he took it with him everywhere. There were always a few bottles in an ice bucket within reach when he was performing. Colonel Tom Parker, who also drank Mountain Valley water, liked to call it "Arkansas champagne." According to Elvis's personal physician, Dr. George Nichopoulos, the star usually drank at least a gallon of Mountain Valley water a day, and Dr. Nick thought the excessive water intake contributed to Elvis's puffiness during the last years of his life.

Moving to Memphis

In 1948 Vernon Presley decided to move his family from East Tupelo, Mississippi, to Memphis, Tennessee—about a hundred miles to the north. Hoping to find regular work in the city and thus lift the Presley family out of its poverty, Vernon packed up the family's few possessions, put them in their 1939 Plymouth, and headed for Memphis. He took his wife, his son Elvis, and his mother, Minnie Mae, who was then living in his household; he was also accompanied by his brother-in-law Travis Smith and Travis's family. After a brief stay in a boardinghouse, the four Presleys moved to a run-down apartment in a poverty-stricken neighborhood on Poplar Avenue.

The quest for increased prosperity in Memphis proved fruitless. Both Vernon and Gladys found various jobs, but the family continued to live at the poverty line until Elvis was able to support his parents on his earnings as a performer.

Muffin

Muffin was the name of Elvis Presley's Great Pyrenees dog. A beautiful white dog, he seemed to have an incurably bad temper, which even obedience school couldn't improve. Visitors learned to give Muffin a wide berth and even Elvis was bitten a few times.

Eddie Murphy

Actor-comedian Eddie Murphy, who also happens to be very serious about his singing career, has an interesting way of warming up at the mike during his recording sessions—he imitates Elvis Presley. According to his producer, "If the lights were out, you wouldn't know it [wasn't Elvis]." Murphy has called Elvis "the greatest entertainer who ever lived." He says he used to lip synch to his Elvis albums when he was a kid, and still likes to pattern some of his actions after those of his idol: "Elvis took care of people and so do I." Eddie's friends reveal that a seven-foot painting of Elvis hangs in his bedroom.

The Music Gate

The main entrance to Graceland is through the Music Gate, a pair of high wrought-iron gates ornamented with a guitar and some musical notes. Whatever the hour of the day or night, when Elvis Presley was in residence at Graceland there were always people waiting outside the Music Gate hoping to get a glimpse of him. As his car drove through the Music Gate he would sometimes slow down, lower his window, and chat with the fans gathered there. Occasionally he handed out small gifts or gave a young woman or child a hug or a kiss on the cheek. He got to know the faces and the names of the regulars and some of them even became members of the Elvis entourage.

The Music Room at Graceland

The music room at Graceland is decorated entirely in red; biographer Albert Goldman said that entering it was like stepping into an immense heart. The focal point of the room is a concert grand piano, which Elvis enjoyed playing.

Musical Tributes to Elvis

Many musicians wrote and performed musical tributes to Elvis Presley, both before and after his death. Among the most memorable:

- *Elvis' Favorite Gospel Songs*, by J.D. Sumner and the Stamps
- *The Guitar That Changed the World*, an album by Scotty Moore, Epic, 1964
- "Concerto for Elvis," a thirty-minute piano concerto written by composer Ben Weisman
- "From Graceland to the Promised Land," a song by Merle Haggard written after Elvis's death, from the album *My Farewell to Elvis*
- "I Remember Elvis Presley," by Danny Mirror
- "The King Is Gone," by Elvis sound-alike Ronnie McDowell
- "The Day the Beat Stopped," by another Elvis sound-alike, Ral Donner
- "D.O.A.," by Tanya Tucker, singing under the name Misty
- "Loving You," by Donna Fargo
- "My Heavenly Father" b/w "What Am I Living For," by one of Elvis's favorite gospel singers, Kathy Westmoreland
- "The Whole World Misses You," by Carl Perkins
- "Graceland," by Paul Simon
- "Elvis and Marilyn," by Leon Russell
- "Hound Dog Man," by Glen Campbell
- "Il Ne Chantera Plus Jamais" (He'll Never Sing Again"), by Petula Clark,
- "Welcome Home Elvis," by Billie Joe Burnette

My Home Movies of Elvis

Joe Esposito, a member of the "Memphis Mafia" and part of Elvis Presley's inner circle for many years, kept his movie camera handy when he was at Graceland. Joe later packaged a selection of candid clips of Elvis—riding his horses, playing with daughter Lisa Marie when she was a baby, romping in the snow with the guys—and sold them as a videocassette entitled *My Home Movies of Elvis*. The Presley estate promptly sued, alleging that they own the rights to all likenesses and images of Elvis and that they have sold the home movie rights to Disney. The forty-five-minute videocassette is currently available only in Great Britain, through the fan club Elvisly Yours. For further information, write: P.O. Box 315; London N.W. 10, England.

"My Way"

The song "My Way," which was written by a trio of Frenchmen and given English lyrics by Paul Anka, became a Frank Sinatra trademark in 1969. Four years later, Elvis Presley recorded the song, which over the years sold more than a million copies. He sang it so often in concert that it became as much Elvis's trademark as Frank Sinatra's.

The Mynah Bird

Among Elvis Presley's many pets was a mynah bird that lived at Graceland. When Elvis returned once from a long stay in Hollywood, the bird—carefully tutored by one of the Graceland insiders—greeted him by saying, "Elvis, go to hell!"

"Mystery Train"

One of Elvis Presley's early hits, recorded on the Sun label, was "Mystery Train," a song that exemplifies his ability to turn what had been called "race" music into the popular mainstream. "Mystery Train" had been written by R&B singer Little Junior Parker with Sam Phillips and recorded at Sun several years before Elvis covered it. Elvis's version, released in July 1955, made it all the way to the number one position on the pop charts.

Mystery Train: The Movie

A 1989 movie written and directed by Jim Jarmusch was *Mystery Train,* named after one of Elvis Presley's hits. It was a series of vignettes linked by a Memphis setting and what one reviewer called "a ghost-of-Elvis aura." The characters are visitors in a cheap Memphis hotel, where each room has a portrait of Elvis. The legend of Elvis is the background for all the stories.

The Naked Gun

The Naked Gun, a movie released in late 1988, stars Priscilla Presley as the female lead. She plays her first comedic role, taking pratfalls, getting sprayed with water, and dressing in a giant condom for a "safe sex" scene. Priscilla told a reporter, "I'm sure everybody thought I would do something safe, something melodramatic, something like *Dallas*. But I'm really known for doing the unexpected."

The Name Presley

The surname Presley is an English cognomen. It comes from the same source as the names Priestly, Priestley, Preslee, Presslie, Pressley, and Prisley, and it means, "a dweller by the priest's wood." In early days it was often given as a nickname to men of priestly appearance or character, and perhaps also to men who were quite obviously *not* priestly.

Naming His Influences

According to Elvis Presley's companion and employee Marty Lacker, Elvis once summed up the people he felt were most influential on his own musical style. "Those who I've always liked and who I try to combine with my own style are Brook Benton, Roy Hamilton, Jess Hess, Arthur Prysock, and Billy Eckstine."

"Nashville Remembers Elvis on His Birthday"

"Nashville Remembers Elvis on His Birthday" was a TV special that aired on January 8, 1978, the first birthday after Elvis Presley's untimely death. The ninety-minute program included recollections of the star by Nancy Sinatra, Stella Stevens, Bill Bixby, Mary Ann Mobley, and Jack Albertson, all of whom had appeared in movies starring Elvis. Carl Perkins and Jerry Lee Lewis, former fellow Sun recording stars, sang, as did Elvis sound-alike Ronnie McDowell.

Bob Neal

Bob Neal was the disc jockey who in the 1950s hosted a program on Memphis station WMPS called "High Noon Roundup." The show featured live performances of country music and gospel, and one of its loyal fans was the young unknown, Elvis Presley, who used to go to the studio in the basement of Memphis's Peabody Hotel on his lunch hour and watch the broadcast. He made friends with the group that sang on the program, the Songfellows, and had hoped he might join the group if one of the members left. That didn't happen before Elvis had made his own first recording at Sun, but Bob Neal kept his eye on the young performer. When it became clear that Elvis was on the brink of real stardom, Bob Neal bought Elvis's management contract from guitarist Scotty Moore, who had been the first to take on that responsibility.

Neal, a man of unflagging energy, ran a record store and operated a management agency in addition to his career as a deejay. He also packaged appearances of country-music and gospel groups that he called "jamborees" and booked them into little auditoriums all over the South; he then advertised the shows on his own radio program. For about six months he arranged for Elvis to travel continuously, polishing his act at every appearance. Neal himself often traveled with Elvis and the band, driving in guitarist Scotty Moore's big old car, and went out onstage to tell a few jokes, warm up the audience, and introduce Elvis and the band.

Neal's greatest coup as manager was booking Elvis Presley, still virtually unknown to a national audience, in a country-music tour over the summer of 1955, along with much better-known performers, including headliner Hank Snow. It was on this tour that Elvis met Snow's manager, Colonel Tom Parker, who took an interest in Elvis and began to advise Neal on how to handle his career. Although Neal's management contract ran until the spring of 1956, he bowed out gracefully when he saw that Parker could do more for Elvis, and by September 1955, Parker was making all the decisions regarding Elvis's career.

Neal later managed various other Sun recording artists, including Johnny Cash, Jerry Lee Lewis, Carl Perkins, and Conway Twitty.

Rick Nelson

Rick Nelson, born in 1940, was one of the young rock stars to emerge during the time Elvis Presley was in the army. Eventually there were many connections between Rick, child star of TV's "Ozzie and Harriet," and Elvis. Rick played football on Elvis's team in Bel Air in the 1960s. The guitarist who replaced Scotty Moore to back up Elvis, James Burton, had formerly played with Rick Nelson. And the Jordanaires, after deciding at the end of the 1960s not to play in Vegas or tour with Elvis, went on to sing with Rick Nelson. Many of the songs Nelson recorded were written by Johnny Burnette, once a kind of mentor for Elvis in the world of Memphis clubs, and his brother Dorsey.

Rick Nelson died in a plane crash on December 31, 1985, enroute to a New Year's Eve concert date.

Neutrogena

Elvis Presley's favorite soap was the transparent hypoallergenic bar made by Neutrogena.

"Never Been to Spain"

"Never Been to Spain" was a song that was a hit for the rock group Three Dog Night in 1971. Elvis Presley recorded it in 1972 and often performed it live. The song was written by Hoyt Axton, son of Mae Boren Axton, who wrote Elvis's first megahit, "Heartbreak Hotel."

A New Home for the New Baby

Late in 1988, Priscilla Presley paid $800,000 for a ranch house in the Los Angeles suburb of Tarzana as a wedding present for her daughter Lisa Marie and new son-in-law Danny Keough, so there would be a secluded refuge for the baby that was on the way. She also arranged to have $150,000 worth of sophisticated high-tech equipment installed for a security system to keep Elvis's grandchild safe.

The New Year's Eve Parties

After he returned from the army in 1960, Elvis Presley began the custom of hosting a lavish party every year on New Year's Eve. Some years the huge parties were held at Graceland, and other years at private clubs in Memphis. The parties were attended by a minimum of several hundred guests who were plied with lavish food and drink. Elvis often hired other singers to entertain the crowd; among the most notable were Ronnie Milsap and B.J. Thomas. The parties usually ended with a dazzling display of fireworks set off by Elvis and his buddies.

Throughout the sixties Elvis seemed to love hosting these New Year's Eve parties, but as the seventies wore on he grew less and less interested in making the effort to be a host. He willingly paid the bills for his friends' food and drink, but he no longer got all dressed up for the occasion and he sometimes stayed at the party for less than an hour. One year he failed even to put in an appearance, much to the disappointment of the assembled guests.

The New York Concerts

In 1972, Elvis Presley gave four concerts at Madison Square Garden in New York. The tickets sold out instantly and among the buyers were such musical celebrities as John Lennon, George Harrison, and David Bowie. The performance was recorded and an edited version was later released as a live album that sold more than a million copies.

Billie Joe Newton

Billie Joe Newton is one of several women who claim to have been married to the young Elvis Presley. According to a story published in the tabloid newspaper *The Globe*, Elvis met Billie Joe when she was eight and she bore him a child the following year (one of the many points of her story that strains credulity). Billie Joe claims to have given birth to two other Presley children and to have married the singer in 1955 when she was fourteen. She further alleges that Colonel Parker made Elvis divorce her the following year to protect his career. Like all the other women who claim to have been Elvis's wife, Newton is unable to produce any of the "lost" documents to support her contention.

N

Wayne Newton

Wayne Newton, one of the most popular of all Vegas entertainers, seems to be hoping to inherit the mantle of Elvis Presley. Certain similarities are obvious—a sexy, macho image, crooned love ballads, and stage shows with lots of glitz and glitter. Newton was an established Vegas institution when Elvis first started appearing there, and Newton befriended the newcomer; he also bought the star's Jet Commander plane when Elvis traded up to a Convair. After Elvis's death, Newton seemed to go out of his way to emphasize his likeness to the King. His current show uses as its opener "That's All Right," and features such other Elvis classics as "Heartbreak Hotel," "Suspicious Minds," and "Are You Lonesome Tonight." He even uses the same song Elvis did to close his show, "Can't Help Falling in Love." In 1987, the *National Enquirer* published an article stating that Newton allegedly claimed that he has several times spoken with Elvis's spirit since his death.

Dr. George Nichopoulos

Dr. George Nichopoulos, or "Dr. Nick," was Elvis Presley's personal physician from 1966 to 1977. Born in Ridgeway, Pennsylvania, in 1927, Nick grew up in Alabama, where his Greek immigrant parents ran a restaurant. An academic overachiever, he earned both a Ph.D. from the University of Tennessee and an M.D. from Vanderbilt University. After his internship Nichopoulos moved to Memphis with his wife Edna and their children to join a partnership called the Medical Group. In Memphis he met his famous patient, Elvis Presley, in 1966, when Elvis caught a cold and his friend George Klein's wife Barbara, then working in Dr. Nick's office, called her employer to ask him to make a house call.

Dr. Nick encouraged Elvis Presley to lead a healthier life. The doctor was himself a racquetball player of championship caliber, and he exerted his influence to make Elvis go on an exercise and fitness regimen that included regular workouts on a luxurious racquetball court the star built behind Graceland. Yet in his attempt to deal with Elvis's multiple physical and emotional problems, it appears that Dr. Nick wrote the prescriptions for the huge numbers and wide varieties of pharmaceutical drugs that Elvis used. More questions about the doctor-patient relationship arose when public records showed that the doctor secured significant personal gain from his patient. Elvis lent Dr. Nick more than $250,000, charging no interest and making the notes payable sometime in the next century. Nichopoulos was also a partner of the star in a business enterprise to open a racquetball court under Elvis's name; Elvis later left the partnership and several lawsuits resulted.

These circumstances raised repeated questions about Dr. Nick's professional ethics. In 1980, a segment reported by Geraldo Rivera appeared on TV's "20/20," dealing with the way Elvis Presley was able to obtain all the prescription drugs he took. Partly in response to that program, Dr. Nick was investigated by the Tennessee Medical Board and barred for a time from further practice in that state. He was then indicted by a Shelby County grand jury for illegally prescribing; he was later found not guilty. Dr. Nick's son, Dean, was a member of the Elvis entourage and often traveled with the star on his concert tours.

Ninja

Ninja was a black Doberman that Priscilla Presley acquired after her divorce. Elvis was never comfortable around Dobermans and used to refer to Ninja as "that devil dog."

Nixon Has an Idea for Elvis

On December 21, 1970, Elvis Presley made a secret visit to President Richard M. Nixon in the White House. Elvis had offered his help in the official fight against drugs, and the president came to the meeting armed with a staff memo that suggested five ways Elvis might contribute to the effort to reduce drug use among young people. One of them read: "Record an album with the theme 'Get High on Life' at the federal narcotics rehabilitation and research facility at Lexington, Kentucky." Nothing ever came of that idea. However, both principals in the meeting were satisfied with its success.

No Jeans

Growing up poor in rural Mississippi, Elvis Presley wore nothing but overalls and blue jeans. When he became rich and famous he refused to wear jeans, even after they were high-style garments. He didn't like to see anyone around him wearing jeans, either.

No "Obey"

When Priscilla Beaulieu married Elvis Presley in 1967, most of the details of the ceremony were arranged by Elvis's manager, Colonel Tom Parker, and they reflected his personality more than they did the bride's. But in the phrasing of her marriage vows, Priscilla insisted on having her own way. She refused to promise to "obey" her husband; in the altered vow she promised to "love, honor and comfort," Elvis.

No White House Concert

In 1970, President Richard M. Nixon asked Elvis Presley to perform in concert for a gala evening at the White House. Elvis's manager, Colonel Tom Parker, promptly asked for a performance fee of $25,000.

When he was told that the White House never paid the performers who appeared there, Parker simply replied that Elvis never performed for free. So there was never an Elvis Presley concert at the White House.

Number One Singles

Fourteen of Elvis Presley's singles reached the top of the pops, the coveted number one position on the list of pop singles. They were

- "All Shook Up"
- "Heartbreak Hotel"
- "Don't Be Cruel"
- "Love Me Tender"
- "Teddy Bear"
- "Are You Lonesome Tonight"
- "Jailhouse Rock"
- "It's Now or Never"
- "Stuck on You"
- "A Big Hunk o' Love"
- "Good Luck Charm"
- "Surrender"
- "Don't"
- "Suspicious Minds"

Numerology

In the last years of his life, Elvis Presley became seriously interested in numerology. According to the numerological system he followed, laid out in Cheiro's *Book of Numbers*, Elvis was an eight, and he attached great significance to that number. A standard interpretation of the nine different numerological personalities indicates that eights are bright, curious, restless individuals. They try to seek out the unusual and like to take risks, while avoiding responsibility and hating to be pinned down. Travel and speculation are popular activities for eights, and they tend to be good at a wide variety of tasks without ever learning to master any particular one. They tend to be self-indulgent and are quick tempered when things don't go their way. One of their major faults can be arrogance.

Elvis once talked about his interpretation of the "eight" personality in a conversation with Red West that Red taped and used in the book he coauthored, *Elvis: What Happened?* "I feel terribly alone, you know, like that number eight. The thing that says they're intensely alone at heart. For this reason they feel that they feel lonely but in reality they have warm hearts toward the oppressed. But they hide their feelings in life but do what they please."

"Nungen"

One of Elvis Presley's terms of endearment for his wife Priscilla was "Nungen," a baby-talk version of "young one."

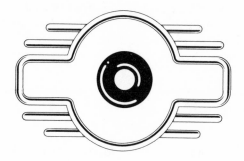

The Official Elvis Presley Fan Club of Great Britain

The Official Elvis Presley Fan Club of Great Britain is the largest Elvis fan club in the world, claiming more than twenty thousand members. It was founded by Albert Hand and run by Todd Slaughter after Hand's death. Among the club's activities are the publication of a subscription-only members' magazine as well as a periodical called *Elvis Monthly*, available at magazine stands in Great Britain or by subscription. For further information about the club and its activities write: P.O. Box 4, Leicester LE3 5HY England.

The Old Lincoln Coupe

The first car that Elvis Presley ever owned was the one he drove in high school, an old Lincoln coupe; it was either a 1940 or 1941 model.

"Old Shep"

"Old Shep" was a country ballad written by Red Foley that was one of the favorite songs of Elvis Presley during his boyhood. As an eight-year-old, he sang it at a talent contest placing second and winning $5; he also sang it in his high school senior talent show. Some people laughed that he sang it so often audiences started to groan when they heard it coming. In December 1956, RCA released a promotional record featuring Elvis singing "Old Shep" to stir interest in the forthcoming album, *Elvis*,

O

on which the ballad was featured. The song so much identified with Elvis's youth was later included on the album *Elvis Sings for Children and Grownups Too*, as well as on a British album called *Elvis Presley Number Two* and on several bootleg collections.

"Old Super Ears"

Elvis Presley's friends and family sometimes called him "Old Super Ears" because of his disconcerting ability to talk to one person attentively and still follow all the other conversations that were going on in the room.

The Oldsmobile Commercial

In 1988, Elvis Presley's daughter Lisa Marie and his ex-wife Priscilla made a commercial for Oldsmobile's fall campaign. Entitled "Not Your Father's Oldsmobile," the commercial shows Lisa Marie complaining, "If I want a new hairdo, my mother puts her foot down." It ends as Lisa says, "I'm sure she'll put her foot down on this car, too." She looks directly at the camera and says, "Uh-oh" in a voice just like her father's as Priscilla floors the accelerator of a sporty new Oldsmobile. Unfortunately the commercial also contains a reference to Lisa's wanting "a new boyfriend," which made the commercial instantly dated, thanks to her October 1988 marriage. The commercial, for which Oldsmobile was reported to have paid the mother-daughter stars $250,000, has been aired infrequently.

Roy Orbison

Elvis Presley once called Roy Orbison the best singer in the world. When Roy, a year younger than Elvis, started out in the music business, he had his own local television show in his native Texas. In 1955, one of the guests on his show was Elvis. Inspired by Elvis's performance and his success story, Roy sent his own demo record to Sam Phillips at Sun Records. Sam responded by offering Roy a contract, and thus Roy was for a time, like Elvis, a Sun recording artist. In the early 1960s, he and Elvis continually battled one another for top position on the music charts; Roy's soulful style in singing such hits as "Only the Lonely" and "Blue Bayou" was an influence on Elvis's rendition of romantic ballads. The two men respected one another and even had somewhat similar performing personas.

In an interview in 1988, Orbison told reporter Bruce Dorminey how he came up with the words to his 1963 hit song, "In Dreams." He dreamed one night that he heard a new hit on the radio. "The song was something about gold," Roy was quoted as recalling. "It was just beautiful, and I said, 'Well, Ol' Elvis has another smash.' Then I woke up and realized Elvis couldn't have sung it; I was dreaming. One night, days later, the lyrics came back to me . . ." He also wrote and sang several songs for the 1980 movie about Elvis, *The Living Legend.*

Roy Orbison died of a heart attack in December 1988, as he was enjoying a comeback that included a hit album made with colleagues Bob Dylan, George Harrison, Tom Petty, and Jeff Lynne, called *The Traveling Wilburys.* Bruce Springsteen said in tribute to Orbison's music, "Roy's ballads were always best when you were alone and in the dark."

Orion

Orion is a novel based on the premise that Elvis faked his own death to escape the burdens of his fame. Republished in 1989, *Orion* was written in 1978 by Gail Brewer-Giorgio, author of *Is Elvis Alive?* Thereafter, singer Jimmy Ellis, an Elvis sound-alike, recorded an album entitled *Reborn* under the name Orion Eckley Darnell, which gave rise to the rumor that the record was actually made by Elvis.

Orpheus Descending

Orpheus Descending is a play by Tennessee Williams that retells the Orpheus myth, about the god with the musical powers who succeeds in taming wild beasts but is eventually torn to pieces by them. The central character of Williams's version of the myth was clearly modeled after Elvis Presley. The play is set in a small town in Mississippi, where the hero, guitar player Val Xavier, lives as a beautiful innocent in the midst of the corruption that finally dooms him to be set upon and killed by the sheriff's dogs.

The play opened on Broadway in March 1957, with Cliff Robertson playing the part of Val. *Orpheus Descending* was revived on the London stage in 1988 and in New York in 1989, with Kevin Anderson as Val. It was made into a movie in 1960, under the title *The Fugitive Kind*; Williams wrote the screenplay and Sidney Lumet directed. Marlon Brando starred in the Elvis-based role and the supporting cast included Anna Magnani, Joanne Woodward, Victor Jory, and Maureen Stapleton.

An Outstanding Young Man of America

In 1971, the thirty-six-year-old Elvis Presley was given an award by the national council of Junior Chambers of Commerce. The Jaycees named Elvis one of the ten outstanding young men of America. He happily accepted the award in person and displayed it prominently at Graceland.

Debra Paget

Debra Paget was Elvis Presley's leading lady in his first movie, *Love Me Tender*. Previously, she had appeared with him in a skit on "The Milton Berle Show." As Berle jokingly warned Elvis that the sophisticated Debra was not in his league and would never go out with him, Debra came out jumping and screaming and carrying

In his movie debut, Elvis romanced Debra Paget. He wanted to do the same off the set of *Love Me Tender*, but she demurred. (Photo from Neal Peters Collection)

on like a typical Elvis fan. In actual fact, though, Berle was probably correct. Although there were rumors of a romance between the two stars when they were working together, both later denied it. Elvis said it was just a publicity gimmick, but most insiders agree he was seriously smitten by his first costar. Paget, born in Denver in 1933 and more than two years Elvis's senior, said, "I didn't even date Elvis. He wasn't really my cup of tea. Too much backwoods, if you know what I mean." Another reason for her lack of interest in Elvis may have been that she was dating Howard Hughes at the time.

Paramount Pictures

In the summer of 1956, Colonel Tom Parker negotiated a movie contract for client Elvis Presley with Hal B. Wallis of Paramount Pictures. The contract called for Elvis to make three movies, at fees that began at $100,000 and could escalate if the movies were successful. The contract was not exclusive, so Elvis also made films at the same time under a separate contract with MGM. Elvis made movies for Paramount off and on throughout his entire film career; the last one was *Easy Come, Easy Go* in 1967.

Parchman Farm

Parchman Farm was a twenty thousand-acre prison farm in the Mississippi delta. Convicts, working in chain gangs watched over by a "boss" riding a tall horse and carrying a shotgun, provided all the labor for what was in essence a gigantic state plantation, cultivated half in cotton and half in corn. In 1938, Vernon Presley was sentenced to three years of labor at Parchman Farm for forging a signature on a check, but managed through good behavior and pleading letters from his wife to win his release in nine months.

The Paris Visit

In June 1959, Elvis Presley was on a week's furlough from the army. Like many other American servicemen stationed in Germany, Elvis decided to spend the time vacationing in Paris. He stayed at the quiet Hotel Prince des Galles, sleeping during the day and going out at night. Several nights in a row he went to the famous Lido Club; one night there he sat at the piano and sang "Willow Weep for Me," and other similar numbers. According to George Bernard, a musician then performing at the Lido, Elvis was a fine piano player who reminded him of George Shearing; his vocal performance of some classic nightclub songs was unexpectedly suave and sophisticated.

Ed Parker

Ed Parker was a California karate instructor who first taught Elvis Presley and then became his bodyguard and confidant. Parker, born in Honolulu, is a cousin of singer Don Ho. Elvis's nickname for him was "Kahuna," which means priest—a name with the same derivation as Presley. In 1978, Parker wrote a book about his friend and boss, *Inside Elvis*.

Marie Mott Ross Parker

The wife of Colonel Thomas A. Parker was Marie Mott Ross Parker. The couple met in Tampa in 1935 at the South Florida State Fair—Parker was there with the American Royal Show and Marie was working in the Hav-A-Tampa cigar booth. Marie, born in 1905, was one of six children of a very poor family and she escaped into marriage when she was nineteen, in 1924. Her first husband was a photographer named Robert Burl Ross, with whom she had a son. They later divorced and Marie took as her second husband, in 1933, the largely unemployed Willett Man Esgler Sayre. At the time Marie met Tom Parker, she had divorced Sayre and was living, along with her ten-year-old son by Ross, with her parents. Sometime in 1935 Tom and Marie became Mr. and Mrs. Parker. According to research by Dirk Vellenga, the Tampa courthouse shows no record of their marriage and Marie's brother confirms there was no wedding party; thus it is not clear whether or not they actually went through the formalities of a wedding ceremony.

Initially the couple traveled together with the American Royal Show, returning to live with Marie's parents each winter in Tampa. When Parker left the carnival life and started managing singers, Marie stayed in the background, although she did act as her husband's bookkeeper. Colonel Parker loved to refer to his wife jokingly as "Miz 'Rie." Mrs. Parker's last years were spent in a coma, as she was cared for at the Parker home in Palm Springs.

Elvis Presley's daughter Lisa Marie was named after Marie Parker.

Pat Parker

Pat Parker was the California waitress and Elvis Presley fan who filed a paternity suit against the star in 1970. She claimed that her son Jason had been fathered by Elvis and asked a judge to award her $1,000 a month in child support. After receiving the results of a blood test and a lie-detector test ordered for Elvis by the court, Parker's lawyer announced she was dropping the suit.

Elvis sits in the office of his manager, Colonel Tom Parker. Just behind his head is a gag photo of RCA's "Nipper" and the "hound dog" Elvis made famous. (Photo from Neal Peters Collection)

Colonel Thomas A. Parker

Colonel Thomas A. Parker claimed to have been born Thomas Andrew Parker, in the United States, but Elvis biographer Albert Goldman was the first to publish the fact that he was actually Dutch. His real name was Andreas Cornelius van Kujik and he was born in Breda, Holland, on June 26, 1909. Andreas, called Dries for short, was the sixth child of Adam and Marie Elizabeth Ponsie van Kujik. As a child he was usually cared for by his three older sisters while his parents both worked to support the family. Dries's father died in 1926 and

the boy then went to live in Rotterdam with his maternal uncle, Jan Ponsie, and Jan's wife.

Andreas came to America when he was eighteen, probably by stowing away on a cruise ship of the Holland-America line and jumping ship when the vessel reached Hoboken, New Jersey. Parker himself confirmed during some court proceedings in 1983 that he had entered the country illegally. He stayed with a Dutch family in New Jersey and then returned to Breda in the fall of 1927. A year and a half later he

P

left Holland again, working as a seaman on a Dutch freighter and simply disappearing when the ship arrived in the Dutch West Indies port of Curaçao. Somehow he made his way to the States and then to Fort McPherson, near Atlanta, where he enlisted in the U.S. Army, perhaps in the hope of getting his American citizenship. He served at Fort Shafter in Hawaii under commanding officer Captain Thomas Parker. Near the end of his hitch he was reassigned to Fort Barrancas, near Pensacola, where he quickly picked up the local accent.

Andreas van Kujik left the army calling himself Tom Parker. In Florida he associated himself with the Johnny Jones Exposition as an advance man and promoter and subsequently worked for the American Royal Show, a huge carnival that traveled to fairs and special events throughout the South. After a brief stint as the county dogcatcher in Tampa during World War II, Parker switched from circuses to country singers. He acted as advance man for Minnie Pearl's traveling show and the Grand Ole Opry, then managed singers Eddie Arnold and Hank Snow.

Elvis Presley met Parker, then a resident of Madison, Tennessee, the home of Eddie Arnold, in the summer of 1955, when Elvis was touring the South as part of a country-music package that included Hank Snow, who was then managed by Parker. Parker was quick to see Elvis's potential for national stardom and he began to advise the young man and to help his manager, disc jockey Bob Neal, book him for appearances. Technically Neal's contract to manage Elvis ran until March 1956, but by the fall of 1955 Colonel Parker was in charge of Elvis's career; in fact Elvis signed his first contract with Parker on August 15, 1955. One of Parker's first management decisions was to move Elvis from Sun Records to RCA,

with RCA buying out Elvis's previous contract and giving the singer a $5,000 bonus for signing.

Elvis and Colonel Parker agreed that Elvis would handle the artistic side of his career while the Colonel would handle the business side from his office in Culver City. Unquestionably the Colonel negotiated some incredible deals for Elvis, making him the highest-paid movie star in Hollywood, the highest-paid live pop performer, and the highest-paid Vegas entertainer. However his decisions about which contracts to sign did in fact impinge on Elvis's creative side, pushing the star to appear in stereotyped roles in second-rate movies and to perform the same musical material over and over. This state of affairs was part of the reason for Elvis's boredom and depression, both of which led to a further diminishing of his artistic instincts.

As Elvis Presley's manager, Colonel Tom Parker received a commission of 25 percent of all Elvis's earnings. The Colonel justified the higher-than-usual fee by the fact that he never worked for more than one client at a time; later, of course, he was able to justify his charges by the huge sums of money he made for Elvis. In fact, even after Elvis's death, the Colonel worked tirelessly to promote his former client's career.

In the early 1980s the Colonel ran into trouble in regard to some of the contracts he had negotiated for his client in the past and he was sued by the Presley estate. An out-of-court settlement effectively removed him from further involvement with Presley affairs.

Parker continues to live in Palm Springs. He acts as a consultant for the Las Vegas Hilton and is reported to be talking to Wayne Newton about managing his career.

P

The Pascagoula Shipyards

Not long after Elvis Presley's father Vernon was given early release from prison in early 1939, he and Gladys and Elvis moved to Pascagoula, Mississippi, a port city on the Gulf, where Vernon found work at the government shipyard, a WPA project. His cousin, Sales Presley, and Sales's wife and children, went to Pascagoula too. They all stayed there for about eight months before returning to Tupelo for unspecified reasons.

The Paternity Suit

On August 21, 1970, a Hollywood waitress named Pat Parker filed a paternity suit against Elvis Presley. She claimed he had made her pregnant, and she wanted the star to pay $1,000 a month in child support for the baby when it was born. For a time the suit was front-page news, although neither Elvis nor his wife Priscilla would comment on it publicly. Eventually the suit was dropped.

Paying the IRS

Elvis Presley was almost certainly the only superstar who routinely asked the IRS to calculate his annual income tax. Early in his career Elvis had once been audited by the IRS and was assessed an additional $80,000 for that year's taxes. The experience greatly alarmed Vernon Presley, who vowed never to let it happen again. Thereafter, he simply reported Elvis's income on the 1040 form and let the IRS tell him how much tax was owed. Elvis himself endorsed this approach to taxpaying and never sought to ameliorate his tax bite by looking for tax shelters or other deductions. "Let's just pay the taxes, Daddy," he said. "I make enough money. I'll make a million dollars and I'll give them half." In fact, half was an underestimate. For most of his career, Elvis was in the 91 percent tax bracket.

Gary Pepper

Gary Pepper, born in 1932, founded the first Elvis Presley Fan Club and remained a loyal supporter of the singer his entire life. Elvis first noticed Gary as a familiar face in the crowd of fans at the gates of Graceland and asked someone why he was in a wheelchair. On learning that Gary was a victim of cerebral palsy, Elvis quickly arranged to provide Gary with live-in assistance, a weekly check, and a car to get around in. (Vernon Presley stopped all these benefits immediately after Elvis's death.)

Gary Pepper was one of the fourteen people invited to Elvis Presley's wedding to Priscilla Beaulieu. Gary's father, Sterling Pepper, was given a job as guard at the gate of Graceland. Gary Pepper outlived his idol by only three years, dying in 1980.

Perfume

There have been two official Elvis Presley perfumes. The first was released in 1957 and was called "Elvis Presley's Teddy Bear Perfume." The second was released twenty years later by Elvis Presley Enterprises and sold at Graceland. Called simply "Elvis," the perfume is packaged in a black spray bottle encased in a pink and black cardboard box with a picture of Elvis on it.

Priscilla Presley intends to introduce her own fragrance, called Priscilla Presley's Moments, in 1990. And Frances Denney Cosmetics has acquired licensing rights for a new Elvis fragrance, to be launched January 8, 1991.

Carl Perkins

When Elvis Presley began to record on the Sun label in late 1954, he was only one of the performers owner Sam Phillips hoped would hit the top of the charts. Another of Sun's promising young recording artists was Carl Perkins. Perkins came from the same kind of background as Elvis and the two young musicians even looked and sounded somewhat alike. One difference was that Carl Perkins wrote most of his own material, while Elvis covered songs that were written by others.

Carl Perkins wrote and recorded "Blue Suede Shoes." Elvis liked the tune and he recorded it also. When Perkins released his record he was asked to sing it on national television; he was booked to appear on both Perry Como's variety show and the "Ed Sullivan Show." On his way to New York for the appearances, Carl and his brother Jay had a bad car accident, forcing the appearances to be cancelled and putting Carl's career on hold while he recovered from his own injuries and watched his brother slowly die. It was during this period that Elvis's version of "Blue Suede Shoes" was released and became a national hit.

Carl Perkins didn't start performing again until 1959, by which time Elvis was already "the King" and Perkins had to struggle against the perception that he was an Elvis clone. He confessed that he had trouble accepting the situation and for a time sought solace in drink. Eventually Perkins won the respect due his own talents, but the composer of "Blue Suede Shoes" had to be content with being viewed primarily as a footnote to the legend of Elvis.

After the death of Elvis Presley in 1977, Carl Perkins wrote a tribute song to his fellow Sun star. He started talking about Elvis onstage, as well as wearing the huge gold belt given to Elvis in 1971 by the International Hotel for drawing record crowds; Elvis gave it to Roy Orbison, who passed it along to Perkins. Perkins once commented on Elvis, "This boy had everything. He had the looks, the moves, the manager, and the talent. And he didn't look like Mr. Ed [the talking horse] like a lot of us did."

In 1988, Perkins appeared in a Cinemax special on TV, and in 1989 he went back into the studio to cut an album. He is once again touring, and playing to full houses.

The Personal Hygiene Problem

According to Dr. George Nichopoulos, Elvis Presley never took a bath. He would sponge himself off but he didn't like to get wet all over. This aversion to soap and water led to problems with bacterial skin infections.

Perugia Way

In 1960, after Elvis Presley got out of the army and had a few months at home to rest and relax, he went out to Hollywood to make a movie, inaugurating a pattern of making three or four every year. Since that schedule meant spending most of his time in California, he decided against living so many months of the year in a hotel. The solution was to rent a house at 565 Perugia Way. It was built in a vaguely Oriental style, with an elaborate garden and waterfall. Supposedly designed by Frank Lloyd Wright, its previous owners included the Shah of Iran and Aly Khan. Elvis's first action after he signed the long-term lease was to tear out the garden and replace it with a rec room for himself and the guys, complete with pool tables and jukebox. The house was located next to the golf course of the Bel Air Country Club, although as far as is known, Elvis never availed himself of its facilities. His neighbors included Pat Boone and Greer Garson. In 1963, Elvis decided the house wasn't large enough and left for Bellagio Road. Within months he moved back to Perugia Way, staying there until 1965, when he moved to Rocca Place.

Dewey Phillips

Elvis historians agree that the honor of playing the first Elvis Presley recording over the airways belongs to fast-talking deejay Dewey Phillips of Memphis station WHBQ, on his program called "Red Hot and Blue," which was broadcast from the mezzanine of the Old Chickasaw Hotel. Like Sam Phillips (no relation) of Sun Records, Dewey thought the young people of America were ready for a singer who sounded black but looked white—and thought Elvis might be what they were waiting for. Not only did

Dewey play the record—"That's All Right (Mama)"—he also conducted the first live interview with the singer. Phillips, born and raised in Arkansas and never to lose his native accent, was also the first deejay to play a Jerry Lee Lewis record on the air. Dewey Phillips died in 1968.

Sam Phillips

Sam Phillips started his career in the music business as a disc jockey, first in his native Alabama, then Nashville, and finally on Memphis radio station WREC. He also taught himself the technical side of the radio show and worked as a recording engineer at the same radio station. In 1950, Phillips got an idea for a side business, opening up the Memphis Recording Studio. He taped speeches and the proceedings of weddings and funerals, and he welcomed anyone who wanted to come into the small studio and make a recording for the modest fee of $4. He also provided professional-quality recording services for black artists in the South who made "race" records.

Initially he sold the masters to Chess Records in Chicago, but in 1953 he started to issue some of the most commercial of these recordings under his own label, Sun Records.

Sam Phillips was a seminal force in the development of rock and roll because he was one of the first in the music business to see that a fusion of black and white musical styles could generate national appeal. His biggest discovery was Elvis Presley but he also discovered and recorded such talents as Roy Orbison, Jerry Lee Lewis, Carl Perkins, and Johnny Cash, as well as black artists Howlin' Wolf and Ike Turner.

The Phony Engagement

Early in 1976, an Alabama newspaper announced the engagement of Mrs. Iladean Tribble, a widowed mother of four, to E.A. Presley, son of Vernon Presley and the late Gladys Smith Presley. The national media somehow got onto the story and the mother of the bride confirmed that her daughter was indeed engaged to the famous star.

Unfortunately when the day of the wedding came there was no groom at the church. One of Mrs. Tribble's sons later explained she had met her fiancé in a Memphis hospital and gullibly accepted the imposter's story that he was the famous entertainer.

Photo Albums

Female fans of Elvis Presley made it a habit to enclose photos of themselves in their letters to the star. His secretaries went through the mail and selected the most attractive to put in a series of photo albums kept in their office. Occasionally Elvis would drop by and leaf through the album; more frequently, his buddies would check out the photos and perhaps pocket one with an address and telephone number on the back. Secretary Becky Yancy says fans also sent nude photos of themselves, which were dumped in the bottom drawer of her desk, which she called "the dirty file." She recalls that Elvis sometimes glanced through the dirty file but usually seemed turned off by the blatant sexuality of most of the photos. Again, it was his entourage who were most interested in those photos.

The Photo of Elvis in His Coffin

On September 7, 1977, *The National Enquirer* ran a photo of Elvis Presley lying in state in his open coffin, which the publication said had been taken by Elvis's cousin Bobby Mann. The photo was controversial because the hairstyle was different from Elvis's 1977 style, resembling instead the way the star wore his hair back in 1960. Some people concluded that Mann and/or *The National Enquirer* had faked the photo; others believed it was additional evidence that Elvis had faked his own death. Later two men were arrested for stealing the negative of this photo and selling it for $20,000.

Photo of Elvis in Vegas

In the fall of 1988, the tabloid paper *The National Examiner* published a photo the editors claimed was taken of Elvis Presley in a recent sighting in Las Vegas. It's a sad spectacle—the man in the picture is paunchy, wearing a dark suit and white shirt open to show the rolls of fat at the neck, and still sporting a greasy pompadour with sideburns. Surely our Elvis would look better than that!

The Piano Player

Although we typically picture Elvis Presley with a guitar in hand, he was never actually a very skillful guitar player. His own favorite instrument was the piano; a good piano was one of the first things he bought when he started to make money. Elvis can be heard playing the piano on his recordings of "Lawdy, Miss Clawdy," "Wear a Ring Around Your Neck," "One Sided Love Affair," and most of the album *How Great Thou Art*.

The Pied Piper of Cleveland

A Cleveland disc jockey named Bill Randle was the star of a documentary made in 1955. It included footage shot at a high school concert in October of that year. The performers were the Four Lads, Bill Haley and the Comets, Pat Boone, and Elvis Presley. Alas for fans, this priceless film has never been released, due to a dispute over its ownership.

The Pink Cadillac

In 1956, Elvis Presley purchased his first brand-new Cadillac, a pink and white streamlined model with big tail fins, with the bonus money he had received for signing a recording contract with RCA. The young singer bought the car as a present for his mother, Gladys, despite the fact that she had no license and couldn't drive. Gladys had once seen a patient drive up to St. Joseph's Hospital, where she worked as an aide, in a pink Cadillac, and it stuck in her mind as a potent symbol of wealth and luxury. As Vernon Presley later liked to point out, the pink Cadillac really was used for the whole family, but it was typical of Elvis to make the sentimental gesture of presenting it to his nondriving mother. The pink Cadillac is still on view at Graceland.

The Pink Harley

Elvis Presley loved motorcycles and motorbikes of all kinds. His friend Ann-Margret once asked him how many he had and he answered, "I don't know, honey. I just can't keep count of them!" It was, however, easy to answer the question of which bike was his favorite. It was a big Harley-Davidson that he'd bought in 1965 and then had customized in hot pink. Elvis was a familiar sight riding around the streets of exclusive Bel Air on that pink Harley, followed by a pack of his buddies, riding the eleven Triumph Bonnevilles that he bought them so they could accompany him. He also bought a Honda Dream 350 for Priscilla.

Pipe Smoking

At home at Graceland Elvis Presley could often be seen smoking a pipe. One of his favorites from his large collection was hand carved in the shape of a lion, with the bowl serving as the lion's head.

Placidyl

In order to get to sleep at seven or eight in the morning after having been up all night, Elvis Presley often took the prescription drug Placidyl. His tolerance for the drug increased with his habitual use of it and he was able to take several 500-mg capsules—enough to put most people out for several days. That's what happened to teenage Priscilla Beaulieu when Elvis gave her two of the capsules to help her get "relaxed" one evening. As she recounts in her book *Elvis and Me*, she was out for nearly three days.

Platinum Albums

Three of Elvis Presley's albums went platinum, having sold more than a million copies. The three were *Elvis Sings the Wonderful World of Christmas, Moody Blue*, and *In Concert*. All three were issued in 1977, as fans rushed to the record stores after Elvis's death.

The Plot to Steal Elvis's Body

On the night of August 28, 1977, three men were arrested by the Memphis police. They were believed to be planning to steal the body of Elvis Presley from the Presley mausoleum at Forest Hills Cemetery and hold it for $10 million ransom. Later events made the story somewhat confusing. It turned out that the person who tipped off the police and enabled the capture was one of the trio, while the other two claimed they thought they were only going to the mausoleum to buy drugs. In the end all three were charged with nothing more serious than criminal trespass since they were arrested before anything happened. Within a few days Vernon Presley applied for and received official permission to remove the bodies of both Elvis and Gladys to the Meditation Garden at Graceland.

The Point of Making Movies

When Elvis Presley was discharged from the army in 1960 and able to take up his career again, manager Colonel Tom Parker had decided that his star's future lay in the movies, which he arranged for the star to turn out with clockwork regularity at the rate of three or four per year. Elvis started his commitment to Hollywood with high hopes for good scripts and a chance to make his mark as an actor. But the Colonel encouraged the producers to make the Elvis movies according to a formula that called for the same plot repeated over and over, with a certain number of instantly forgettable songs dropped into every script. Elvis was severely disillusioned and eventually became bored and depressed.

But the Colonel resolutely deflected all efforts to make the movies more creative. As he told one director, "All we want is songs for an album."

Polaroid Pictures

In her book *Elvis and Me*, Priscilla Beaulieu Presley revealed that before she and Elvis were married he liked her to dress up and enact sexual fantasies with him, of which they made Polaroid pictures. Priscilla's role was always that of the ingenue—the young student, the innocent secretary.

Polypharmacy

Some time after the death of Elvis Presley, a spokesperson for Baptist General Hospital in Memphis, where the star had been pronounced dead, officially stated that the underlying cause of the entertainer's death was probably "polypharmacy," meaning the chemical problems caused by taking too many pills of too many different kinds. It was revealed that in the last seven months of his life Elvis had been prescribed more than five thousand pills (although there is evidence that some of those pills may have been taken by members of his entourage rather than by Elvis himself), and at the time of his death there were ten different medications in his body.

The Pompadour

An Elvis Presley trademark at the beginning of his career was the tall pompadour and the long sideburns. It was not a popular hairstyle when the singer first attracted national attention—most young men his age were wearing square waxed-up crewcuts —and many people made fun of it. Elvis had worn his hair that way even back in high school, which made him the victim of some mean-spirited teasing from the other kids. One friend from that period, Red West, remembered, "If he had a regular haircut like the rest of us, he probably wouldn't have been bothered. But I guess the other kids thought he was trying to show off or something. I have never known any other human being to take more time over his hair. He would spend hours on it, smoothing it and combing it."

Elvis used Royal Crown Pomade, a hair grease sold in the black neighborhoods of Memphis, to keep his high pompadour in place. According to one account, he modeled his hairdo on that of screen star Tony Curtis. Another explanation, made years later by Elvis, was that the pompadour was a style greatly favored by southern truck drivers, which is what he had wanted to be when he got out of school. "Dad mostly drove trucks, and when he used to bring them home, I used to sit in them."

Poplar Avenue

When the Presley family moved to Memphis in 1948 their first home, after a brief period in a boardinghouse, was at 572 Poplar Avenue. It was a single room on the ground floor of a run-down house in one of the poorest areas of the city, for which they paid $35 a month. Vernon, Gladys, Elvis, and Minnie Mae (Vernon's mother) all shared one bathroom with fifteen other families, and had nowhere to cook. The Presleys stayed on Poplar Avenue for about a year, until they qualified for a low-income housing project, Lauderdale Court, providing larger quarters for the same rent.

Porcelain Fillings

His years of childhood poverty had given Elvis Presley an aversion to the flashes of silver and gold fillings he had seen so often in the members of the Smith and Presley families. In his own mouth all the fillings were replaced by porcelain inlays and he insisted that Priscilla Beaulieu do the same thing.

The Post Office Considers an Elvis Stamp

Fans of Elvis Presley have campaigned for a number of years for a postal stamp to honor the superstar's memory. The U.S. Postal Service has vetoed the idea of an Elvis stamp several times, using a variety of excuses—that the Presley estate might not approve, that a 1987 stamp commemorated another singer (classical tenor Enrico Caruso), that it would be hard to decide how to portray Elvis, and that stamp honorees must be proved dead for ten years. Novelist James Michener wrote a joking letter to the New York Times pointing out that since Elvis had supposedly been seen in a supermarket in Waco, Texas, in September 1988, the sighting moved the earliest possible date of Elvis's eligibility for a stamp back to 1998. Some have complained that the government ought not to honor a man who "died from the addictive consumption of drugs and alcohol"; others point out that many of the world's most important artists have had the same problem and that we celebrate their works, not their life-styles.

Although no Elvis stamp is presently being planned, Postmaster General Anthony Frank went on record in 1988 as saying that an Elvis stamp "sounds like a good idea." Chances look good that if the fans continue to press for the stamp, we will eventually be sending out letters with

P
___
209

the King on the envelope. To tell the Post-master General your opinion about the matter, write him at U.S. Postal Service headquarters, 475 L'Enfant Plaza SW, Washington DC 20250-6700.

Post-Wedding Press Conference

After Elvis Presley married Priscilla Beaulieu on May 1, 1967, causing heartbreak to millions of fans who had secretly imagined themselves in the role of Mrs. Elvis, the nervous groom held a press conference. He told reporters, "Priscilla was one of the few girls who was interested in me, for me alone. We never discussed marriage in Germany, we just met at her father's house, went to the movies, and did a lot of driving—that's all. I waited for her to grow up. We shall continue to live in Memphis, and we hope to spend a lot of time on my new horse farm in Mississippi."

Potomac

The yacht *Potomac* was a 165-foot ship that served as President Franklin D. Roosevelt's "floating White House" from 1935 until his death in 1944. Elvis Presley bought the *Potomac* when the government put it up for sale and donated her to St. Jude's Children's Hospital in Memphis. St. Jude's sold her to raise money, and the ship later fell on hard times; used by drug smugglers, she was seized by the government in San Francisco Bay, where she promptly sank. Today, the *Potomac* is in Oakland, and a combination of Federal funds and private donations is financing a complete restoration.

Precision Tool Company

After Elvis Presley graduated from L.C. Humes High School in 1953, his first job was working on an assembly line at the Precision Tool Company in Memphis. Elvis may have gotten the job because his father had also worked there. Elvis was paid $1.65 an hour for helping to make shell casings for the army; his average weekly earnings were about $65. But he found the work boring and quit after a few months to take a job as a truck driver for Crown Electric. The pay at his new job was only $41 a week, but Elvis apparently thought the increased freedom was worth the reduced income.

Preparing for the Show

In the last years of his life, whenever Elvis Presley was scheduled to perform live in Las Vegas or on tour, he prepared for the work through a fixed routine. He would diet to get his weight down while exercising to build his endurance for the physical demands of performing. He would visit his dentist to make sure there would be no problem with his teeth, and he even had his ingrown toenails clipped to prevent any possible discomfort onstage.

The President's Tribute to Elvis

When Elvis Presley died in August 1977 President Jimmy Carter paid a brief tribute to the man who had changed the face of American popular music:

> Elvis Presley's death deprives our country of a part of itself. He was unique, and irreplaceable. More than twenty years ago, he burst upon the scene with an impact that was unprecedented and will probably never be equaled. His music and his personality, fusing the styles of white country and black rhythm-and-blues, permanently changed the face of American popular culture. His following was immense, and he was a symbol to people the world over of the vitality, the rebelliousness and the good humor of his country.

Andrew Presley, Jr.

Andrew Presley, Jr., was the grandson of the first of Elvis Presley's ancestors to move to the New World. He fought in the Revolutionary War and in 1781 took part in the battle of Eutah Springs, the last major engagement fought in the South, which forced the British to retreat to Charleston. Presley later claimed to have had several close encounters with musket balls, but nothing more than his clothing was injured.

Davada "Dee" Elliott Stanley Presley

Davada "Dee" Elliott Stanley was the second wife of Vernon Presley and thus for a time Elvis Presley's stepmother. Born Davada Elliott, she had married a man named William Stanley and then followed her husband to Germany when he was an army officer stationed there. The couple had three sons, William Jr., Richard, and David. In 1959 Dee met Vernon Presley, a recent widower living with Elvis in Germany, fulfilling his promise to his late wife to stay close to their son. Not long afterward the troubled Stanley marriage ended in divorce.

Dee and Vernon Presley were married on July 3, 1960 and spent their honeymoon in Panama City, Florida. Official statements to the press depicted Elvis as rejoicing in his father's new happiness. In private the star was extremely angry, and his anger erupted when Dee moved into Graceland and judiciously began redecorating. Shortly thereafter Dee and Vernon moved to a house of their own.

Dee and Vernon separated in 1974 and were divorced three years later. Dee later married Lewis Tucker. In 1979 she and her sons wrote a book about her famous stepson, called *Elvis, We Love You Tender.*

David Presley

David Presley was the first of the Presley family to come to the New World. A Scots-Irish blacksmith, he emigrated to North Carolina around 1745. His great-grandson Dunnan was Elvis Presley's great-great-grandfather.

Dunnan Presley

Dunnan Presley was Elvis Presley's great-great-grandfather. Born in 1827, he fought for the Confederacy in the Civil War, in Ham's Regiment of Mississippi Cavalry, deserting twice. He also managed to get married four times without any intervening divorces. His granddaughter told Presley biographer Albert Goldman, "My mother told me that when she and her sister were just little babies, their grandparents had taken them to church one Sunday and when they came back, their father, Dunnan, was gone. He went back to his other wife and child." Dunnan Presley died in 1900.

Gladys Love Smith Presley

Gladys Love Smith was the fourth child (and fourth daughter) of a farm family in Tupelo, Mississippi, born on April 25, 1912. Her pretty mother, nicknamed Doll, was a semi-invalid, and her father died when Gladys was in her late teens. At that time, she took a job working as a sewing machine operator at the Tupelo Garment Company to help support her mother and younger brothers and sisters. Gladys Smith married Vernon Presley, whose family lived down the road from hers, in similarly poverty-stricken conditions, in 1933, when she was twenty-one and he was seventeen. Two years later Gladys gave birth to twin sons, one of whom was stillborn; the other was named Elvis Aron Presley. The Presleys had no other children.

A photo taken in Gladys Presley's mid-twenties, when her son Elvis was only two, shows her to have been an attractive young woman who looked very much like Elvis at the time he first achieved national stardom. Her son's fame brought Gladys the

Elvis posed for pictures with his father Vernon and mother Gladys after he finished his basic training. Gladys, only 46, looked old and ill, and it was only a few months later that she died. (Photo from Neal Peters Collection)

first comfortable circumstances of her life but by that time she was already suffering from depression, liver problems, overweight, and possibly alcoholism. Her own health and emotional problems, combined with her worry over the demands of stardom on her son, robbed Gladys of the chance to enjoy wholeheartedly Elvis's success.

Gladys Presley died at the age of forty-six on August 14, 1958, in the Methodist Hospital at Memphis. She was being treated there for acute liver problems when she had a sudden heart attack. Elvis, then in the army and stationed at Fort Hood, Texas, was distraught with grief. Gladys was buried at Forest Hills Cemetery in Memphis, only a few miles from Graceland. In 1977, a few weeks after her son Elvis's death, Vernon Presley moved the bodies of both Elvis and Gladys to the Meditation Garden at Graceland for greater security.

Jesse D. McClowell Presley

Jesse D. McClowell Presley, usually called J.D., was Elvis Presley's grandfather. Jesse was born in Itawamba County, Mississippi, in 1896, a son of free-spirited Rosella Presley and a father she refused ever to identify. In 1913, when he was seventeen, J.D. married Minnie Mae Hood and the couple moved to East Tupelo. According to

P
———
213

those who remembered him in his younger days J.D. was a hard drinker and a mean drunk. He spent many nights in the county jail and when he was sober he was usually spending nights in the company of some woman other than his wife. It should have been a relief to Minnie when J.D. finally left for good in 1946 and filed for divorce the following year. Yet he was not forgotten by the family and his son Vernon named one of his sons—Elvis's stillborn twin Jesse Garon—after him. J.D. later married Vera Pruitt and the couple lived in Louisville, Kentucky. They sometimes visited Elvis in Memphis, but because Minnie Mae Presley lived in the east wing of Graceland, J.D. and Vera always stayed at Vernon's house, located nearby on the mansion's grounds. J.D. Presley died in 1973.

Jesse Garon Presley

Elvis Aron Presley was a twin; his brother, Jesse Garon, was the first of the babies to be born in the two-room Presley home in East Tupelo, Mississippi, on the afternoon of January 8, 1935. According to legend, which was in large part created by Vernon Presley in later years, the doctor who attended Gladys Presley had not realized she was carrying twins until her labor continued after the birth of the first boy. But friends of Gladys remember that she knew for months that she would give birth to twins.

Jesse Garon Presley, named after his paternal grandfather, was stillborn. His tiny body was placed in a makeshift cardboard coffin in the same front room where Gladys and the second twin, Elvis, were resting. The baby was buried the next day in an unmarked grave in nearby Priceville Cemetery. Years later, after the death of Elvis Presley, a small monument was erected near his grave in the Meditation Garden at Graceland in memory of his stillborn twin.

Lisa Marie Presley

Lisa Marie Presley, the only child of Elvis and Priscilla Presley, was born on February 1, 1968 at 5:01 P.M. in Memphis, Tennessee. The baby, who weighed six pounds, fifteen ounces, became an instant celebrity. Millions of fans anxiously awaited full details of the new little Presley and their first glimpse of Elvis as a father.

Lisa Marie's childhood was divided between Graceland and various homes in California. Her parents separated when she was not quite five and although her mother Priscilla was awarded custody of the little girl, she continued to see her father regularly, both in California and Tennessee. In fact, Lisa Marie was visiting Graceland in August 1977 at the time Elvis died. Accompanied by her mother, she said a private farewell to her beloved father before the funeral.

As the daughter of one of the most famous men in the world, Lisa had to be protected throughout her childhood and security was always a concern. Fans and

Newlyweds Lisa Marie Presley and Danny Keough after their surprise wedding in Hollywood October 3, 1988. (Photo from AP/Wide World).

reporters alike were asked not to take pictures of her so she would not be recognizable, and until she was a grown woman the only photos released of her were long shots that did not reveal her face. Despite the unusual circumstances, Priscilla Presley was determined to try to give Lisa a normal childhood and to a great extent succeeded in her task. It was perhaps made easier by living during Lisa's school years in Los Angeles, where many children have rich and famous parents.

As a teenager Lisa was introduced by her mother to the Church of Scientology, which has since played an important role in her life. Although she went through the typical rebellious period of a teenager she avoided the problems of drugs and alcohol

P

that shadow the lives of so many young people. It was also through the Church of Scientology that she met Danny Keough, the man who became her husband in a ceremony at the Church in October 1988.

At the moment, Lisa's plans for the future revolve around raising Elvis's grandchild Danielle, born on May 29, 1989. As time passes she will probably begin to play a role in administering the estate of Elvis Presley, of which she is the major heir. Her inheritance is expected to be upwards of $50 million—and at the rate that Elvis Presley records, movies, and memorabilia continue to sell, it may be many times that figure in Lisa's lifetime.

Minnie Mae Hood Presley

Minnie Mae Hood Presley was Elvis's grandmother. It is certain that she was born on June 17, but there is some debate about the year of her birth. Minnie Mae claimed that it was 1893, but some family members suspected her of shaving off a few years and alleged she was really born five years earlier, in 1888. Writer Elaine Dundy, who researched the Presley family meticulously for her own book, *Elvis and Gladys*, accepts the earlier date as correct. Whatever the year, Minnie Mae Hood was born in Fulton, Mississippi, and according to Dundy was socially several levels above her husband, Jesse D. Presley, whom she married in 1913. Sometime soon thereafter the Presleys moved to East Tupelo, where J.D. became a sharecropper. They lived in a four-room house on Saltillo Road with their six children: Vester, Vernon, Delta, Nashville, Lorene, and Gladys.

By all accounts, J.D. Presley was a difficult husband for Minnie Mae to live with. He drank, he got in trouble with the law when he was drunk, and he womanized when he was sober. It seems that it should have been a relief when he left home in 1946, but the following year, when J.D. filed for divorce—on the ludicrous grounds that his wife had deserted him—Minnie Mae contested it. Without money from her husband she was forced to give up her own home, moving in with her son Vernon and his family.

In later years, Minnie Mae, a tall lanky woman lacking the softness that is stereotypical of grandmothers, liked to reminisce about her famous grandson's childhood in rural Mississippi. After Elvis's mother died in 1958 and his army unit was sent to Germany, his grandmother traveled overseas to live with him in the house he rented off the army base. "My grandmother cooks all my favorite dishes," he told reporters. "You know, good simple food just like my mamma used to make."

When Elvis finished his tour of duty, Minnie Mae Presley moved into Graceland with him, while Vernon lived nearby with his new wife Dee. Minnie Mae decorated her room with a selection of the presents sent to Elvis by his fans, and in one corner sat an organ given to her by Elvis, on which she would occasionally play a rousing gospel song. Called "Grandma" by most of the Presley entourage and "Dodger" by Elvis, Minnie Mae, who wore dark sunglasses day and night, was a favorite with everyone. Minnie Mae Presley outlived both her son Vernon and her famous grandson, dying on May 8, 1980. She is buried in the Meditation Garden at Graceland.

Priscilla Presley announcing pregnancy attended by daughter Lisa Marie and live-in Marco Garibaldi (1986). (Photo from AP/Wide World)

Priscilla Ann Beaulieu Presley

Priscilla Ann Beaulieu was born in 1945. Her mother Ann had been a photographer's model before her wartime marriage to Lieutenant James Wagner, a handsome Navy pilot. Wagner was killed in a plane crash when daughter Priscilla was just six months old. Ann Wagner remarried about two years later. Her second husband was also a career military man, Air Force officer Joseph Paul Beaulieu, who officially adopted Priscilla. Ann and Paul Beaulieu were to give Priscilla five brothers and sisters—Don, four years younger than Priscilla; Michelle, nine years younger; Jeff, twelve years younger; and twins Tim and Tom, fifteen years younger.

Priscilla grew up like most Army brats, moving frequently, and was thus perhaps closer to her family, the constants in her life, than most kids her age. At the time she graduated from junior high in Austin, Texas, her father was transferred to a base at Weisbaden, Germany. There, in 1959, she met Elvis Presley, also stationed in Weisbaden. The singer was discharged and went back to the States the following spring, and Priscilla flew over to visit him in California two years later in the summer of 1962. In 1963 Priscilla's parents gave in to her insistence that she be allowed to move to Graceland to finish her high school education in Memphis.

For four years, Priscilla Beaulieu was one of Elvis Presley's best-kept secrets. She lived in his home but the relationship was never publicized; officially she was described as a child whose parents wanted her to be able to go to high school in America, a wish their friend Elvis had granted. Unofficially, Priscilla was Elvis's girlfriend—but as she was to find out in painful confrontations, so were a number of other women.

Priscilla's patience was rewarded at last when she married Elvis Presley on May 1, 1967. Their daughter Lisa Marie was born nine months later. As Priscilla has re- counted in her own book, *Elvis and Me*, the marriage suffered from a lack of privacy and eventually from a lack of intimacy as well. Priscilla surprised the world in late 1972 when she left the idol of millions, divorcing him in 1973. Many Elvis fans still cannot forgive her for what they see as "betraying" their idol.

After the divorce Priscilla opened a clothing boutique called Bis and Beau in Hollywood with partner Olivia Bis. At about the time Elvis died, she embarked on an acting career. She modeled in Wella shampoo commercials and was a cohost of TV's "Those Amazing Animals." In the fall of 1983 she won the role of Jenna Wade on "Dallas," which gave her national stardom in her own right. For a number of years she was involved in a relationship with model-actor Michael Edwards.

In 1986 Priscilla Presley began living with Italian actor Marco Garibaldi. Their son Navaronne was born in 1987. She has recently costarred in the feature film *The Naked Gun* and acted as executive producer for a TV-movie version of her best-selling book, *Elvis and Me*. She became a grandmother in 1989, when daughter Lisa Marie gave birth to her own daughter Danielle.

Rosella Presley

Rosella Presley was Elvis Presley's great-grandmother. Born in 1862, she was the daughter of Dunnan Presley by one of his four (simultaneous) wives. Her father left her mother when she was a young girl and Rosella grew up to be an independent woman who lived her life according to her own standards. She never married but had ten children without telling any of them who their fathers were. One of them later commented to Presley biographer Albert Goldman, "I can't remember anyone ever talking about who our father was. It was a big mystery when we were children." Another of those fatherless children, all of whom she gave the Presley surname, was Jesse D. McClowell Presley, born in 1892, the grandfather of Elvis Presley. Rosella Presley died in 1924.

Sam Presley

Sam Presley was Vernon Presley's first cousin. Sam ran a gambling club on the Alabama-Mississippi border called the Sage Patch, in partnership with T.B. Richard- son, who later went to Vegas, where he signed Elvis to appear at the New Frontier Hotel in 1956.

Vernon Elvis Presley

Vernon Elvis Presley was the father of Elvis Presley. Vernon was born in 1916 on a farm near East Tupelo, Mississippi. In 1933, he married Gladys Smith, daughter of a neighbor and at twenty-one, four years older than himself. The newlyweds had so little money they had to start their married life sleeping on the floor in the home of a relative, and Vernon never succeeded in lifting his family out of the poverty they were born into. He worked on other people's farms as a sharecropper or a laborer, sometimes riding the bus long distances to find another job during the Depression, which hit the small farmers of Mississippi hard. At one time he worked for a dairy farmer in Tupelo, delivering milk door to door, and he asked his boss to help him finance a little two-room house (now open to the public as the Elvis Presley boyhood home). When his son Elvis was just three, Vernon was charged by that same dairy farmer with forging a check on his bank account. Vernon was sentenced to three years of hard labor at the notorious Parchman Farm, although good behavior and pleading letters from his wife reduced his sentence to only nine months.

In 1948, Vernon Presley moved his family (which by that time included his mother, Minnie Mae Presley, abandoned by her husband) to Memphis in search of increased economic opportunity. But even in the city, prosperity continued to elude him. He got a steady job at the United Paint Company in 1951 but made only about $3,000 a year. It was not until Elvis's success as a recording artist in 1955 that the Presley family was able to move out of cramped and inadequate housing. Soon thereafter Vernon quit his low-paying job and took on the responsibility of handling his son's finances, which he continued to oversee— not very professionally—for the rest of his life.

Vernon Presley became a widower when Gladys died in August 1958. Keeping a promise to his late wife to stay near their son always, Vernon and his mother Minnie Mae went to Germany to live in the house Elvis rented off base while his army unit was stationed near Hamburg. There Vernon met Davada "Dee" Elliott Stanley, an American married to an army officer. Vernon began a courtship, Dee divorced her husband, and on July 3, 1960 Vernon and Dee were married. Dee lived at Graceland for a short time and acted as Priscilla Beaulieu's chaperone when the young girl first arrived at Graceland. Then, along with Dee's three sons from her previous marriage, Ricky, Billy, and David, the Vernon Presleys moved into a home of their own in Memphis, at 1850 Nolan Road, near Elvis but not under the same roof.

Vernon separated from Dee in 1974 and

the two were divorced in 1977. By that time he had already found a new companion. She was Sandy Miller, an attractive blonde from Denver whom he had met while traveling to Las Vegas with Elvis. Sandy had moved to Memphis with her three children in 1974, about the time of Vernon's separation from Dee. According to some reports, Vernon took Sandy as his third wife; other sources say the couple never went through the formality of marriage.

Vernon Presley outlived Elvis by two years, dying on June 26 1979, and was buried beside his son and his first wife Gladys at the Meditation Garden at Graceland.

Vester Presley

Vester Presley was Elvis Presley's uncle, a brother of his father Vernon. According to Presley legend it was Vester who first taught young Elvis to play a few chords on the guitar. In 1935, the year Elvis was born, Vester married Clettes Smith, the sister of Elvis's mother Gladys, and thus their daughter Patsy was Elvis's double first cousin. In the early 1940s, Vester and Vernon shared a two-family house on Reese Street in East Tupelo; later Vester moved his family to Memphis to be near Vernon and Gladys, and Vester worked for a time at the Precision Tool Company, which also employed both Vernon and Elvis at various periods. Like many of Elvis's relatives, Vester eventually wound up on the payroll at Graceland, serving as a gate guard for many years. He wrote a book, on sale at Graceland, about the family, called *A Presley Speaks*, short on fact but long on legend about his famous nephew.

Presley Air Force

Elvis Presley owned a number of airplanes to help make the constant travel required by his career more comfortable. His largest plane was a former commercial airliner, a Convair 880, that he'd had remodeled for his personal use. He also owned a nine-seat Lockheed Jetstar, later leased to a private airline, for short hops. At one time Elvis owned a twin-engine jet Commander, which he later sold to Vegas star Wayne Newton for $300,000. After he bought the Convair, he sold his Gulfstream twin-engine jet to a construction company in Mississippi for $690,000.

Presley Center Courts

In 1976, Elvis Presley invested money in a racquetball court in Memphis, called Presley Center Courts. His partners in the venture included his doctor, Dr. George C. Nichopoulos; his road manager, Joe Esposito; and a local real estate developer. Before the business was one year old Elvis backed out and withdrew the right to use his name. Shortly thereafter his partners in the venture sued him for failing to live up his agreement to lend the business both his name and his capital.

A conversation Elvis had with Red West that Red taped and used in the book he coauthored, *Elvis: What Happened?*, indicated that the problems of Presley Center Courts and the legal tangles with his friends had gotten Elvis down in the last year of his life. "You know that racquetball thing?" he asked Red unhappily. "Two courts for a million three hundred thousand dollars. My understanding was that we were going to just use my name. And that's all and that was the contract I signed. I did it as a favor for Dr. Nick and Joe . . .

It started off kinda innocent. I was told one thing, like I wouldn't have to put up a dime . . . What would happen was that we would be out and they would start hitting me for ten thousand, one thousand. I thought, are you guys putting up that kind of money? . . . I didn't want to crush their dreams, I tried to hang in there with them . . . What started out as a friendship and favor and they turned it into a million-three-hundred-thousand-dollar project . . . I'm in the process of getting out of it. You know, I don't even care that much for racquetball." Apparently the problem did not damage Elvis's relationship with either Joe Esposito or Dr. Nick, both of whom continued to be a part of the Presley entourage, but it did depress Elvis about the meaning of friendship.

The Presley Estate

After Elvis Presley died in 1977, his father, Vernon, was the first executor of his estate. When Vernon died two years later, new executors were appointed—Priscilla Presley, Joe Hanks (Elvis's former accountant), and the Memphis National Bank of Commerce. At an appearance in probate court a judge became interested in why the estate was paying so much money to Colonel Tom Parker, Elvis's former manager, and he appointed Memphis attorney Blanchard Tual to look into the matter. Tual's report pointed to greed and mismanagement by Colonel Parker, and the court directed the estate to stop all payments to Parker. Later the new executors of the Presley estate brought suit against both Parker and RCA for an agreement in which RCA bought back the rights to all Elvis's recordings made before March 1973. The suit was settled out of court in the

summer of 1983. Thereafter the estate regained full control of the rights to all the profits of Elvis Presley's career.

The major heir of the Elvis Presley estate is his daughter, Lisa Marie Presley Keough. Originally she was to have inherited the principal on her twenty-fifth birthday in 1993. According to insider reports, she has signed an agreement to defer her inheritance for another five years, until 1998. At the time Elvis died, the estate was estimated to be worth perhaps no more than $5 or $6 million. Thanks to Elvis's continued popularity and the court actions that removed Colonel Parker from active involvement in the estate, it has greatly increased in value. Informed estimates suggest the Presley estate might be worth more than $75 million today, bringing in at least $15 million a year in income.

The actions of the Presley estate today

frequently ruffle the feathers of dedicated Elvis fans. In a sweeping campaign to stop the unlicensed reproduction of the image and likeness of Elvis, the estate has moved against the publications of some of the fan clubs, prevented at least one English fan club from accepting American members, removed an Elvis bear from the market, and attempted to stop the broadcast of various radio and TV shows containing references to Elvis. Many fans consider the estate's efforts overzealous and misguided.

The Presley Estate Sues the Colonel

In 1981, the executors of the Elvis Presley estate brought legal action against Colonel Tom Parker, who then countersued the executors. The case revolved around the Colonel's handling of Elvis's affairs—in particular his negotiation of the 1973 agreement through which RCA bought back the rights to more than seven hundred songs recorded by Elvis, giving the Colonel the lion's share of the payment. The estate also brought suit against RCA. Before the case went to trial it was settled out of court in June 1983. The Colonel gave up all claim to future income from the career of Elvis Presley, in return for 50 percent of all record royalties earned before September 1982, plus a cash payment of $2 million from RCA. Thereafter all monies earned in any way by the talent of Elvis Presley would be paid directly to the estate.

The Presley Family Cookbook

One of the books on sale at Graceland is the *Presley Family Cookbook*, written by Elvis Presley's Uncle Vester in collaboration with Graceland cook Nancy Rooks. There are recipes for such Elvis favorites as ham hocks, black-eyed peas, and cornbread.

Presley Heights

Today, East Tupelo, Mississippi, the poor section of Tupelo where Elvis Presley was born and grew up, is called Presley Heights. Despite the new name, it is still considered the "wrong" side of the tracks.

Presley Plastic

In September 1988, applications were mailed to more than a million people for the Elvis Presley MasterCard. The card is issued by the Leader Federal Savings &

Loan of Memphis, under an agreement with the Presley estate that will give half of the $36 annual fee plus a percentage of the 17.88 percent interest charge to the Elvis Presley Memorial Foundation, to be used for the upkeep of Graceland and also for the scholarship fund established by Elvis. The black charge card features a picture of the young Elvis wearing sideburns, a sport jacket, and two-toned shoes, wailing away with his guitar.

Pretty Wild Clothes

Everyone who met Elvis Presley in the early days of his performing career remembers the same striking fact about the young singer—he wore some pretty wild clothes. A high school classmate recalled, "We all wore Levis, but I remember Elvis had two pairs of pants, both made of gabardine: one pair was black with a white stripe down the side, and the other was black with a pink stripe." Singer Johnny Burnette recalled, "He always seemed to be wearing purple pants or else striped black pants with a white sport jacket and white buck shoes." Scotty Moore remembered that when he first saw Elvis he was wearing a pink shirt and pink trousers and had a black DA hairstyle. Drummer D.J. Fontana recalled how Elvis loved clothes and colors. "White shoes, white belt, black pegged pants. He was like that from the first day I met him. That was the way he dressed. He'd put together colors that would look awful on you or me, but he could pull it off."

Prince Albert in a Romance—With Lisa Marie

In the fall of 1988, rumors began to circulate of a romance between Lisa Marie Presley and Prince Albert, heir to the throne of Monaco. It was a fairytale fantasy of a future for America's little princess, but the fiction was soon revealed when Lisa Marie married Danny Keough only weeks after the gossip began.

Priscilla's First Christmas at Graceland

Elvis Presley invited Priscilla Beaulieu to come to Graceland for the Christmas of 1962. The teenager was met in New York by Elvis's father Vernon and his second wife Dee, who traveled with her to Memphis in the role of chaperons. The beauty and bounty of Christmastide at Graceland made an indelible impression on Priscilla, who fervently wished she would never have to leave. By the end of the visit she and Elvis were making plans for her to return that spring as a permanent guest at Graceland —a status she would hold until their marriage in 1967.

Priscilla's First Visit to Elvis in the States

Two years after Elvis Presley said goodbye to fifteen-year-old Priscilla Beaulieu in Germany, he called her and asked her to come visit him in Los Angeles, where he was just finishing another movie. After some difficulty in persuading her parents to allow her to go, Priscilla arrived in June 1962 for a two-week stay with her "friend." Although her parents had arranged to have her carefully chaperoned, Elvis, in charge of the arrangements, circumvented all their plans.

During the visit, he took Priscilla to Las Vegas in his customized bus, accompanied by his cousin Gene Smith. There Elvis introduced Priscilla to sexy clothes and heavy makeup that made her look years older, and amphetamines that helped her keep up with the Presley night life. In her book Priscilla remembers clearly the shock and distress of her parents when their teenage daughter returned to them looking like a Vegas hooker.

Priscilla's Tuna Salad Secret

One of Priscilla Beaulieu Presley's favorite foods was tuna salad, but Elvis hated fish of any kind and didn't even like to smell it on her breath. So whenever Elvis was away,

Priscilla liked to make herself a huge tuna salad, which she ate with lots of crackers and hot tea.

A Prisoner in Her Own Home

Elvis Presley and his parents, Gladys and Vernon, moved into Graceland on May 1, 1957. Shortly thereafter Gladys began to complain that she was a virtual prisoner there. She said she couldn't go do her own grocery shopping, cook in her own kitchen, go see her old friends, or even go out in the backyard and feed her own chickens.

Part of the reason was Elvis's desire to protect his mother from any hardships or difficulties, part of it was the fact that Gladys's spontaneous behavior—exacerbated by her drinking problem at that time—was considered by those around him to be bad for Elvis's image.

Nashville Presley Pritchett

Nashville Presley Pritchett was a sister of Vernon Presley, Elvis's "Aunt Nash." Aunt Nash was a minister of the Assembly of God Church and her impassioned pulpit style was an early influence on Elvis that was later reflected in the vitality of his own stage performance. When he became a star Elvis helped build Aunt Nash her own church in Walls, Mississippi. She married Earl Pritchett, and after Elvis bought Graceland, Aunt Nash and Uncle Earl Pritchett lived in a comfortable mobile home on the property. Earl was put on the payroll as groundskeeper.

According to family insiders Aunt Nash was deeply upset in 1988 when her great-niece Lisa Marie Presley was married in the Los Angeles Church of Scientology. Apparently Aunt Nash had for years dreamed that when Lisa Marie got married she herself would perform the ceremony.

Aunt Nash has recently written a book about the Presley family, revealing Elvis's background and passing along nuggets of family history. Called *One Flower While I Live*, the book can be ordered directly from Rev. Nash Pritchett, 702 Dover Road, West Memphis AR 72301

The Privacy Issue

Priscilla Presley has commented that one of the reasons her marriage to Elvis failed was that they never had any privacy. Elvis had fallen into the habit of surrounding himself with an entourage; even when Priscilla and Elvis went on vacations they were accompanied by a group of his buddies. "Somebody's always there, everywhere we go," she complained. "A bunch of guys and their wives are always around. We never have any privacy." Although she tried repeatedly to arrange their lives so they could be alone together, Elvis usually circumvented her plans by inviting along a number of other people.

Prom Date

In 1953, Elvis Presley, then a senior, attended the prom at L.C. Humes High. According to the recollections of his date, Regis Wilson, he wore a dark suit and suede shoes—which she swears were blue! She had met him at the Lauderdale Court housing project, where they both lived, and dated him a few times before prom night. He brought her a pink carnation corsage to match her dress, and drove her to Memphis's Peabody Hotel in the 1942 Lincoln that was the Presley family's only car. In an article in *People*, Regis recalled that he told her he didn't dance, so they just sat and drank Cokes all night. She also remembered Elvis as "a good kisser."

"The Promise"

Elvis Presley went through a period of bitterness and anger after his wife Priscilla left him and embarked on a liaison with karate instructor Mike Stone. According to Red and Sonny West, the star spoke to them on several occasions about having Mike Stone killed, and other insiders confirm that he was for a time prey to an ugly desire for retribution. In the end, however, Elvis's true character dictated his actions. He got down on his knees and prayed, and then he wrote out a short document he called "The Promise"—a vow never to do anything to hurt Priscilla, Lisa Marie, or Mike Stone. It was a promise he kept.

Juliet Prowse

The talented dancer Juliet Prowse costarred with Elvis Presley in *G. I. Blues* and for a brief period their names were linked romantically. Juliet was also seeing Frank Sinatra at that time, so the headlines played up the notion that Elvis was stealing Frank's girl. Elvis said about Juliet, "She has a body that would make a bishop stamp his foot through a stained-glass window." Prowse later confessed that she had been very attracted to Elvis, but thought that his fame was too great a drawback, making it impossible for them to go anywhere together. Interestingly she didn't seem to think the same problem existed with Frank Sinatra.

Psychic Healing

In his later years Elvis Presley believed he had powers of psychic healing. When members of his entourage were hurt he would lay his hands on the injured area and explain that the pain would soon leave their bodies and pass into his fingertips. In their desire to please Elvis most of them would quickly agree that they were getting better. As Red West put it, in the book *Elvis: What Happened?*, "It's just that he is so certain of these powers, you don't want to throw it up in his face. It's like spoiling someone's fun and we just went along." Elvis even tried his psychic healing on strangers, such as a woman in labor, and they too seemed to believe that the magic of the superstar's presence made them forget about their pain.

A Psychic Link Between Elvis and Gladys

When Elvis Presley began his career as an entertainer his road trips took him away overnight for the first time in his life. His mother, who had kept him close to home throughout high school, was worried and anxious during his frequent absences. One night in early 1955, while Elvis was driving down the highway to a gig, his car, a used Cadillac that he'd had painted pink, caught on fire and he narrowly escaped being blown to bits. At that exact moment, Gladys Presley sat up in bed and screamed. She'd had a nightmare in which she saw the car burning and Elvis in mortal danger.

"Put a Dog in It"

The screenwriters responsible for *Spinout*, Theodore Flicker and George Kirgo, recall that they were working on an assignment from MGM to write a feature film for Sonny and Cher when they got a call from the studio telling them to switch to Elvis Presley instead. After Flicker and Kirgo finished the first draft of the script they were summoned to a meeting with Elvis's manager, Colonel Tom Parker. He told them he loved the script and thought it needed only one change. "Put a dog in it," decreed the Colonel. And so they did.

The RCA® Contract

Late in 1955, Colonel Tom Parker, who had taken over the management of Elvis Presley's career that fall, approached his friend Steve Sholes at RCA about a recording contract for Elvis. Parker had concluded that Sam Phillips's Sun label was too small and too local to be able to launch his client as a national star, so he thought Elvis should move on to a label with more clout. Thanks to Sholes's efforts, RCA, in cooperation with the music publishing company Hill & Range, finally offered Phillips $35,000 for Elvis's contract and the rights to the five Presley singles Sun had already recorded and released, a large sum for the contract of a new performer. Sam Phillips felt he should take the offer and use the money to help launch some of the other talents he had signed to his label, such as Carl Perkins, Jerry Lee Lewis, and Johnny Cash, so he agreed to the deal. As part of the new contract Elvis himself received a $5,000 bonus at the time of the signing. Some reports say the money came from RCA, whereas other accounts suggest the sum was a final payment from Sun Records for all royalties owed at the date of the signing. Wherever the money came from, Elvis used it to buy a new pink Cadillac, which he formally presented to his mother—who didn't drive. The RCA contract was actually signed on November 21, 1955.

ROTC

While Elvis Presley attended L.C. Humes High School in Memphis he became a member of the school's Reserve Officer Training Corps, posing for a photo with other ROTC members in 1953. However, when he was inducted into the army five years later, he entered as plain Private Presley.

Rainbow Skating Rink

In the 1950s and early 1960s one of Elvis Presley's favorite activities was roller skating. It was his custom to rent the Rainbow Skating Rink in Memphis after it closed to the public at midnight and to spend the rest of the night skating there with his buddies. They often played tag or chose teams for a roller derby, identifying themselves by colored bandannas in their hip pockets. Even tough guys like Red West commented on the ferocity of these contests. Before Elvis went into the army in March 1958, he rented the Rainbow skating rink for eight consecutive nights of skating parties.

Reasons for the Divorce

After Elvis and Priscilla Presley were divorced, she happened to be in Las Vegas when he was giving a performance. She sat in the audience with their daughter Lisa Marie, and Elvis introduced the two from the stage. About Priscilla, he told his audience, "We are the best of friends and always have been. Our divorce came about, not because of another man, but because of circumstances involving my career. And nothing else! Regardless of what you have read, or have been led to believe. I don't think it was fair on Priscilla, with me gone so often and traveling so much."

A Record for Gladys's Birthday

In 1953, the eighteen-year-old Elvis Presley, then driving a truck around Memphis for the Crown Electric Company, decided to make a recording to give his mother for her birthday. At least that's the way the legend goes; some Presley researchers have suggested Gladys's birthday was nothing more than a convenient pretext. At the Memphis Recording Studio, owned by Sam Phillips (who also released records under the Sun label), anyone who wanted could make one copy of a ten-inch 78-rpm record on an Ampex 350C for only $4. Gladys had been urging Elvis to make a record for months, and so had a bass player in local clubs, Bill Black, who thought Sam Phillips might be interested in the young singer. Elvis walked in with his guitar and recorded two songs that had been big hits for the Ink Spots—"That's When Your Heartaches Begin," and "My Happiness." Gladys loved her record but more significantly, so did Sam Phillips's secretary, who just happened to hear the teenager making the recording. She played part of it for Sam; several months later he telephoned Elvis and asked the young man to come in and rehearse a few numbers with Black and guitar player Scotty Moore for a Sun recording. That's the way a star was born.

Rumor has it that the record Elvis cut that first day he walked into the Memphis Recording Studio still exists and is now in the hands of a friend of Elvis's from high school, Ed Leek. The story goes that Elvis gave the record to Ed for safekeeping. Ed has reportedly sold the rights for a commercial release for the recording to Shelby Singleton, to be marketed on the Sun label. What a treat *that* would be for all of us!

A Record Library for the Elvis Fan

The Complete Sun Sessions (RCA 6414-1-R) This is a two-record set that contains not only the master recordings of sixteen of Elvis's early Sun records but many alternate takes as well.

Elvis Aron Presley (RCA CPL8-3699) In 1980, RCA released this boxed set to commemorate the twenty-fifth anniversary of Elvis's signing with the label. Each of the eight records has a different theme—early live performances, an early benefit performance, gold hits from movies, the TV specials, Las Vegas years, lost singles, Elvis at the piano, later concert years.

Elvis's Christmas Album (RCA AFM1-54-86; also available on compact disc) This is the digitally remastered version, pressed on green vinyl, of the 1957 hit album on which Elvis sings a number of Christmas classics—a must for the holidays.

Elvis's Golden Records (RCA AFM1-5196; also available on compact disc) In 1985, RCA rereleased this album in honor of Elvis's fiftieth birthday. The digitally remastered record includes such classics as "Hound Dog," "All Shook Up," "Don't Be Cruel," "Teddy Bear," and "Love Me Tender."

Essential Elvis—The First Movies (RCA 6738-1-R; also available on compact disc) This album is a compilation of seventeen songs from Elvis's first three movies, a good way to remember the young and handsome King.

A Golden Celebration (RCA CPM6-5172) This six-record set was released in 1984 and contains taped versions of Elvis's appearances on TV with the Dorsey brothers, Milton Berle, Steve Allen, and Ed Sullivan; it also includes his 1956 appearances at the Mississippi-Alabama Fair and Dairy Show.

How Great Thou Art (RCA AQL1-3758; also available on compact disc) This is the 1967 gospel album for which Elvis was awarded his first Grammy.

Moody Blue (RCA AQ11-2428; also available on compact disc) This album was released less than a month before Elvis's death and contains live concert recordings of a number of sentimental ballads—the best of the late Elvis.

The One-Million-Dollar Quartet (Sun Records S-5001) A bootleg album containing thirty-nine tracks from the famous Sun impromptu recording session on December 4, 1956, featuring its "Million-Dollar Quartet" of Elvis Presley, Carl Perkins, Jerry Lee Lewis, and Johnny Cash.

Rocker (RCA AFM1-5182; also available on compact disc) If you want to remember Elvis as the King of Rock and Roll, this is the album for you—all of his classic rock singles and nothing else.

Records Released in 1955

In 1955, Sun released four Elvis Presley singles, following up on the success of the first record that was issued in late summer 1954. All four continued the same successful pattern, with a blues song on one side and a country song on the other. The 1955 singles were:

- "Good Rockin' Tonight" B/W "I Don't Care If the Sun Don't Shine"
- "Milk Cow Blues" B/W "You're a Heartbreaker"
- "Baby, Let's Play House" B/W "I'm Right, You're Left, She's Gone" (a mistake in the label; the song was actually titled "You're Right, I'm Left, She's Gone")
- "Mystery Train" B/W "I Forgot to Remember to Forget"

Records Released in 1956

In 1956, the first year that Elvis Presley began to record for RCA, the company released eleven singles, six EPs, and two LPs. Four of the singles reached the number one spot on the charts—"Heartbreak Hotel," "Don't Be Cruel," "Love Me Tender," and "Hound Dog." The first LP, *Elvis Presley*, remained in the top spot for ten weeks. The second, *Elvis*, entered the charts in the number one position and stayed in the top ten for more than half the year.

The Recording Session in the Army

During the time Elvis Presley was in the army, he was able to enter the recording studio only once. It was on June 11 and 12, 1958, after it became obvious that his unit would soon be sent overseas. Elvis was able to obtain a weekend pass and he went to the RCA studios in Nashville to record. Five sides came out of that session. The first of them to be released was "Such a Fool As I."

The Red Corvair

When Priscilla Beaulieu graduated from high school in June 1963, Elvis Presley gave her a present of a shiny red Corvair.

R

"Reflections"

"Reflections" was a newsletter about Elvis Presley, published for a time after his death by Charlie Hodge, Elvis's long-time valet, and Dick Grob, Elvis's former chief of security at Graceland.

"Return to Sender"

"Return to Sender" was a song recorded by Elvis Presley for the soundtrack of *Girls Girls! Girls!* in 1962. Written by Otis Blackwell and Winfield Scott, it was released as a single even before the movie came out and was another of Elvis's gold records. It reached the number two slot on the pop charts.

The Revised Budget

When Priscilla Presley discussed the financial arrangements of her divorce from Elvis she agreed that she could live on $1,000 a month alimony. But when she actually began living on her own she quickly learned how inadequate that sum would be. Although she didn't want to live the way she had as Mrs. Elvis Presley she did want to have some degree of comfort and privacy. Here is the revised budget of monthly expenses she submitted to the court in the spring of 1973:

Rent	$700
Property insurance & taxes	400
Maintenance of residence	500
Food & household supplies	1,000
Utilities	150
Telephone	400
Laundry & cleaning	300
Clothing	2,500
Medical	200
Insurance	300
Child care	500
School	300
Entertainment	500
Incidentals	1,500
Transportation	1,000
Auto expenses	500
Installment payments	1,350

Kang Rhee

Kang Rhee was a karate master, a Korean immigrant, who lived in Memphis. Elvis Presley studied the psayu style of karate with Rhee for a time and always addressed him respectfully as "Master." Rhee explained his personal philosophy to Elvis biographer Jerry Hopkins. "My school in Memphis basically about self-refine, self-reform and self-respect. Not trying to raise champion, but help the weak and to build confidence, to make better human beings. I'm teaching here as an art, in the traditional manner." Rhee attempted to use his influence over his famous student to keep Elvis physically and mentally fit and drug free, but not even his urging succeeded in bringing about permanent changes in Elvis's life-style.

Dane Rhudyar

Dane Rhudyar was the astrologer who worked out Elvis Presley's personal chart. Elvis was, of course, a Capricorn.

Rising Sun

Rising Sun was a big golden palomino horse that belonged to Elvis Presley. Before Elvis bought him in 1966, the horse had worked in horse shows and rodeos and it seemed that he loved to be admired. Elvis fell in love with Rising Sun the minute he saw him and quickly got into the habit of riding every day at Graceland. But with just thirteen acres, Graceland was not designed to be a horse farm. So early in 1967, Elvis decided to buy the Circle G Ranch in Mississippi, where he could keep Rising Sun and other horses as well. Rising Sun returned to Graceland when the Circle G was sold, and he outlived his owner by ten years, remaining on the grounds of the mansion for some years as a tourist attraction after Graceland was opened to the public.

The Road Not Taken

Elvis Presley fans can only lament some of the chances their hero never took. Among the movie roles he—or Colonel Tom Parker on his behalf—turned down were the lead in *West Side Story*, the role played by Kris Kristofferson in *A Star Is Born*, the Paul Newman role in *Sweet Bird of Youth*, the role of the hustler in *Midnight Cowboy*, the Tony Curtis role in *The Defiant Ones*, the Robert Mitchum part in *Thunder Road*, and the role of Hank Williams in the movie made about his life, later played by George Hamilton. As if all this weren't enough to make you weep, think about the records he never made. Louis Armstrong wanted to make a record with him; so did Arthur Fiedler of the Boston Pops.

R

Mrs. Edna Robinson

The name of the midwife who attended Gladys Smith Presley during the birth of her twin sons was Mrs. Edna Robinson of Tupelo.

Rocca Place

In 1965, Elvis Presley moved out of his leased house on Perugia Way, in the exclusive Los Angeles community of Bel Air, and into a modern house at 10050 Rocca Place, in the same general area. It was located in Stone Canyon, near the Bel Air Hotel. Elvis rented this house until after his marriage to Priscilla in 1967, when they decided to buy a house in Trousdale Estates that offered better security.

The Rolls-Royce

It was completely predictable that Elvis Presley, the lover of expensive cars, would eventually buy himself a Rolls-Royce. In 1961, he bought a Phantom V from a dealer in Beverly Hills and for a time he rode in it frequently, usually with Sonny West at the wheel. However Elvis really preferred the look and feel of America's luxury car, the Cadillac, and in 1964 he gave the Rolls to be auctioned off for the benefit of charity. Two decades later, in the summer of 1986, that same Rolls was once again on the auction block, and was sold by the prestigious London firm of Sotheby's for £110,000, or about $200,000.

"The Roots of Elvis"

Interestingly Elvis Presley's grandfather, Jesse D. Presley, once made a record. It was called "The Roots of Elvis" and featured J.D. singing three songs: "The Billy Goat Song," "Swinging in the Orchard," and "Who's Kickin' My Dog Around." The record was released on the Legacy label in the late 1950s, riding on the coattails of J.D.'s grandson's success.

Kurt Russell

Kurt Russell, born in 1951, made his movie debut as a child when he kicked Elvis Presley on the shin in *It Happened at the World's Fair* in 1963. Fifteen years later Russell starred in the TV movie *Elvis*, playing the title role. The following year he married Season Hubley, who played the role of Priscilla in the same movie. In one final twist of life imitating art, Kurt later divorced Season.

Leon Russell

Leon Russell played piano on several of the soundtracks for Elvis Presley's movies in the 1960s. In addition to Russell's own solo career, he has also backed Jerry Lee Lewis, the Rolling Stones, and Bob Dylan.

Nipsey Russell

Black comedian Nipsey Russell worked for several years as Elvis Presley's opening act.

Sheila Ryan

Sheila Ryan was a Chicago model and *Playboy* cover girl (October 1973) who briefly dated Elvis Presley in the mid-1970s. Although her name was frequently linked with his in the news media and she sometimes traveled with the star, in January 1976 she married actor James Caan.

St. Jude's Children's Research Hospital

The St. Jude's Children's Research Hospital was founded by entertainer Danny Thomas and is located in Memphis. Elvis Presley was a generous supporter of St. Jude's, which provided advanced medical care for children regardless of their parents' ability to pay for it. In 1961, Elvis performed at two benefit concerts in Memphis that helped raise funds for St. Jude's, and he usually wrote the hospital a sizable check every year. He also made them a gift of the former presidential yacht, the *Potomac*, which he purchased for that purpose.

Satchmo Says

Jazzman Louis "Satchmo" Armstrong heard that Elvis had remarked that he wanted to make a record with him. Satch said, "You'd be surprised what we could do together." Alas for music lovers, the duet never came off.

"Sattnin"

A term of endearment much loved by Elvis Presley was the word "Sattnin." He and his mother used it for one another and it subsequently became a term of special intimacy between Elvis and his wife Priscilla. Elvis later used it with Linda Thompson as well. The derivation of this unusual term is not clear.

"Saturday Jamboree"

In the 1940s, the single radio station in Tupelo, Mississippi, WELO, broadcast a live program from the county courthouse on Saturday afternoon between 1:00 and 4:30 P.M., called "Saturday Jamboree." It was a showcase for amateur talent and local kids would stand in line waiting for their turn to go on in front of the studio audience, often as many as 150 people. From the age of eight until his family left Tupelo, Elvis Presley often appeared on the program. The song he sang most often was "Old Shep," the sentimental ballad by Red Foley about a dog. It was with this song that he won his first talent contest.

Scatter

Scatter was a chimpanzee that Elvis Presley kept at Graceland as a pet. Elvis bought the animal from Captain Bill Killebrew, owner of a Memphis TV station on which the chimp sometimes appeared. Elvis and the Memphis Mafia thought it was funny to teach the chimp to pinch attractive young women and grab at their skirts. They also encouraged Scatter to drink bourbon while sitting on a barstool alongside his human friends. Scatter's antics often made front-page news in Memphis but he was an unpopular pet with most visitors to Graceland. In his latter years Scatter became very difficult to control and was confined to a cage on the grounds of Graceland. Although Scatter was even then carefully tended, there were few tears shed when he finally died.

Jerry Schilling

Jerry Schilling, born in 1943, was one of the members of Elvis Presley's entourage from the time they met playing touch football in Memphis in 1964 to the time of the star's death. Jerry, a former football player for Arkansas State University, was for a while on Elvis's payroll and he joined Elvis in studying karate, earning from the star the martial arts nickname "The Cougar." Jerry left his position with Elvis to pursue a career as an actor and then got into the management end of the music business. He is a one-time manager of the Sweet Inspirations, a black female vocal group that frequently backed up Elvis, and his second wife is Myrna Smith, a member of the group. He later managed Billy Joel and the Beach Boys. Jerry Schilling was one of the pallbearers at Elvis's funeral, and currently he serves as creative affairs director for the Presley estate, as well as co-producer of the TV series "Elvis: Good Rocking Tonight."

Screen Test

On April 1, 1956, Elvis Presley made a screen test for Hal B. Wallis of Paramount Pictures. For the test Wallis had selected a scene in which a young man, played by Elvis, confronts the father who has been holding him back, played by Hollywood veteran Frank Faylen. Faylen later remembered that Elvis at first acted too nice and had to be encouraged to make the scene truly confrontational. According to biographer Albert Goldman, Wallis remembered the test as electrifying. "I felt the same thrill I experienced when I first saw Errol Flynn on the screen. Elvis, in a very different, modern way, had exactly the same power, virility, and sexual drive. The camera caressed him." The result of the test was that Elvis was signed to a contract for seven years and three pictures.

Second Only to Mickey Mouse

At the time of Elvis Presley's death, according to his biographer Albert Goldman, Elvis's was the second most commonly reproduced face in the world. The first was that of Mickey Mouse.

Second Only to Mao Tse-Tung

According to a research project of the early 1970s, the most recognized person on the planet at that time was Chinese leader Mao Tse-Tung. Second only to Mao was Elvis Presley.

Peter Sellers

One of Elvis Presley's favorite actors was British comedian Peter Sellers, and the Sellers film he loved the most was *Dr. Strangelove*. John Lennon remembered their shared love of Sellers's work as an immediate bond between them when they met in 1965.

Selling Elvis Stories

In 1988, Joe Smith published a book called *Off the Record*, interviews with the biggest names in pop music. According to Smith, "Over and over, the names people mentioned as having inspired them were the Beatles, Elvis Presley, and Bob Dylan." Smith approached Colonel Tom Parker to ask for an interview about his client. Par-

ker responded by offering to sell him ten Elvis stories for $2,500 apiece. No interview with Parker appears in the book.

Sergeant's Stripes

At the press conference held when Elvis Presley was discharged from the army, he was wearing his uniform and the insignia of the rank to which he had been promoted at the end of his tour of duty—a sergeant's stripes. As it happened, the stripes he was wearing were the yellow stripes of a staff sergeant, although he had only attained the lower rank of buck sergeant. He later explained that the tailor put the stripes on by mistake in the mad rush to get his uniform ready to return home to the reporters.

Elvis poses for a beefcake picture wearing his dog tags with the serial number his fans knew by heart. Although no movies and only a few new songs were released while he was in the army, his popularity remained undiminished. (Photo from Neal Peters Collection)

S

Serial Number

When Elvis Presley was drafted by the United States Army it didn't take reporters long to discover and publish his serial number. It was 533-1076-1. During his army hitch the star often received mail with nothing more than the serial number for an address.

Jurgen Seydel

When Elvis Presley was in the army and stationed in Weisbaden, Germany, he took karate lessons from a black-belt instructor named Jurgen Seydel. Seydel happened to live near Elvis's home in Bad Nauheim, and he was reputed to be one of the best karate instructors in Germany. Red West also trained with Seydel.

Shakerag

Shakerag was the name of the black ghetto in Tupelo, Mississippi. Elvis Presley recalled that he used to hear black men sitting out on their porches, playing the guitar and singing the blues. Stylistically the music would no doubt have belonged to the school known as the delta blues, with simple chord changes, spare instrumentation, and a real emotional wallop.

Cybill Shepherd

In 1970, Elvis Presley secretly began seeing actress Cybill Shepherd. The blonde beauty had been born in Memphis in 1950 and left the city after winning a modeling contract in a Miss Teen Age America beauty contest. Cybill met Elvis in 1970 and according to one report she took four days off the filming of *The Last Picture Show* to spend with Elvis, who at the time was still married to Priscilla. In her book, *Elvis: Precious Memories*, Sue Wiegert quotes a fellow fan about an experience at Elvis's Palm Springs house while he was dating Cybill: "When Cybill climbed out of the pool and laid on a chaise lounge next to Elvis, he leaned over to kiss her. Then he began to kiss her throat, her neck, and on down to her stomach, where he gave her several little butterfly-type kisses around her navel." According to the fan, Cybill didn't even bother to open her eyes and look at Elvis!

Cybill, the mother of three children, starred in the hit TV series "Moonlighting," which left the air in 1989.

Sherlock

Sherlock was the basset hound used in publicity photographs of Elvis Presley when he was promoting his 1956 hit record "Hound Dog." A composite picture, created by splicing together negatives of Sherlock and the RCA dog, Nipper, hung for years on the wall of Colonel Tom Parker's office; it showed the basset hound as about half the size of the little Nipper, and looking up at him adoringly.

The Shirts off His Back

Elvis Presley always enjoyed his fans' reactions to him and his music. When a reporter asked him if he wasn't annoyed by the fans' desire to touch him and grab his clothes (a common attitude of those who have finally achieved their goal of enormous success), Elvis answered, "I've never been seriously hurt. I've had my hair pulled, and a few scratches. I've lost a few suits of clothes too. But as far as I'm concerned, if they want my shirt they can have it. After all, they put it on my back to start with!"

This picture of Elvis with some of his fans dates from before he went into the army, and is characteristic of his attitude toward the people who made him famous. He never complained about the desire of fans to be near him. (Photo from Neal Peters Collection)

Steven Sholes

Steven Sholes was the head of RCA's country music division in the late 1940s, when Colonel Tom Parker was managing Eddy Arnold, who had a recording contract with RCA. Parker became close friends with Sholes, who would later be the one to work out the contract between RCA and Parker's new client, Elvis Presley. Sholes remembered that when he learned the amount of money Sun was asking to release Elvis from his contract with them, he "drew several deep breaths. This boy could be the making of RCA, I thought, or the breaking of me!" His gamble, the largest amount ever offered an unknown pop singer, paid off in handsome profits for RCA for decades to come.

Steve Sholes was elected to the Country Music Hall of Fame in 1967. He died the following year.

Shopping in Vicksburg

In 1987 a woman shopping at Felpausch's Supermarket in Vicksburg, Michigan, saw a man standing in line who she believed was Elvis Presley. That sighting led to a rash of others in the area, as well as a number of jokes about Elvis's life after death. A rival supermarket advertised "Jimmy Hoffa Shops Here" and a local eatery served "Don't Be Cruel" bean soup. The whole fuss put Vicksburg (population 2,800) on the map.

The Sideburns Issue

When Sergeant Elvis Presley was released from the army, he held a press conference to field reporters' questions. One of the first addressed an issue uppermost on the minds of many of his fans: Now that Elvis was once more free to wear his hair the way he wanted to, would he let his sideburns grow again? He answered, "I'm gonna let my sideburns grow a little, but I doubt if they'll be as long as they were. I've gotten over that kick." By the late 1960s, however, his sideburns had crept back down his cheeks in response to prevailing fashions.

Signing with Colonel Parker

The first contract Elvis Presley signed with Colonel Tom Parker was dated August 15, 1955. At that time Elvis still had an existing contract with his former manager Bob Neal, so the new contract did not refer to Parker as Elvis's manager, nor did it give Parker a share of Elvis's earnings. Instead he was to be paid a flat fee of $2,500 plus all his expenses for his efforts "to assist in any way possible the build-up of Elvis Presley as an artist." The contract was signed by Elvis and also by his father Vernon, since Elvis was still a minor at the time. Interestingly Colonel Parker signed on behalf of "Hank Snow Jamboree Attractions" rather than as an agent in his own right.

The first contract was superceded by a second one, signed on November 21 of that same year, which officially made Colonel Parker Elvis's manager, in exchange for payments to Neal that would continue until March of 1956, when Neal's contract as manager would have expired. Elvis then signed a third contract with Parker on March 26, 1956, after he had turned twenty-one. He agreed to pay the Colonel 25 percent of all his earnings, in a contract that had no termination date. That contract was still in force at the time of the star's death.

Simple Arrangements

When Elvis Presley went into the studio to make a recording he always told his backup musicians that he didn't want them to play anything fancy. His intention was to keep the music very simple. "I want every band in every club across the country to be able to play these songs. I want everybody to hear these songs."

Frank Sinatra

What Frank Sinatra was to the young women of one generation, Elvis Presley was to their daughters. Elvis admired Frank's vocal talents, but at first Frank had only negative comments to make about Elvis's music: "His kind of music is deplorable, a rancid-smelling aphrodisiac," he pronounced. Sinatra called rock "the most brutal, ugly, degenerate, vicious form of expression it has been my displeasure to hear." He added, "It fosters almost totally negative and destructive reactions in young people. It smells phony and false. It is sung, played and written for the most part by cretinous goons, and by means of its almost imbecilic reiterations and sly, lewd—in plain fact—dirty lyrics, it manages to be the martial music of every side-burned delinquent on the face of the earth."

However by 1960 Sinatra had recognized the enduring popularity of the style and he invited Elvis, newly discharged from the army, to appear on his TV special that March. The show was broadcast from the Fontainbleau Hotel in Miami Beach and featured a brief duet by the two heartthrobs.

Nancy Sinatra was Elvis's co-star in the 1968 movie *Speedway*. In the past, they had been linked romantically, but by the late sixties they were just old friends, and Nancy was giving Priscilla Presley her baby shower before the birth of Lisa Marie. (Photo from Neal Peters Collection)

Nancy Sinatra

Nancy Sinatra, the daughter of Frank Sinatra born in 1940, became a close friend of Elvis Presley. Perhaps because her father had been the teen idol of a previous generation, Nancy had a special understanding of the problems and pressures of Elvis's enormous fame and hence she was one of his most sympathetic confidantes. When Nancy met the star at the airport on his return from Germany in 1960 after his army discharge, and then also made a cameo appearance with him on her father's TV special a few weeks later, rumors of a romance were rife. Priscilla Presley admitted in her book *Elvis and Me* that she had feared the rumors were true.

Nancy also played one of Elvis's love interests in the 1968 movie *Speedway*. She was for a time married to singer Tommy Sands, something of an Elvis clone, who was also for a time managed by Colonel Parker. One more footnote: It was Nancy Sinatra who gave Priscilla Presley her Hollywood baby shower when she was pregnant with Lisa Marie.

"Sinful Music"

When the Presley family moved to Memphis Elvis began listening to the music on the local black radio stations, which featured such outstanding blues artists as Muddy Waters and B.B. King. He later commented, "I dig the real low-down Mississippi singers, mostly Big Bill Broonzy and Big Boy Crudup, although they would scold me at home for listening to them. 'Sinful music,' the townsfolk in Memphis said it was. Which never bothered me . . ."

Sing Along with Elvis

In the early days of his fame Elvis Presley loved to put his own records on the jukebox that stood on the patio at Graceland and then sing along with himself, giving visitors the treat of Elvis in stereo. Sadly, as his career gradually turned singing into work instead of play, the Elvis singalongs became a thing of the past.

Sing, Boy, Sing

A 1958 movie entitled *Sing, Boy, Sing* was based on the Elvis Presley story—or at least as much of it as was known at that date. Derived from a TV drama called *The Singing Idol*, the 20th Century-Fox movie was directed and produced by Hollywood veteran Henry Ephron. It starred Tommy Sands in the Elvis role (which he also played on the TV show) and Edmund O'Brien as his Colonel Parker-type manager. The soundtrack album was released on Capitol Records. Elvis Presley had originally been offered the role played by Sands but turned it down.

Singles That Went Gold

1956
- "Heartbreak Hotel"
- "I Was the One"
- "I Want You, I Need You, I Love You"
- "Hound Dog"
- "Don't Be Cruel"
- "Love Me Tender"
- "Any Way You Want Me"

1957
- "Too Much"
- "Playing for Keeps"
- "All Shook Up"
- "That's When Your Heartaches Begin"
- "Teddy Bear"
- "Loving You"
- "Jailhouse Rock"
- "Treat Me Nice"
- "Don't"
- "I Beg of You"

1958
- "Wear My Ring Around Your Neck"
- "Hard Headed Woman"

- "I Got Stung"
- "One Night"

1959
- "A Fool Such As I"
- "I Need Your Love Tonight"
- "A Big Hunk o' Love"

1960
- "Stuck on You"
- "It's Now or Never"
- "A Mess of Blues"
- "Are You Lonesome Tonight?"
- "I Got to Know"
- "Wooden Heart"

1961
- "Surrender"
- "I Feel So Bad"
- "Little Sister"
- "His Latest Flame"
- "Can't Help Falling in Love"
- "Rock-a-Hula Baby"

1962
- "Good Luck Charm"
- "Anything That's Part of You"
- "She's Not You"
- "Return to Sender"
- "Where Do You Come From?"

1963
- "One Broken Heart for Sale"
- "Devil in Disguise"
- "Bossa Nova Baby"

1964
- "Kissin' Cousins"
- "Viva Las Vegas"
- "Ain't That Loving You, Baby"
- "Blue Christmas"

1965
- "Crying in the Chapel"
- "I'm Yours"
- "Puppet on a String"

1966
- "Tell Me Why"
- "Frankie and Johnny"
- "Love Letters"
- "Spinout"
- "All That I Am"
- "If Every Day Was Like Christmas"

1967
- "Indescribably Blue"
- "Big Boss Man"

1968
- "Guitar Man"
- "Stay Away"
- "We All Call on Him"
- "Let Yourself Go"
- "Almost in Love"
- "If I Can Dream"

1969
- "In the Ghetto"
- "Charro"
- "His Hand in Mine"
- "Clean Up Your Own Backyard"
- "Suspicious Minds"
- "Don't Cry Daddy"

1970
- "Kentucky Rain"
- "The Wonder of You"
- "Mama Liked the Roses"
- "I've Lost You"
- "You Don't Have To Say You Love Me"
- "Patch It Up"
- "I Really Don't Want To Know"

1971
- "Where Did They Go Lord?"
- "Only Believe"
- "I'm Leavin' "
- "It's Only Love"

1972
- "An American Trilogy"
- "Burning Love"
- "Separate Ways"

1973
- "Raised on Rock"

1974
- "Take Good Care of Her"
- "It's Midnight"

1975
- "My Boy"
- "T-R-O-U-B-L-E"

1976
- "Hurt"

1977
- "Way Down"
- "My Way"

Sivle Yelserp's Secret

As soon as Elvis Presley was released from the army he went into the RCA studio in Nashville to record some new songs that could be released to his eager fans. The recording session took place on March 20, 1960 amid conditions of greatest secrecy. RCA was afraid the studio would be mobbed if it became known that Elvis was working there, so they told all the session musicians they hired that they would be backing up country singer Jim Reeves. On the studio log, the session was coyly listed as being for "Sivle Yelserp."

As usual Elvis began the session by warming up with some gospel numbers with the Jordanaires. It wasn't until the wee hours of the morning that he started to sing the numbers he had gone there to record. His backup musicians included Scotty Moore, D.J. Fontana, and Floyd Cramer; Chet Atkins was the session producer. Although Atkins was concerned that the months in the army might have made Elvis rusty—Elvis later confessed he'd shared the same worry—the recording session went well. As Elvis told reporters afterward, "After a couple of hours, it came natural again. And it has to be natural . . . if I couldn't feel it, I wouldn't do it." The first single to be issued from that session was "Stuck on You," which went gold before it was even released.

The Six-Door Mercedes

One of the many automobiles Elvis Presley owned during a lifetime of car collecting was a specially built six-door Mercedes-Benz. It was seen briefly in his film *Elvis on Tour*. Elvis kept the car on the West Coast and when he wasn't using it he sometimes rented the car out to other celebrities.

The Sixty-five-Cent Army Haircut

On the morning of March 25, 1958, Elvis Presley's first full day in the United States Army, all new recruits at Fort Chaffee, Arkansas, were scheduled to get their army crewcuts. The base was besieged by reporters and photographers who wanted to record for posterity the moment that the beloved sideburns and pompadour bit the dust. Elvis paid the barber, James Peterson, the standard fee of sixty-five cents for the haircut that transformed him from a rock-and-roll star into Private Presley. Fans waiting outside hoped for a lock of Elvis's hair, but strict orders had been given that the famous locks were to be mixed with the shavings from other recruits and disposed of promptly. The pictures of Elvis getting his haircut were on the front page of nearly every paper in the United States the next day.

S

The most famous G.I. haircut in the world—the moment Elvis Presley lost his pompadour and sideburns. The pictures made the front pages of newspapers all over the world. (Photo from Neal Peters Collection)

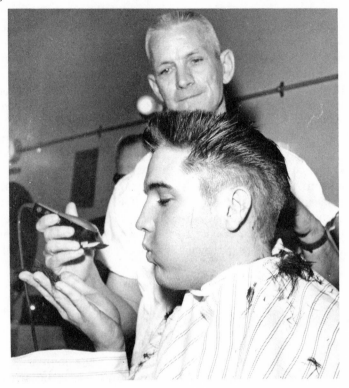

Sleeping Pills

In order to maintain his preferred life-style of sleeping until mid-afternoon and then staying up all night, Elvis Presley relied heavily on sleeping pills and barbiturates. Among his favorites were Placidyls, Seconals, Quaaludes, and Tuinals.

Sleepwalking

From the age of three or four until his late teens Elvis Presley experienced repeated episodes of sleepwalking. He sometimes left the house during these episodes; they were one of the reasons his mother was constantly fearful that something might happen to him. She too was a sleepwalker on occasion, so Elvis may have inherited the tendency from her. Psychiatrists believe that sleepwalking may often be caused by some emotional upset—such as the one young Elvis could have experienced when his father was sent to prison, an episode that coincided with the onset of his sleepwalking.

S

Billy Smith

Billy Smith was the youngest of the three sons of Travis Smith, Gladys Presley's brother, and a first cousin of Elvis Presley. Billy was somewhat younger than Elvis, whose attitude toward him was always paternalistic. As soon as Billy was old enough to work, he, like many other members of the family, went on Elvis's payroll and he remained a constant companion of his cousin until Elvis's death. Billy then took his wife and children to Mississippi to make their home in his native state.

Gene Smith

Gene Smith was one of Elvis Presley's cousins on his mother's side; Gene's father was Gladys Presley's brother, Travis Smith. Gene and Elvis had known each other since they were children, and as young men they had worked together briefly on an assembly line at the Precision Tool Company, until Elvis quit to take a job driving a truck. When Elvis first started his career in show business his mother asked Gene to stay near Elvis and look after him. For a number of years Gene Smith was on Elvis Presley's payroll and he and his wife lived in the garage apartment at Graceland. In 1962, Elvis and Gene had a misunderstanding and they drifted apart, although Gene later occasionally visited his cousin at Graceland.

Junior Smith

Junior Smith was Elvis Presley's cousin, the second son of Gladys Presley's brother, Travis Smith. Junior suffered what appeared to be an emotional breakdown during his army service in the Korean War and shot an entire family of Korean allies for no apparent reason. For a time he was on Elvis's payroll, serving as a bodyguard and a security guard at Graceland. Junior Smith died before he was thirty, of a seizure.

Octavia Luvenia Mansell Smith

Octavia Luvenia Mansell Smith was Elvis Presley's maternal grandmother. Born the third daughter of White and Martha Mansell in northeastern Mississippi in 1876, she was always called "Doll" because of her pretty face and childlike ways. In 1903 Doll married her cousin Robert Lee Smith, the son of her aunt Ann Mansell and Ann's husband Milege Obediah Smith. Robert and Doll settled on a farm in the hills of Mississippi's Lee County and had nine children: Effie (1904), Lillian (1906), Levalle

(1908), Elvis's mother Gladys (1912), Travis (1915), Tracy (1916), Clettes (1919), and John (1922). Doll was tubercular and an invalid for most of her life, although she actually outlived her husband, who died in 1932. She died three years later at the age of fifty-nine.

Robert Lee Smith

Robert Lee Smith was Elvis Presley's maternal grandfather. He was the third son of Ann Mansell (1849–1935) and her husband Milege Obediah Smith, born on a farm in northeastern Mississippi in the late 1870s. He married his cousin Doll Mansell in 1903, and they had nine children, one of whom was Gladys, Elvis's mother. Doll was a life-long invalid and thus able to contribute little to the family welfare. Bob Smith worked as a sharecropper but couldn't make ends meet because he had too few sons to help him in the fields and too many daughters to feed. He occasionally supplemented his income by making moonshine. The family, which settled in Gilvo, Mississippi, lived most of the time in dire poverty. Bob Smith died of pneumonia in 1932. He was buried in an unmarked grave in the Spring Hill Cemetery in Mississippi.

Travis Smith

Travis Smith was Elvis Presley's uncle, the younger brother of his mother, Gladys Smith Presley. Travis had always been close to his sister's family, so when Elvis, Gladys, and Vernon moved to Graceland in 1957, Travis and his wife Lorraine and son Billy accompanied them, living in a small house at the back of the property. Travis acted as a gate guard for many years, sharing stories of the Presley family with the many Elvis fans who thronged the Music Gate and occasionally befriending some, who were invited to his home for supper. Travis Smith died in the 1980s, and his wife Lorraine died of a heart attack on November 11, 1988. Both are buried in the Forest Hill Cemetery.

Snakes

There were a lot of snakes in East Tupelo, Mississippi, where Elvis Presley grew up. The star told Marty Lacker he remembered that snakes often got in their house and his father had to kill them. Elvis's childhood experiences led to a life-long fear of waking up to find a snake in his bed, as well as an obsession with the subject of snakes, about which he was unusually well informed.

Sneering the Elvis Way

Perhaps the most famous of all Elvis Presley trademarks was his sneer. Those who imitate Elvis depend principally on their mastery of the sneer (along with a little hip-wiggling); the sneer was so thoroughly associated with the performer that even he made jokes about it. For example in his 1968 TV special he laughs that he can't remember how to do the sneer anymore, and manipulates his lip in a variety of contortions as he tries to recapture his trademark expression. The sneer was a part of his performing persona, that ineffable combination of tough guy and polite young man, simultaneously attracting and threatening.

The first photo of Elvis in existence, taken when he was only three and wearing a slouch hat, is often produced as the initial example of the sneer. Yet Presley insiders have claimed that the beloved grin in the photo was merely the result of Elvis's attempt to conceal a peanut in his mouth at the moment the picture was snapped.

Snoopy and Brutus

Snoopy and Brutus were a pair of Great Danes that Elvis Presley bought as a gift for his wife Priscilla. The two huge dogs went everywhere with her, always acting as her gentle protectors. Brutus can be seen playing the role of the Great Dane Albert in the movie *Live a Little, Love a Little* (1968). The dog died not long after Elvis and Priscilla were divorced. Snoopy later became Lisa Marie's dog, following the little girl like a faithful shadow. Priscilla commented, "They understand each other completely. Some adults have trouble with Snoopy, but Lisa just gives a command and Snoopy heels in a hurry."

Hank Snow

Clarence Eugene "Hank" Snow was a very successful country-and-western singer who was for a time managed by Colonel Tom Parker. Snow was a Canadian, born in 1914 in Liverpool, Nova Scotia, who loved country music and idolized vocalist Jimmie Rodgers. While still in Canada, Snow managed to get an RCA recording contract, and when his records began to sell in the United States he went to Nashville to appear on the Grand Ole Opry. By the time Hank met Colonel Parker in early 1954 he was already an Opry regular with one enormous hit to his credit—"I'm Moving On." Snow turned to the Colonel to help consolidate his career and expand his business interests into the field of talent management. Together the two men developed the Hank Snow Jamboree Attractions, a touring show that was also one of the major booking agencies for country-and-western artists.

It was when Elvis Presley was booked to appear on the Hank Snow Jamboree tour in the summer of 1955 that Elvis met Colonel Parker. Apparently at the time that the Colonel first began to pursue Elvis as a client, Hank Snow was led to believe that Parker was acting not on his own but on behalf of the Jamboree. In fact Elvis's first contract with Parker was signed by the Colonel as a representative of Jamboree. But a few months later the Colonel signed Elvis to a personal contract with no reference to Jamboree, and that caused a break between Parker and Snow. Hank Snow later sued the Colonel for a share of Elvis's earnings, claiming that he was the one who brought Elvis to Parker's attention and that he was the one who really arranged Elvis's RCA recording contract. The suit was later dropped.

After Elvis's death Hank Snow said, "I have nothing but good things to say about Elvis, as I knew him. At that time he did not smoke, drink, or take the Lord's name in vain and was a perfect example of an all-American boy." Snow added, "My personal thoughts on the untimely death of this giant was that it was due to the constant pressure he was under." Snow didn't specify whether the source of the pressure he had in mind was Elvis's manager.

The Soda Fountains

In Graceland, there were two complete soda fountains where one of Elvis Presley's friends, relatives, or employees could make him a soda, milk shake, or sundae at any hour of the day or night. One soda fountain was in a corner of the trophy room, the other downstairs in Elvis's den.

Something for Everybody

The Elvis Presley album called *Something for Everybody* was issued by RCA in June 1961 and soon reached the number one spot on the album charts. Although it contained no songs that we remember today as Elvis hits, it nevertheless remained in the Top 100 for twenty-five weeks.

"Sooties"

"Sooties" was the baby-talk word Elvis used for feet. Apparently he had picked the word up from his mother, and he used it in his love talk with both Priscilla Beaulieu and Linda Thompson.

Souvenirs from Graceland

For Elvis Presley fans who want something to remember their idol by, Graceland sells a wide variety of souvenirs at the gift shop on the grounds and through a special catalog. Among the available items are an Elvis doll with a concealed microcassette that plays one of his great hits; a commemorative plate; a satin pillowcase silk-screened with his face; wrapping paper with pictures of Elvis; the Elvis board game; and the Presley family cookbook. For further information, write Graceland Gifts, 3797 Elvis Presley Blvd., Memphis TN 38116.

Speedway

Speedway was the twenty-seventh movie Elvis Presley made, in which he played a race-car driver. Ironically much of the plot of the 1968 Elvis vehicle revolves around the star's troublesome manager, whose greed and incompetence gets him into trouble with the IRS. Of course that wasn't all bad, since the IRS agent on his case is Nancy Sinatra, with whom he eventually falls in love. It would be interesting to know how Colonel Parker viewed the recurring motif of the greedy manager in his client's movies. The soundtrack album for *Speedway* is unique in that it features a solo by Nancy Sinatra, singing "Your Groovy Self." Although the album contained a bonus of a color photo of Elvis it reached no higher than number eighty-two on the charts.

Spending Another $4

Elvis Presley made his first recording in the summer of 1954, supposedly as a present for his mother. In January 1954, he returned to the Memphis Recording Studios to make a second record at his own expense. On his second visit he recorded two country-and-western songs, "Casual Love Affair" and "I'll Never Stand in Your Way." On this occasion Sam Phillips was at the recording controls, but the head of Sun records remained noncommittal, telling Elvis only that he would call him if something came up. The call finally came that May.

Split Pants

On his concert tours Elvis Presley always traveled with one or two changes of clothes handy. One reason was that he wore his pants so tight they often split. He also found that his fans could be hard on his clothes, ripping and tearing his shirts in their eagerness to reach out and touch him.

S

The Stamps

The Stamps were a white male gospel group, headed by J.D. Sumner, that worked with Elvis Presley from 1972 until his death. The members of the Stamps, in addition to J.D. Sumner, were Donnie Sumner, Bill Blaize, Ed Knoch, Richard Staborn, and Ed Wideman.

Stamps Honoring Elvis

The first nation to honor Elvis Presley with a stamp bearing his likeness was the little Caribbean country of Grenada, which issued its stamp in 1979.

Germany has also issued an Elvis stamp.

In 1988, Dominica (another small Caribbean country) included an Elvis stamp in a series on entertainers, and Madagascar featured Elvis in a series on musicians.

Billy Stanley

William "Billy" Stanley, born in January 1953, is the oldest son of William Stanley and his wife Dee, who later divorced Stanley and married Vernon Presley. Billy Stanley lived for a time at Graceland and joined with his brothers and mother in authoring the tell-all book, *Elvis, We Loved You Tender*. He subsequently authored a second book, *Elvis, My Brother* (1989).

David Stanley

David Stanley, born in 1954, was one of the three sons of Dee Stanley, the second wife of Vernon Presley, and her first husband, William Stanley. When Dee married Vernon and moved first to Graceland and then to a separate house near the mansion, David and his brothers were part of the household and came to know their famous stepbrother Elvis. David, who has admitted that he himself had a drug problem, also alleges that he saw Elvis use a number of drugs, including cocaine. The Stanley brothers, along with Dee Presley, later wrote a book about Elvis entitled *Elvis, We Loved You Tender*, and for several years David collected fees for coaching various Elvis impersonators. In 1988, Dave Stanley announced he was making a movie version of the Stanleys' story. According to his announcement, he has raised $24 million from backers in Texas to produce the movie.

Ricky Stanley

Richard "Ricky" Stanley was Elvis Presley's stepbrother, the son of Vernon Presley's second wife, Dee Elliott Stanley. Ricky, not yet in his teens when his mother remarried, idolized his famous stepbrother and then tried to imitate him. In 1975, when Ricky was twenty-one, he was arrested for attempting to obtain the prescription drug Demerol from a hospital pharmacy in Memphis, using a forged prescription. Eventually the charge was reduced to malicious mischief and the young man was given a small fine and a suspended sentence. According to one report by a Memphis police officer, Elvis appeared at police headquarters to lecture his stepbrother on his involvement with drugs. "He told him that is the one thing he hates—anything to do with drugs," said the officer. "He said he thought Stanley was disturbed to get into any trouble like this." Elvis recommended psychiatry for the young man, who was hooked on heroin.

Ricky Stanley later became a minister, after studying at the Christian Center in Florida. He now gives full credit to Elvis for saving him from a life of drug addiction or worse.

Barbara Stanwyck

Barbara Stanwyck costarred with Elvis Presley in the 1964 movie *Roustabout* and, like most of the other actors on the set, Elvis called the glamorous star of such films as *Stella Dallas* and *Sorry, Wrong Number* by the respectful nickname of "Missy." In *Roustabout* Stanwyck played the role of Maggie Morgan, the owner of a carnival that Presley joined, and she vowed to teach him the value of hard work. (Interestingly, the role was first offered to Mae West, who turned it down.) Stanwyck recalled, "When Hall Wallis called and said he had a part in a picture and mentioned Elvis Presley, I wondered what on earth I would do in a Presley film. I can't sing. I can't dance." One contemporary reviewer characterized Stanwyck's performance as "pluckily holding her own under less-than-ideal conditions."

The veteran actress, born in 1907 and once the highest-paid woman in Hollywood, had nothing but praise for her young costar. "He was a wonderful person to work with. He asked for nothing. So many people expect the other—swelled head and all that. So did I, frankly. But it was not the case. Elvis was a fine person. His manners are impeccable, he is on time, he knows his lines."

A Star Is Born

Elvis Presley was born in a small house in East Tupelo, Mississippi, on the afternoon of January 8, 1935. Gladys Presley was attended first by a local midwife, Edna Robinson, and then by Dr. William Robert Hunt from Tupelo. At about 4 P.M. Gladys

In *Roustabout*, Barbara Stanwyck co-starred with Elvis as the owner of the circus where he worked. The classy "Missy" Stanwyck thought Elvis was a nice young man. (Photo from Neal Peters Collection)

gave birth to the first baby, a stillborn boy named Jesse Garon. Half an hour later, at 4:35, the second boy, Elvis Aron, was born. Shortly thereafter Gladys began to hemorrhage and the doctor had his hands full trying to stabilize her. At the same time, he was worried about the surviving twin, so he sent mother and baby to the Tupelo Hospital. Since the family couldn't afford to pay, Gladys and Elvis were placed in the charity ward, where they stayed for three weeks. They were likewise unable to pay Dr. Hunt his $15 fee, which he eventually collected from welfare.

The Star on His Film Career

By the 1960s, Elvis Presley was creatively isolated and emotionally defensive about his career as a singer and actor, two factors that virtually prevented any future artistic growth. An example can be seen in his attitude toward his film career, which was beginning to sag by 1963. He commented publicly at that time about the situation:

I've had intellectuals tell me that I've got to progress as an actor, explore new horizons, take on new challenges, all that routine. I'd like to progress, but I'm smart enough to realize that you can't bite off more than you can chew in this racket. You can't go beyond your limitations. They want me to try an artistic picture. That's fine. Maybe I can pull it off some day. But not now. I've done eleven pictures and they've all made money. A certain type of audience likes me. I entertain them with what I'm doing. I'd be a fool to tamper with that kind of success.

Red West, in his book, quoted Elvis talking privately about his movie career in a very different vein. Red recalled that Elvis was generally disgusted whenever he saw himself on the screen. He would say, "Who is that fast-talking hillbilly sonofabitch that nobody can understand? One day he is singing to a dog, then to a car, then to a cow. They are all the damned same movies with that Southerner just singin' to something different."

The Starlight Wranglers

The Starlight Wranglers were a country-and-western band that had attracted Sam Phillips's attention and that he once recorded on the Sun label. He got to know the Wranglers' bass player Bill Black and guitarist Scotty Moore, and he sometimes used them as studio musicians. He assigned them to rehearse with unknown singer Elvis Presley before his first recording session. When Elvis's first release was a local hit all three musicians began to appear together, and at first there was some idea that the fees would be split, with Elvis getting 50 percent and Scotty and Bill each getting 25 percent. But it was quickly apparent that Elvis was the star the crowd wanted to see and Scotty and Bill recognized they were not part of a hit group but simply Elvis's backup musicians—and accepted payment accordingly.

Statue of Elvis in Germany

On October 1, 1988, a life-size statue of Elvis Presley was set down on a dock in Bremerhaven, Germany, to commemorate the day, exactly thirty years earlier, that Elvis and his military unit had arrived at the same dock. The statue was later transported to Bad Nauheim where it is to be permanently sited. The commemorative statue was a joint undertaking by German fan clubs and the English club, Elvisly Yours.

Statue of Elvis in Vegas

In 1978, Elvis Presley's father Vernon and his ex-wife Priscilla unveiled a bronze statue of Elvis, wearing a jumpsuit and holding a microphone, at the Las Vegas Hilton. The statue was sculpted by Carlo Romanelli and it still stands in the hotel's lobby.

S

Stax Studio

The Stax Recording Studio in Memphis was famed for its productions of black rhythm-and-blues records. Elvis used the studio in 1973 for two recording sessions.

Staying Close to Home

When Elvis Presley was a boy in East Tupelo, Mississippi, he usually stayed very close to home. This was largely due to the insistence of his mother, who had been shaken by the death of Elvis's twin brother at birth and by the knowledge that she couldn't have any more children. She probably also felt insecure because her husband Vernon had to leave the family for more than a year to serve a jail term. Gladys always worried that something might happen to her adored and protected only child. Elvis later recalled, "My mama never let me out of her sight. I couldn't go down to the creek like all the other kids. Sometimes when I was little, I used to run off. Mama would whip me, and I thought she didn't love me."

Staying with the G.I.s

According to fellow soldier and later Presley insider Charlie Hodge, Elvis Presley always wanted to be treated as an ordinary soldier during the time he was in the service. Charlie has recalled how Elvis was once asked by a colonel to go on a public-relations junket on behalf of the army, touring several European cities and ending with a meeting with the pope. It was the middle of winter and Elvis's unit was on maneuvers at the time, camping out in the snow in sleeping bags. Elvis told the top brass, "There's fifteen thousand men out there that are sleeping in the snow and for me to leave and go to a nice warm comfortable place and then to come back and work with the guys, I just couldn't face them, so I think I'll just stay here."

"Steadfast, Loyal and True"

"Steadfast, Loyal and True" was a song written by Jerry Leiber and Mike Stoller and sung by Elvis Presley for the soundtrack of *King Creole*; it was supposedly his school song. It is now the official anthem of the International Elvis Presley Appreciation Society.

S

Stealing Elvis

Any city with a street named "Elvis" or "Presley" can expect to spend a considerable sum replacing stolen street signs. For example, city workers report that the sign on Elvis Drive, in San Jose, California, always disappears within hours of each replacement (at a cost of $75-$100).

Stealing more authentic Elvis memorabilia is also popular. For example, in the summer of 1989, Elvis impersonator Charlie Stickerod reported that burglars had broken into his home to steal the cape and suit worn by Elvis in *Aloha from Hawaii*. Stickerod, who said he had paid $7,500 for the outfit, offered a reward of $5,000 for its return.

Connie Stevens

While Elvis Presley was in Hollywood for the filming of *Kid Galahad* in 1962, his regular date was actress Connie Stevens.

Still Selling After All These Years

For Christmas 1988, MGM arranged to issue six of Elvis Presley's movies from the 1960s on videocassette at the low price of $19.95 each. The movies, which included *Kissin' Cousins* and *Girl Happy*, were among the most popular gifts of the season.

Mike Stone

Mike Stone was a Hawaiian-born karate teacher who worked in the early 1970s at a school in Los Angeles operated by Chuck Norris. Elvis Presley, himself a black belt in karate, urged his wife Priscilla to try the sport. She took lessons with Mike Stone, who had once worked as Phil Spector's bodyguard. After a time it became obvious to many Presley insiders that the two had embarked on a romantic relationship. It seemed that Elvis remained unaware of the situation until early 1972, when Priscilla moved out of their home in Holmby Hills and into an apartment of her own. Shortly thereafter Mike Stone's wife sued him for divorce. He became a free man in the summer of 1972 and Elvis filed for a divorce from Priscilla six months later. The relationship between Priscilla and Mike Stone broke up not long afterward, as she struck out to achieve genuine independence. For a time Elvis was preoccupied by feelings of anger against Mike Stone, but eventually he recognized—as did Priscilla—that his wife's relationship with Stone was a symptom of the breakdown of intimacy in the Presley marriage rather than a cause of it.

Stranger than Truth

In 1979, a book was published called *Elvis Presley Speaks*, by psychic specialist Hans Holzer. It purported to be Elvis's messages from beyond the grave, as delivered through the medium of a New Jersey housewife.

"Stuck on You" B/W "Fame and Fortune"

As soon as Elvis Presley was released from the army in March 1960, he entered the RCA recording studio in Nashville to make a new single. The company had orders for more than a million copies of the new Presley record before anyone—including Elvis—even knew what would be on it. The session was backed up by guitarists Scotty Moore and Hank Garland, pianist Floyd Cramer, drummers D.J. Fontana and Buddy Harmon, and, on vocals, the Jordanaires. The single that emerged from that session was "Stuck on You," a fast rocker written by Aaron Schroeder and J. Leslie McFarland. It was backed with "Fame and Fortune," a slow ballad by Fred Wise and Ben Weisman. Needless to say the record was an instant hit. It reached the number one spot on the charts, staying there for four weeks, and sold more than two million copies.

A Student at the Jo Haynes School of Dancing

Priscilla Beaulieu Presley studied ballet in Memphis at the Jo Haynes School of Dancing. She first enrolled when she was still a high school student, continuing to study even after she and Elvis were married. Priscilla appeared in several of the dance school's recitals, but she used a fictitious name, so no one in the audience realized they were watching Mrs. Elvis Presley.

Stuff

Stuff was the name of a black poodle that lived at Graceland. Stuff belonged to Elvis Presley's Aunt Delta Mae Biggs, but Elvis grew as fond of the dog as its owner was.

S

Stunt Work

Elvis Presley did many of his own stunts in his movies. There was usually a fight in every picture, and although directors offered Elvis a stunt double, the star always chose to do the fight scenes himself, making them much more realistic. One of the actors Elvis fought on screen was Gary Lockwood, himself a former stuntman.

Gary remembers initially being apprehensive about the damage he might accidentally do to the studio's most valuable star. But he later recollected, "I needn't have worried. Elvis quickly proved he could take care of himself with his fists, and I soon began to reckon he might have made a boxer if he had wanted to."

"The Ed Sullivan Show"

When Elvis Presley appeared on "The Milton Berle Show" early in 1956 and was publicly criticized for his hip-swinging gyrations, Ed Sullivan, the host of the most popular variety show on television, commented sanctimoniously that he wouldn't touch Elvis with a long pole. But before the year was out he had apparently found a pole long enough. Ed booked Elvis for three appearances on the show and paid him the top fee of $50,000. The reason for his change of heart was obvious when the ratings of the first show, on September 9, 1956, were released—the Elvis shows drew more than 80 percent of the viewing audience.

Actually Ed Sullivan himself was absent from the first show on which Elvis appeared, having been injured in a car accident, so it was hosted by English actor Charles Laughton. Elvis's second appearance came on October 28, when the regular host was back on the job, but Ed did no more than introduce the new teen sensation. It was not until Elvis's third appearance on the show, on January 6, 1957, that Elvis and Ed actually spoke together on the air. After Elvis had sung four songs, Ed came out to stand by him and told the viewing audience, "I wanted to say to Elvis Presley and the country that this is a real decent fine boy, and we've never had a pleasanter experience on our show with a big name than we've had with him." Ironically it was for that third show that the famous edict was issued, ordering that Elvis be filmed only from the waist up, avoiding broadcasting his sexy gyrations.

Elvis finished that show with two more songs, "When My Blue Moon Turns to Gold Again" and "Peace in the Valley." One of the other guests on the program was the young comedienne, Carol Burnett.

J. D. Sumner

J. D. Sumner was a gospel singer with a magnificent bass voice whom Elvis Presley had listened to when he was a little boy. They met because Elvis kept hanging around the places gospel singers appeared, and when Sumner learned the young fan didn't have the money for admission to the gospel show, he began to sneak him in. For twelve years, from 1954 until 1965, Sumner sang with the Blackwood Brothers, one of the best-known white gospel groups; before that, he had his own group called the Sunshine Boys. When the Jordanaires, Elvis's original backup group, decided to stop traveling with him, Elvis hired Sumner, along with his new group called The Stamps, for backup vocals in recording sessions and at performances. Sumner recalls that in the middle of the first show they ever did together, at the International Hotel in Las Vegas in January 1972, Elvis walked over to him and gave him a diamond ring off his own finger; the ring proved to be worth more than $40,000. Later when the Stamps had to leave Graceland after a rehearsal session and head for the airport to catch a plane, Elvis threw Sumner the keys to his own $55,000 Lincoln stretch limo and told him the vehicle was his. Sumner later discovered that he could rent out the stretch limo at the rate of $1,000 a weekend. After Elvis's death Sumner recorded a tribute to him for RCA, entitled *Elvis Has Left the Building.*

Sun Records

Sun Records was a by-product of the Memphis Recording Studio, established by Sam Phillips in Memphis in 1950. He had seen a commercial opportunity in the fact that there was no place in the entire south for black performers to make recordings, so he opened the studio.

In the beginning Phillips sold the masters he recorded of black performers to Chess Records in Chicago, taking a few cents royalty on each record Chess sold. But in 1953 he decided to press and distribute some of the masters himself under the label of Sun Records. Sun's race records, made by such artists as Howlin' Wolf, B.B. King, and Bobby Bland, sold reasonably well, but Phillips had an idea about how Sun could be even more successful. In those days, recordings by black artists had sales and airplay only in the black community; they were not yet part of the cultural mainstream. Phillips reasoned that the key to success was to find a white singer who had the spirit and energy of the black performers. "If I could find a white man who had the Negro sound and the Negro feel, I could make a billion dollars."

The performer he found to fit this formula was Elvis Presley.

In 1953, Elvis walked into the Memphis Recording Studio to cut a record, intended, according to legend, as a birthday present for his mother. The office manager of the studio, Marion Keisker, heard the young man's amateur efforts and realized he was what her boss was looking for. She kept the scraps of the tape Elvis made and played them for Sam. "This is what I heard in Elvis," she explained, "this . . . what I guess they now call 'soul.' So I taped it. I wanted Sam to know."

Sam Phillips too recognized Elvis's potential. In the early summer of 1954 he asked Elvis to come to the three-room Sun Studio at 706 Union Street and make a recording. As a result, Phillips issued the first Elvis Presley record on the Sun label, disc number 209, only weeks later. On one side was "That's All Right," written by blues singer Big Boy Crudup, and on the other side was a wild version of "Blue Moon of Kentucky," a hit associated with the King of Bluegrass, Bill Monroe. In the following year, 1955, Sun recorded and issued four more singles by Elvis Presley, two of which made it onto the country charts.

Sun Records discovered and recorded a number of other young talents in addition to Elvis Presley. The list includes Johnny Cash, Conway Twitty, Carl Perkins, Roy Orbison, Jerry Lee Lewis, and Charlie Rich. In 1955, through an approach by Elvis's new manager, Colonel Tom Parker, RCA offered Sun a total of $35,000 to buy Elvis's contract and the rights to the five recordings already issued by Sun. Phillips decided to take the money and use it to promote some of his other performing artists. He accomplished his goal when he issued hot singles by Perkins, Lewis, and Cash, but in comparison with the amount of money Elvis Presley was to earn for RCA over the years, Phillips probably made a bad deal.

The Sun Sound

The early recordings of Elvis Presley on the Sun label are part of the legendary "Sun Sound," pioneered by Elvis, Carl Perkins, Jerry Lee Lewis and Johnny Cash—the label's famed Million-Dollar Quartet. The Sun Sound featured raw energy, sparse instrumentation, and echoes and distorted sound, due as much to the shortcomings of the Sun recording studio as to the intent of producer Sam Phillips. Once the Million-Dollar Quartet left the Sun label none of them ever recaptured that early sound—although most of them sold more records.

"Surrender"

"Surrender" was based on an old Italian song, "Come Back to Sorrento," with new words by Doc Pomus and Mort Shuman. Elvis Presley recorded the song in the fall of 1960 and on its release it quickly climbed to the number one spot on the charts. "Surrender" has the distinction of being the shortest of Elvis's gold records, clocking in at just one minute, fifty-one seconds.

"Suspicious Minds"

"Suspicious Minds" was a song Elvis Presley recorded in early 1969 in a session at American Studios in Memphis. Written by Mark James, the song was released as a single by RCA and rose to the top of the charts.

It was Elvis's first number one record since the early days of the decade. It was also the last Elvis single that would ever make it to the number one position.

The Sweat-Stained Scarves

A feature of Elvis Presley's live performances that specially delighted fans was the moment when he took off the scarf he was wearing around his neck and threw it out into the audience. It began as a spontaneous gesture, but it was such an obvious crowd-pleaser that the star incorporated it as part of his act. His dresser, Charlie Hodge, was equipped with a large stock of inexpensive scarves and as soon as Elvis threw one to the crowd Charlie draped another around his neck. Even in Vegas, where audiences largely consisted of middle-aged couples sitting sedately at small tables, anticipation of the moment when a scarf would be tossed to fans was extreme.

The Sweet Inspirations

For his first appearance in Las Vegas in 1968, Elvis Presley hired the Sweet Inspirations, a black female group, to warm up the audience before he went on and then to sing backup vocals during his own act. The Sweet Inspirations had often sung with Aretha Franklin and had the gospel-soul sound that Elvis felt comfortable with. The members of the group were Myrna Smith, Estelle Brown, Sylvia Stenwell, and Cissy Houston (the mother of pop singer Whitney). Elvis often referred to the ladies affectionately as the "Sweets."

Sweet Pea

Sweet Pea was a tiny dog that Elvis Presley gave his mother Gladys in 1956. After Gladys's death, Elvis continued to care for the dog. He was on one occasion photographed with the diminutive Sweet Pea on his shoulder.

"TCB"

Elvis Presley's motto was "TCB," or Taking Care of Business. All of his male employees were given gold necklaces bearing the TCB insignia bisected by a bolt of lightning. He also gave everyone sunglasses with TCB stamped in gold on the earpiece. The motto is still used by fans in their efforts to keep the memory of Elvis alive, an endeavor they refer to as "TCB-ing."

"TLC"

Elvis Presley loved the motto "TLC," or Tender Loving Care, which he thought appropriate for the women around him (as opposed to TCB, Taking Care of Business, which he applied to the male of the species). The wives and girlfriends of his buddies all received gold necklaces with the letters TLC. An interesting symbolic feature of the necklaces was that they had no clasps. Elvis explained to one friend that it meant there were no catches to his feelings.

Take-Offs on Elvis Presley

Over the years Elvis Presley has furnished material for scores of comics. Among some of the more memorable Elvis take-offs were:

- Tom Gibson as Elvin Pelvin, singing "Brown Suede Combat Boots," on the "Phil Silvers Show"

- Stan Freberg, with his parody of "Heartbreak Hotel," using so much echo you can't hear the words
- Homer and Jethro, singing "Hart Brake Motel" and "Two Tone Shoes"
- Puneet Singh Sira, a Sikh, in a commercial for a brand of Indian food aired on

British TV, singing, "Get your gums off my poppadums" to the tune of "Blue Suede Shoes"
- John Belushi as a blimpy Elvis filming a sequel to *Viva Las Vegas*, in which he plays a singing busboy, on "Saturday Night Live"

- Ferlin Husky, recording under the name Simon Crum, singing "Don't Be Mad," a parody of "Don't Be Cruel"

Taking the Boy out of the Country

When Elvis Presley was in the army he was sent to Germany, the first—and last—time in his life that he was to spend more than a few days in another country. When he returned to pick up his career he was a different performer. He was less sexy, less raunchy, less vital—it seemed that he had finally joined the cultural mainstream. The change led one reporter to quip, "When they took the boy out of the country, they apparently took the country out of the boy."

Taking the Divorce Hard

All those who were close to Elvis Presley at the time his wife Priscilla asked for a separation agreed that he took it very hard. Part of the difficulty was that he had no inkling that the blow was coming; it also hurt that she was already involved with another man, karate instructor Mike Stone. According to Elvis biographer Jerry Hopkins, Elvis one night poured his heart out to friend Ed Parker, saying, "She has everything money can buy, Ed—cars, homes, an expense account. And she knows that all she has to do is ask, and I'll get her whatever she wants. I can't understand, Ed. I love that woman." Another clue to Elvis's feelings came when he added a new song to his Vegas act, "You Gave Me a Mountain," by Marty Robbins, about the sorrows of a man whose wife has left him.

The Talent Contest in Tupelo

When Elvis Presley was eight years old and attending school in East Tupelo, Mississippi, one of his teachers, who had heard him sing at school, entered him in the talent contest at the annual Mississippi-Alabama Agricultural Fair. According to legend little Elvis climbed on a wooden chair and sang a sentimental ballad written by Red Foley about a dog, "Old Shep," which moved the audience nearly to tears. He won second prize—$5 and all the rides he wanted to go on while he was at the fair.

Norman Taurog

Norman Taurog was the movie director with whom Elvis Presley worked most frequently; in all, they made nine movies together. Taurog, born in 1899, was a former child actor who became a skillful director of comedy, working with such stars as Jerry Lewis and Dean Martin, Bing Crosby, and Judy Garland. In 1931, Taurog won an Oscar for his direction of *Skippy*, starring young Jackie Cooper. Taurog claimed that one way he achieved success with young stars such as Elvis was to reward them for good performances with one of the candy bars he kept in his pockets. He said of Elvis, "I was always proud of his work, even if I wasn't too proud of his scripts." Taurog died in 1981.

Teacher's Pet

The Class Will of the class of 1953 at L.C. Humes High School in Memphis mentioned Elvis Presley in one clause: "Donald Williams, Raymond McCraig and Elvis Presley leave hoping there will be someone to take their place as *teacher's pet*." Elvis's high school friend Red West later commented, "I think she [the teacher] had a soft spot for Elvis because he was so polite to her."

"Teddy Bear"

In the 1957 movie *Loving You*, Elvis Presley sang the song "Teddy Bear," which was then released as a single, with "Loving You" on the flip side. Written by Kal Mann and Bernie Rowe, the song was quickly linked to Elvis's interest in the stuffed animals, which made the record go gold almost instantly—and caused Graceland to fill up with teddy bears. "Teddy Bear" spent seven weeks in the coveted number one position on the pop charts in 1957.

Teddy Bear of Zi-Pom-Pom

Teddy Bear of Zi-Pom-Pom was a pedigreed poodle given Elvis Presley by an adoring fan when he was in the army in Germany. Apparently the dog never made it back to the States when Elvis returned.

Teddy Bears

In 1957, Elvis Presley recorded the song "Teddy Bear," which eventually hit the number one spot on the charts. At that time he revealed to the press that he personally loved teddy bears and never traveled without one. Although his passion for teddy bears was undoubtedly exaggerated by his manager, Colonel Parker, to hype the hit record, there was a grain of truth underlying all the publicity. Elvis did indeed like teddy bears and pandas and he usually had a number of them around him. Fans obligingly sent him hundreds of the cuddly creatures, and close friends were always on the lookout for a special bear to give Elvis as a present.

Temper Tantrums

Elvis Presley was given to temper tantrums, a trait he inherited from his mother Gladys, who would occasionally hurl an iron skillet at her husband when he made her mad. In Elvis this tendency to blow up in anger was exacerbated by the use of drugs that undermined his emotional stability. He would scream and shout, throw things, shoot up the television set, fire people or insult them, and then stomp off to his room in disgust. Typically he would later apologize for his outburst, blaming it on his tiredness or the pressure he was under. Then he would make some extravagant gesture to patch things up.

Sister Rosetta Tharpe

Sister Rosetta Tharpe was a gospel singer popular throughout the south in the 1930s and 1940s. Elvis Presley used to listen to her singing and later cited it as an influence on his own vocal styling and choice of music. Elvis sang a song written by Tharpe, "Saved," in his 1968 TV special.

"That's All Right" B/W "Blue Moon of Kentucky"

The first recording of Elvis Presley ever released was Sun Records disc number 209, issued on July 19, 1954. On the *A* side of the disc was "That's All Right (Mama)," written by blues singer Arthur "Big Boy" Crudup and first recorded by him as a race record in 1946. Two days after Elvis's first studio recording session, on July 5, Sam Phillips gave a dub of "That's All Right" to his friend, local deejay Dewey Phillips of station WHBQ. When Dewey first aired the song he got so many telephone requests for an encore that he ended up simply playing the record over and over for the rest of the show—a total of thirteen times. On the same program Dewey held an interview with Elvis, who had to be fetched by his mother from a movie theater where he was hiding to avoid the suspense of the airing of his first record.

Within a few days Sun had orders for seven thousand copies of the record, which had not yet been manufactured. In a second session on July 10 the B side of the record was added. That was Bill Monroe's bluegrass hit, "Blue Moon of Kentucky," moved down into Elvis's vocal range with a few blues licks added for good measure. The record was ready for release nine days later. Eventually it sold more than twenty thousand copies in the Memphis area, pioneering a new style of music that was later labeled "rockabilly" and that soon turned into full-blown rock and roll.

"They Definitely Weren't Wax"

Terry Mike Jeffrey, one of the stars of the 1988 production *Elvis: An American Musical*, and also its musical director, had been an admirer of Elvis during the time he was growing up in Memphis. When Terry Mike started a band there some years later he got to meet Elvis and they became friends. Terry Mike was one of the few outsiders invited to the private funeral of the star he had idolized. He later attempted to quash reports that Elvis had faked his own death by telling reporters about his recollections of the event. "At one point we were left in the room with Presley's body in the casket. I went over and touched his face, his sideburns. They definitely weren't wax."

This Is Elvis

In 1981, *This Is Elvis* appeared in movie theaters. Delving into the life and career of Elvis Presley, it was made with the co-operation of Colonel Tom Parker by the producing-directing team of Malcolm Leo and Andrew Solt, specialists in rockumentaries. David Wolper was executive producer; he would collaborate with Solt again on the 1988 documentary about John Lennon, *Imagine.*

This Is Elvis contains some of the best of Elvis's performances of his classic songs, such as "Hound Dog," "Don't Be Cruel," "Heartbreak Hotel," "Blue Suede Shoes," and "Love Me Tender." It also includes several of the most successful production numbers from his movies, as well as his early TV appearances with the Dorsey brothers, Milton Berle, and Ed Sullivan. The movie is organized around the gimmick of a narrative, supposedly by Elvis and performed by singer Ral Donner, that connects the series of clips. A videocassette version of the film includes material not seen in the theatrical version, such as home movies of Elvis on the set taken by Dolores Hart,

T

Elvis's costar in the 1957 movie *Loving You* and candid clips of Elvis relaxing taken by Priscilla Presley.

Reviewer Pauline Kael described *This Is Elvis* as a horror movie in which "we witness the transformation of a young whirlwind performer into a bloated druggie with dead eyes." Kael complained that the re-creations of Elvis's life in the movie denied the singer "his singularity, his drive, and his tragedy," but concluded that Elvis himself still rose above the material: "There's an authentic mystery about him."

Linda Thompson

In 1972, when Elvis Presley's marriage was on the verge of breaking up, he began dating Linda Thompson. Their relationship lasted four years. At the time they met Linda was the reigning Miss Tennessee in the Miss Universe Pageant, a tall dark-haired beauty who had been born and raised in Memphis. She was an English major at Memphis State University who had accumulated three and a half years of credits before dropping out to become Elvis's constant companion. She met Elvis at the Memphian Theatre in the summer of 1972 when she was invited by one of his friends to join the gang there on a night Elvis rented the theater. After Priscilla left Elvis, Linda became the woman he was closest to. In the course of their relationship Elvis gave her a Lincoln Continental, a fur coat, and her own American Express card, and he also let her charge whatever she wanted to his accounts. He bought her a house near Graceland and later bought houses in Memphis for her parents and her brother as well.

The outgoing Linda seemed to enjoy Elvis's celebrity life-style, and most of his inner circle agree she was a good influence on him during an increasingly difficult time in his life. The reasons for the couple's breakup in 1976 were not clear, and they continued to be friends as long as the star lived. Linda's relationship with Elvis was the subject of a 1981 TV movie she authorized, called *Elvis and the Beauty Queen*. In 1981 Linda married Olympic decathlon champion Bruce Jenner. They separated in 1987.

Willie Mae (Big Mama) Thornton

Willie Mae Thornton was a classic blues singer, nicknamed "Big Mama," born in Alabama in 1926. She recorded during the 1940s and early 1950s. In 1953 Peacock Records, a Houston label, issued her recording of "Hound Dog," a song written for her by Jerry Leiber and Mike Stoller, who were later to write many hits for Elvis Presley. Thornton's single reached the number one spot on the rhythm-and-blues charts and stayed there for six weeks, but she received only a flat payment of $500 for making the record. In 1956, Elvis Presley recorded "Hound Dog" and his version was an immediate hit, staying on the charts for more than half a year and selling more than six million copies that year alone. Thornton was understandably bitter about the difference in the two versions' success.

"Those Amazing Animals"

"Those Amazing Animals" was the television series of which Priscilla Presley was a cohost. The program, which debuted in 1980, features live animals, film clips of animals, and some human guests, such as Jacques Cousteau, talking about animals. Burgess Meredith was the host, Priscilla and country singer Jim Stafford the cohosts. The show did well enough to remain on the air for the entire season but not well enough to be renewed for a second season.

Tired of Being Elvis Presley

Elvis Presley's last recording session took place in the late spring of 1977, only months before his death. During the session, he turned to his producer Felton Jarvis and said, "I'm sort of getting tired of being Elvis Presley."

Those who believe that Elvis faked his own death to find some peace and privacy often cite this comment as evidence of his motive. Those who believe Elvis died because he was tired of living also point to the remark as telling.

The Title of Colonel

"Colonel" was an honorary title bestowed on Tom Parker in 1948 by Governor Jimmy Davis of Louisiana, thanks to one of the Governor's staff members who had worked with Parker in the American Royal carnival. Thereafter Parker saw to it that everyone addressed him by his honorary title. In 1953 he was made an honorary Colonel by the governor of Tennessee for his help in a political campaign.

To Elvis, with Love

A nurse named Lena Canada wrote a book about one of her patients, a young girl suffering from cerebral palsy. Identified only as "Karen," the girl wrote to Elvis Presley, who answered her letter and began a regular correspondence that lasted until her death—which took place immediately after writing her last letter to the star.

The Tooth Fairy

When young Lisa Marie Presley was visiting her father during one of his Las Vegas engagements, she lost one of her baby teeth. The next morning the little girl awoke to find that the tooth fairy had left her five dollars. Priscilla later scolded Elvis for this prodigality, explaining that the fairy usually left only fifty cents. Elvis just laughed; as Priscilla concluded, "Who would expect Elvis Presley to know the going rate for a tooth?"

Touch Football

Elvis Presley's old friends say that in his teens he liked to play football and went out for the high school team, although he didn't succeed in making it. Years later he still liked to play a rousing game of touch football, and during the years that he spent most of his time in Hollywood he had a team of his own, called the Elvis Presley Enterprisers. They played regularly every weekend against teams of other stars.

Touched by Love

Touched by Love was a 1980 movie starring Deborah Raffin as a teacher and Diane Love as an emotionally withdrawn teen who is obsessed with Elvis Presley. The teacher uses that obsession to help the girl. In the course of the plot Elvis becomes the girl's penpal and is briefly seen on screen when the girl goes to an Elvis movie. The clip used in the production is actually not from a movie but from Elvis's 1956 appearance on "The Ed Sullivan Show."

The Tour Machinery

Elvis Presley's tours in the late 1960s and 1970s were miracles of logistic planning. First to arrive were the advance team, which consisted primarily of Elvis's manager, Colonel Tom Parker, and Parker's assistants. They would check security at the hotel, prepare the star's room with its customary aluminum foil at the windows to help him sleep, finalize arrangements at the concert venue (where they would pick up a check for the gate receipts), set up interviews, and make sure records were available for purchase. Next to arrive were Elvis and his entourage. Elvis would eat a huge meal from room service, pop some pills, and fall asleep. Meanwhile his entourage scurried around to make sure everything would be just the way he liked it when he awoke and got ready to perform that evening.

As Elvis slept a big plane—usually a four-engine jet Electra 99—would land, carrying musical instruments, sound equipment, singers, musicians, and roadies; usually no fewer than forty people were an integral part of the concert. Most of the concert veterans who went on tour with Elvis agreed that it was one of the smoothest operations they had ever been part of.

Tours of Graceland

Hundreds of thousands of Elvis Presley fans have toured Graceland every year since it was opened to the public in 1982. The tour of the mansion includes the main floor, whose highlight is the concert grand piano completely covered in gold leaf; the lower level with its billiard room and Elvis's "jungle" den; the trophy room; the cars in the garage, including the famous pink Cadillac; the racquetball building; the grounds and the horses still kept there; and the Meditation Garden, Elvis's final resting place. For an additional fee visitors may also tour two of Elvis's airplanes—the *Lisa Marie* and the Jetstar—and his customized bus, as well as the Elvis Museum.

The tours are such a big business that there is now a Howard Johnson's and a Quality Inn nearby on Elvis Presley Boulevard, and it is often necessary to make reservations at Graceland in advance to guarantee a particular date and time for the tour. There is a special Christmas festival with choirs, arts and crafts, gingerbread and hot chocolate, and extravagant lighting and decoration all over the mansion and grounds—just the sort of lavish holiday production Elvis always loved (although some fans who attended the 1988 Christmas display complained that most of the Christmas music played over the public address system was sung NOT by Elvis but by artists such as Nat Cole and Bing Crosby).

Also on the grounds at Graceland is the Heartbreak Hotel Restaurant, which usually serves dishes made from recipes found in the Presley family cookbook, available at the gift shop.

Tour packagers have gotten in on the action too, offering airfare, rental car, hotel for two nights, and the full tour of Graceland, with a side trip to the Sun Studios and their photographic "Wall of Fame."

Despite the commercialization of Graceland it is still a home. Elvis's daughter, Lisa Marie, told a reporter from *Life*, "There's just an incredible feeling about that house even now that it's open to the public. I go there three or four times a year. At night, when we're alone in the house, and the same maids are cooking corn bread and black-eyed peas for us like they always did—if feels just the way it used to, when my dad was alive."

For information about tours of Graceland, write: Graceland, 3764 Elvis Presley Blvd., Memphis TN 38116.

Traveling in Scotty Moore's Wife's Car

When Elvis Presley first began to make live appearances he traveled all over the South —clubs, schools, shopping center openings —with his backup musicians, Bill Black and Scotty Moore. Scotty recalled that the first six months the group did all their traveling in his wife's car. "She was the only one that had a job, working at Sears, and making enough for a car. It was a brand-new 1954 Bel Air with gold and white trim and I think it collapsed after about 40,000 miles."

The Trophy Room at Graceland

In the trophy room at his Memphis home, Graceland, Elvis Presley displayed the hundreds of awards he had won during his career. These included all his gold records (more than any other single recording artist), his three Grammy awards, and even the cup won by a softball team in Memphis that he sponsored. The trophy room had once been a patio, then a room devoted to the slot cars that Elvis and his friends raced for a time. It was converted to its present use in one of Elvis's frequent remodelings of Graceland.

Trousdale Estates

Not long after Elvis Presley married Priscilla Beaulieu he decided to move out of his leased house on Rocca Place, in a Los Angeles suburb, and buy a home of his own in California. He chose a fully furnished four-bedroom house at 1174 Hillcrest, in Trousdale Estates, a posh development that appealed to Priscilla because of its privacy and seclusion. The house, six years old at the time and built in an imitation French regency style, had six bathrooms, a guest cottage, and an Olympic-size pool. The development was home to other stars, such as Danny Thomas, and it had excellent security, an important consideration for Elvis and Priscilla, who were expecting their first child and had to consider the possibility of the most famous baby in America being kidnapped.

Blanchard Tual

Blanchard Tual was a Memphis lawyer who was appointed by the probate court in 1980 to represent the interests of minor Lisa Marie Presley in regard to the Elvis Presley estate. After Elvis's death his executor, Vernon Presley, had agreed to continue doing business as usual with manager Colonel Tom Parker on Parker's notably steep terms, and after Vernon died the new co-executors, Priscilla Presley, Joe Hanks (Elvis's former accountant), and the Memphis National Bank of Commerce, also seemed willing to carry on as before. But the probate judge found Parker's fees inordinate and appointed Tual to look into the matter.

Tual made his first report late in 1980 and filed an amended analysis six months later. He accused Parker not only of mismanagement but of conspiracy, fraud, misrepresentation, and collusion. A few months later, on August 14, 1981, the judge of the probate court embraced most of Tual's report and ordered the Presley estate to stop making any further payments to the Colonel.

Presley Tanita Tucker

In 1989, country singer Tanya Tucker, sometimes called a female Elvis, gave birth to a baby girl she named Presley Tanita Tucker. She has refused to say who the father is.

Tupelo

Tupelo, Mississippi, is a town of about six thousand people in the northeast corner of Mississippi. The name comes from a Chickasaw Indian word, although there is disagreement about the word's real definition. Surrounded by farms, Tupelo achieved prosperity when the St. Louis–San Francisco Railroad was built through the town in the 1880s. The east side of Tupelo, where Elvis Presley was born and raised, was separated from the rest by the train tracks and some cotton fields, and it has always been considered the wrong side of the tracks.

Tupelo Garment Company

When Gladys Smith was nineteen years old her father died. It was the depths of the Depression, her mother was ill, and she had several younger sisters still at home. So Gladys had to look for full-time work to help bring in the money the Smith family, then living in East Tupelo, Mississippi, needed so desperately. In December 1932, the young woman found a job in nearby Tupelo as a sewing machine operator at the Tupelo Garment Company. Gladys earned $2 a day and probably considered herself lucky to get the job. She was still working at the Tupelo Garment Company when she met and married Vernon Presley.

T

The Tupelo Tornado

In the second year of Elvis Presley's life the town of Tupelo, Mississippi, was struck by a catastrophic tornado. Several hundred people were killed, and the property destruction was enormous. By good fortune the Presleys and their home were completely untouched.

Turning Night into Day

Elvis Presley always liked to stay up at night and sleep during the day. Perhaps this habit began in 1954 and early 1955, when he was on the road so often and had no choice but to sleep in the day while he was traveling to get ready for a late night. Once Elvis became a big star he began to keep a schedule that deliberately turned night into day. He rarely rose before two o'clock in the afternoon. Afternoons and early evenings were usually spent quietly, taking care of business matters, reading the newspaper, and going for a ride. Around midnight the Presley entourage would gather and things would start to happen.

At home in Memphis, Elvis might rent the roller-skating rink, take over a local movie theater, or simply hold open house at Graceland for dozens of friends. In Bel Air, California, he might go out for a ride on his motorcycle or shoot pool and listen to his jukebox. It wasn't until the sun came up that Elvis was ready to go to bed.

Unfortunately staying on this unnatural schedule required a regimen of sleeping pills and stimulants. He used both and he also gave them liberally to friends, employees, and anyone else who wanted to keep him company on his unusual schedule.

The TV Special with Frank Sinatra

Elvis Presley fans had waited anxiously for their first chance to see their hero perform again after he was discharged from the army. The opportunity came on March 21, 1960, when Elvis was the featured guest on a Frank Sinatra TV special called "Welcome Home, Elvis," broadcast from Miami Beach's Fontainbleau Hotel. His manager, Colonel Tom Parker, had negotiated a fee of $125,000 for a six-minute appearance during which Elvis sang two songs, "Fame and Fortune" and "Stuck on You."

Then Sinatra and Presley duetted on "Witchcraft" and "Love Me Tender." Other guests on the show were Sammy Davis, Jr., Peter Lawford, Joey Bishop, and Frank's daughter Nancy. Although Sinatra had been one of Elvis's outspoken detractors in the early days, he apparently had changed his mind about both rock and roll and its leading exponent. The TV special also presaged a change in Elvis's own image, which began to move closer to the cultural mainstream.

"The Twelve"

Elvis Presley sometimes referred to his entourage as "The Twelve," an ironic comparison to the twelve disciples of Christ.

"The Twilight Zone"

When the TV series "The Twilight Zone" was revived in 1986, one of the episodes on the first show was about Elvis Presley. Called "The Once and Future King," it tells the story of an Elvis imitator who accidentally kills the real Elvis.

U2 Tours Graceland

In the 1988 movie starring rock group U2,
Rattle and Hum, the group tours Graceland
to pay homage to Elvis Presley.

The Variety Show at Humes High

In his senior year of high school Elvis Presley entered the annual variety show held in the school auditorium on December 20, 1952. One of thirty acts, Elvis sang "Cold Cold Icy Fingers" and probably also his standard crowd-pleaser in those days, the tear-jerking ballad "Old Shep." As the student who had obviously received the most applause, Elvis was the one chosen to perform the only encore. The teacher in charge of the show remembers that Elvis came off the stage saying over and over in wonderment, "They really liked me, they really liked me."

Vernon's First Heart Attack

In the spring of 1975, Vernon Presley had his first heart attack. He was admitted to Baptist Memorial Hospital in Memphis by Elvis's personal physician, Dr. George Nichopoulos. Vernon recovered from the mild attack quickly, but even with the best of care he continued to have heart trouble, dying four years later of a massive coronary.

Vernon's Prison Term

In early 1938, when Elvis Presley was only three years old, his father Vernon Presley either altered or forged a check written on the bank account of Orville Bean, a local dairy farmer who was both Vernon's employer and landlord. The story goes that Vernon had sold Farmer Bean a hog and then received in return a check for just $4, much less than Vernon had expected to get. In collusion with his brother-in-law Travis Smith and a friend named Lether Gable, Vernon decided to alter the check to a sum he considered more appropriate. Bean, outraged by what he viewed as an outright theft, pressed charges.

Vernon was arrested and then held for months in the Tupelo jail because his family either couldn't or wouldn't post bail for him. The trial took place on May 24, 1938 and all three men were sentenced to three years of hard labor on the notorious Parchman Farm. Gladys and Elvis had to move out of the house where Elvis was born and into the home of her cousin, Frank Richards, in South Tupelo. Gladys took in laundry so she and her son could survive. It was probably this episode in his childhood that made Elvis Presley, who became in effect the man of the house while his father was away, so protective of his mother.

Yet it seems that neither Gladys nor Elvis ever held this escapade against Vernon. Gladys stood by him at the time and Elvis treated his father with respect for the rest of his own life. Thanks to Vernon's good behavior and Gladys's stream of letters on his behalf, Vernon was given an early release from Parchman on February 6, 1939, after serving only nine months of his sentence.

When Elvis became a star, this aspect of the Presley family past was of course kept hidden, both to safeguard Elvis's career and to protect the feelings of his mother and father. There have been suggestions that knowledge of Vernon's prison term was one of the holds Elvis's manager, Colonel Tom Parker, had over his client. According to this theory, implied threats to reveal Vernon's disgrace made Elvis agree to stay with the Colonel and accept many of the Colonel's decisions that were not in Elvis's own best interests.

Video Versions of Elvis

Fans regret that Elvis Presley's stardom occurred before the days of music videos, since Elvis was one of the most dazzling live performers ever and would surely have been the King of the video. Elvis fans will have to content themselves by watching the few videocassette versions available of his performances.

The video that belongs in every Elvis fan's library is "Elvis: Comeback '68," the video version of the 1968 TV special (chosen in a 1989 article in *TV Guide* the best rock performance ever to air on TV). It is available from Media Home Entertainment. The Cinemax cable TV special entitled "Elvis '56" is also available on videocassette; it was one of the top ten sellers in 1988. David Wolper's film for Warner Brothers, *This Is Elvis*, has been released on videocassette in an expanded version that is forty minutes longer than the movie.

If you still can't get enough of Elvis, most of his films are now available on videocassette.

Visiting Jesse Garon's Grave

When Elvis Presley was a small child in East Tupelo, Mississippi, his mother Gladys would frequently take him to the nearby Priceville Cemetery to visit the grave of his stillborn twin brother, Jesse Garon. Together, Gladys and Elvis would talk to Jesse about family activities and recent events. Gladys habitually referred to Jesse in the present tense, as if he were a present part of the Presley household. Many have since wondered at the psychological effect this emphasis on Elvis's missing twin had on the star.

Visiting the Morgue

According to Priscilla Presley, Elvis liked on occasion to pay a visit to the Memphis morgue to make detailed observations of the bodies lying on slabs. He explained that the experience could make a person feel peaceful and realize how temporary life is, how easily it could end without warning.

Viva Las Vegas

Viva Las Vegas was an Elvis Presley movie released in 1964. It is special among Elvis vehicles because it contains a truly passionate romance between the star and his leading lady, Ann-Margret, who can sing, dance, and emote so well that she becomes a real character in her own right, rather than just another pretty face whose only function is to give Elvis a chance to sing. According to Hollywood gossip Elvis and Ann-Margret were also romancing off the screen at that time; at the very least, they were "good friends." *Viva Las Vegas* grossed more than $6 million, but its soundtrack EP stayed on the album charts for only one week.

WDIA

When Elvis Presley was a teenager in Memphis, he spent hours listening to the music played on radio station WDIA. Aimed at the black community, the 250-watt station first went on the air in 1948, the year the Presley family moved to Memphis, and it played blues, black gospel music, and rhythm-and-blues records. Its success with programming all-black music and using hip black deejays caused WDIA to grow into a 50,000-watt station by 1954. Called the "Mother Station of the Negroes," WDIA not only acquainted Elvis with the full range of what was then termed "race" music, but also with the street language of the urban blacks in the South. One of WDIA's deejays for a time was blues great B.B. King. Elvis himself was the first to acknowledge his debt to the sounds he heard on WDIA, and when he began to earn good money as a performer he made regular contributions to the station to help keep it on the air.

According to former WDIA deejay Rufus Thomas, a singer himself, the manager of WDIA did not want to air Elvis Presley's records when they first began to appear on the Sun label because he thought a black audience would not like to hear a white singer. Thomas defied the edict and played the records—which his listeners loved.

WLVS

After the death of Elvis Presley in 1977, Sam Phillips changed the call letters of his Memphis Radio station to WLVS, in tribute to his one-time protégé on the Sun label.

Alice Walker's "1955"

Writer Alice Walker (*The Color Purple*) published a short story about the life of Elvis Presley, titled "1955." Her fictional account of a young singer's sudden and enormous fame focused on the emptiness of the Elvis legend and the sadness of his secluded life.

Hal B. Wallis

Hal B. Wallis was a veteran Hollywood director and producer, involved in more than four hundred films in his lifetime, who helped launch Elvis Presley's film career. It was Wallis who tested young Elvis in 1956 and then signed him to a three-movie contract at Paramount. Wallis later said he did it on the basis not of the test but of seeing Elvis perform on the Tommy and Jimmy Dorsey variety show on TV. There was some talk that Wallis would cast Elvis in a male ingenue role in *The Rainmaker*, starring Burt Lancaster and Katharine Hepburn, but Elvis's first role was as the star of *Love Me Tender*, for which Wallis put him on loan to Twentieth Century-Fox.

Looking back on the nine pictures he made with Elvis, Wallis explained tactfully, "Of course, the Elvis films . . . were filmed for strictly commercial purposes." He said his own favorite was *King Creole* (1958), and his biggest regret was that he had been unable to carry out his idea for a movie starring John Wayne as a veteran gunfighter and Elvis as his young protégé —an idea vetoed, no doubt by Colonel Parker, on the grounds that it wouldn't give Elvis a chance to sing. Hal Wallis died in 1986.

Andy Warhol Paints Elvis

In the early 1970s, Andy Warhol painted a huge silkscreen of multiple images of Elvis Presley with a pistol in his hand. It was later sold at the prestigious Parke-Bernet Galleries for the highest price paid to that date for any piece of pop art. An earlier (1956) work of Warhol's was a "shoe portrait" of Elvis, featuring a single boot.

Warm-Up Routine

When Elvis Presley went into the recording studio he had a particular routine that he used to warm up for the session. He liked to play and sing gospel music along with his backup band and his vocalists— often the Jordanaires, an accomplished

W

283

group of gospel singers. The gospel singing might go on for hours, but it was the way Elvis got psychologically and musically prepared to record.

When Elvis was in Hollywood to record his movie soundtracks he followed the same system. It was apparently upsetting to studio moguls, who thought the star was simply wasting expensive time. When Elvis was recording *King Creole*, executives at MGM approached his backup vocalists, the Jordanaires, during a break and told them they had to stop singing gospel music with Elvis because the time thus spent was costing the studio too much money. When the Jordanaires didn't rejoin Elvis at the piano after the break, he asked them what the trouble was and they explained their instructions. An angry Elvis said, "Look, if I want to bring you guys to Hollywood to sing spirituals all day long, that's what we'll do," and left the studio for the rest of the day. Thereafter no one tried to interfere with Elvis's gospel singing.

Watching Movies with Elvis

In the late 1950s and 1960s, when Elvis Presley felt in the mood for seeing a movie, he simply rented a movie theater in Memphis. Then he would borrow films from a local storage depot, usually brand-new movies that weren't yet in general release, and show them for his friends or anyone else who wanted to join the group. Not all the audience enjoyed these evenings at the movies because Elvis was in complete control of the projection room. If he didn't like a film or got bored with it he would order the projectionist to switch to something else. He sat front and center—and of course no one sat in front of him. When he rented the movie theater he always asked the owners to keep the concession stand open so he and his guests—often as many as two hundred people—could have all the popcorn, candy, and sodas they wanted. Pizza was brought in too, and sometimes the evening ended with a food fight.

The Wedding

On May 1, 1967, Elvis Presley, the idol of millions of women all over the world, married Priscilla Beaulieu in a secret ceremony at the Las Vegas Aladdin Hotel. Elvis's wedding was presided over by Justice of the Nevada Supreme Court David Zenoff and took place in the private suite of the hotel's owner, Milton Prell, an old friend of Colonel Parker. The service took only eight minutes. The maid of honor was the bride's thirteen-year-old sister Michelle. The groom had two best men; Joe Esposito and Marty Lacker. The guests at the private ceremony were:

- Harry Levitch, Elvis's favorite Memphis jeweler, and his wife Frances
- Patsy Presley Gambill, Elvis's cousin, and her husband Gee Gee, Elvis's chauffeur
- George Klein, Elvis's friend since high school, and his fiancée Barbara Little
- Major and Mrs. Joseph P. Beaulieu, the bride's parents
- Donald Beaulieu, the bride's brother
- Vernon Presley, Elvis's father, and his wife Dee
- Colonel Tom Parker, Elvis's manager

Elvis and his bride, Priscilla, sharing their happiness with guests and the media at the reception following their Las Vegas wedding. Colonel Parker was in charge of all the arrangements. (Photo from Neal Peters Collection)

Wedding Attire

For Elvis Presley's wedding to Priscilla Beaulieu, he chose to wear a black brocade jacket and matching vest. Plain black trousers completed the ensemble.

The bride wore a traditional white gown made of silk organza, trimmed in seed pearls with a six-foot train. Her three-quarter-length tulle veil was held in place by a rhinestone tiara. She bought the gown off the rack in a store in Los Angeles.

The Wedding Breakfast

The wedding of Elvis and Priscilla Presley was followed by a reception and champagne breakfast at the Las Vegas Aladdin Hotel. Among the dishes served were suckling pig and southern-fried chicken, as well as such elegant fare as oysters Rockefeller. The bride and groom cut a six-tiered wedding cake decorated with red and pink hearts that were studded with tiny pearls. The band played many of Elvis's hits, including "Love Me Tender." One of the celebrity guests was comedian Redd Foxx.

The Wedding Reception at Graceland

When Elvis Presley married Priscilla Beaulieu, it was in a secret ceremony arranged by his manager, Colonel Tom Parker, in Las Vegas, to avoid the mobs of fans that presumably would have gathered if the wedding plans had been made public. The wedding's secrecy and its out-of-town location excluded many of Elvis's friends in Memphis from one of the most important moments of his life. To soothe their hurt feelings Elvis decided to hold a second wedding reception when he and his new bride returned to Graceland. The bride and groom wore their wedding clothes and stood in a formal receiving line. There was a band, a roving accordion player, a huge spread on the buffet table, and a never-ending stream of champagne.

Wedding Rings

When Elvis Presley married Priscilla Beaulieu, the couple exchanged rings. Priscilla's was a three-carat diamond surrounded by twenty smaller diamonds that Elvis bought from his friend and jeweler Harry Levitch for $4,000. Priscilla gave Elvis a plain gold band that he later lost somewhere on the grounds of the Circle G ranch.

The Wedding That Never Was

In 1976, the news media carried a story about impending wedding plans for Elvis. According to the UPI story, a vice president of RCA Records named Allan Wexler had announced that Elvis would be married in a civil ceremony in the next few days. The bride was to be a young woman named Alexis Skylar, identified as a former RCA secretary who had quit her job in 1973 to work for Elvis. The story was confirmed by the manager of the Kirk of the Heather Chapel in Las Vegas, who said she had been told to prepare for Elvis's wedding there the following afternoon.

Somewhere, someone was laughing over the success of this hoax. There was no Alexis Skylar, no Allan Wexler, and no wedding.

The Weight Problem

By the mid-1970s, one of Elvis Presley's most serious health difficulties was his fight against fat. He had been a sex symbol for a generation, and like most sex symbols, he could not be allowed to age or change or get fat. He struggled to keep his weight down but many of his dieting strategies were unsuccessful and others had the effect of decreasing his energy, which caused problems with his performances. In fact his ill-advised attempts to manage his weight no doubt contributed to his ongoing problems with both weight and health. Elvis got into the "yo-yo syndrome," gaining thirty-five or forty pounds quickly and then dieting them off too fast, eating virtually nothing for a time. Much of the medication he began to take so heavily was aimed at solving his weight problem too—injections to help him lose weight, or stay on a diet, or to make him feel more energetic while he was living on a drastically reduced caloric intake. Elvis was still trying to get his weight under control when he died.

Bobby "Red" West

A long-time member of the so-called Memphis Mafia was Bobby "Red" West. Born in 1936, Red was a fellow student of Elvis Presley's at Humes High in Memphis and an All-Memphis football player. On several occasions Red intervened when kids were making fun of Elvis's unusual pompadour hairdo—according to a story he tells himself, once preventing a group of guys from giving Elvis an impromptu haircut in the bathroom. Red went on to attend Jones Junior College on a football scholarship and to play in the Junior Rose Bowl.

Red traveled occasionally with Elvis in 1954 and early 1955 as the young singer was booked in venues all over the South. When Elvis's sudden enormous fame made him a virtual prisoner in his own home he turned to Red for companionship and fun.

Red, along with another of Elvis's buddies, Lamar Fike, even went to live in Germany while Elvis was stationed there. When Elvis returned to Graceland Red was put on the star's payroll as a bodyguard, driver, and general factotum; in 1961 he married Elvis's secretary, Pat Boyd.

Red was a man of many talents. While in Hollywood with Elvis, he worked as a movie stuntman. He was also a successful songwriter, penning several of Elvis's hits, among them "Separate Ways" (1973), about Elvis's split with Priscilla, "Holly Leaves and Christmas Trees" (1971), and "If Every Day Could Be Like Christmas" (1966). He was for a time a regular cast member of the TV series "The Wild, Wild West." He remained close to Elvis until he was fired by Vernon Presley, supposedly in an economy drive, in 1975. Then Red and his cousin Sonny helped write a book that exposed the darker side of Elvis Presley's life—in order, they claimed, to send a message to Elvis that he had to change if he wanted to survive. The only message Elvis got was the bitter one that his former friends had been disloyal. After Elvis's death Red West occasionally appeared in the supporting cast of Robert Conrad's TV series, "Baa Baa Black Sheep" as Sergeant Andy Micklin; Conrad was one of Red's close friends, to whom he had often turned when the pressures of life in Elvis's entourage got to be too much for him. Most recently, he had a small part in the 1989 movie *Roadhouse*, starring Patrick Swayze.

Delbert "Sonny" West

Delbert "Sonny" West, born in 1937, was Red West's cousin. Like Red, Sonny was for a time also on Elvis Presley's payroll, working as a guard, driver, and whatever else Elvis needed at the time. Sonny was fired along with Red by Vernon Presley in 1975. Sonny then collaborated with his cousin in writing the book *Elvis: What Happened?* that was published just before the star's death and revealed the darker side of his life, such as his drug use and related emotional problems. In the 1980s Sonny was arrested in Los Angeles for "possession or intent to sell" of cocaine.

Pat Boyd West

Pat Boyd was one of Elvis Presley's first secretaries, working out of an office at Graceland to help the young singer deal with the financial aspects of his sudden enormous success. In 1961, Pat married one of Elvis's close friends, Bobby "Red" West, whom he had met in high school and later put on his payroll. Two years after her marriage Pat quit her job to have a baby.

Kathy Westmoreland

Kathy Westmoreland was a gospel singer, much admired by Elvis Presley, who eventually joined his payroll and toured with him. Elvis often introduced Kathy as "the little girl with the high voice." She sometimes sang backup for the star and also performed her own solo material before he came on. In the mid-1970s the friendship between Elvis and Kathy apparently crossed the border into romance, and on occasion his introductions of the singer from the stage could be embarrassingly personal. Kathy sang at Elvis's funeral, choosing one of his favorite gospel songs, "My Heavenly Father Watches Over Me"; she later recorded the song as a tribute to Elvis. In 1988, she wrote a book about her personal recollections of Elvis, called *Elvis and Kathy*. It can be ordered from the publishers: Glendale House, 249 North Brand Blvd., Suite 440, Glendale CA 91203

Whammies

Whammies were ice cream desserts that Elvis Presley learned to love in the mid-1970s. The freezers at Graceland were always well stocked with Whammies.

What the Critics Said About Elvis

When Elvis Presley first became a national star, critics in general had few kind words for the new teen phenomenon. Among the insults hurled Elvis's way in the early days were:

• An unutterable bore
• Unspeakably untalented and vulgar
• Can't sing a lick
• A menace to young girls
• No discernible singing ability
• Obscene
• Oversexed

What Elvis Said About the Critics

Elvis Presley was invariably courteous in public, even under conditions that could make most people's tempers flare. When Elvis was viciously attacked by the critics at the beginning of his career his response was a characteristically mild one. "Critics have a job to do," he said, "just like anyone else. I got no reason to get mad about it."

What Happened to Elvis's Fans?

Paul Stanley, lead guitar player for the rock group Kiss, told *People* what had happened to the fans of Elvis Presley: "The problem is some kids who grew up loving everything Elvis stood for are now journalists who have become what they feared most—parents."

What Teri Garr Learned from Elvis Presley

Interviewed on the "Today" show on November 25, 1988, Teri Garr said she had danced in nine Elvis Presley movies without any credit. One of them was *Viva Las Vegas*, starring Elvis and Ann-Margret, in which Garr was a member of the chorus, a position she described as "one step above being a cocktail waitress." In another 1988 interview Garr said she learned by watching Elvis that fame alone wasn't enough to make a person happy. Her analysis of his problem was that "Elvis tried to be like everybody else and he couldn't. He went from this guy who was a truck driver to enormous fame, and it just wrecked him." Garr also commented that she thought if Elvis had lived, he would be a health nut today.

What Would Elvis Look Like Today?

If Elvis Presley *were* alive today, how would we recognize him? The answer depends, of course, on what he might have been doing with himself in the past decade. People who claim to have sighted him have seen a man who looks just like Elvis did in 1977, just a little older. According to these reports he has long dark hair with sideburns, a heavy face, and in some instances a figure tending toward the portly.

But why would Elvis fake his own death in order to resume his former problems? We think that the Elvis of the 1990s would be a man who had gained control of his life. His figure would be trim and he would be incredibly fit. With his somewhat obsessive concentration on each of his interests, if Elvis ever took up the cause of fitness, you just know he would go all the way. The new Elvis would wear his hair a little shorter and he would also have stopped dyeing it—black is too harsh for an older face. Exercise and fresh air would have let the sun lighten his natural dark blondness into the color of Robert Redford's hair—a nice combination with the tan he would have acquired at the same time. He would dress casually now that he is out of the public spotlight, but with the distinctive flair that was always his own. The trend toward more colorful clothes for men would definitely suit him.

Oh, yes, we'd know how to recognize him!

Whatever Happened to Elvis Bearsley?

A special delight for Elvis fans of all ages was the teddy bear called Elvis Bearsley, dressed in a jump suit and carrying a microphone. The bear sold briskly until the Presley estate put pressure on the manufacturer for its unlicensed use of Elvis's likeness and the bears had to be withdrawn from the market.

Whatever Happened to Elvis's Old Clothes?

Anything that Elvis Presley ever wore has become a collector's item. Even before his death fans tried to get their hands on his garments—and one of his albums, *Elvis: The Other Sides*, was promoted by including with each record one square inch of some article of his clothing. It was his theatrical wardrobe, and especially the heavily sequinned jumpsuits, that were most sought after, and some of those were donated to charitable causes to be auctioned off for sums in the thousands of dollars. Elvis gave one of his most famous outfits, his diamond-studded gold lamé suit, to his hairdresser, Gil Gilliland. Many of his clothes, including items from his stage wardrobe, can be seen today at Graceland; others are on display at the Country Music Hall of Fame in Nashville.

Where to Look for Elvis

Since Elvis Presley's death in 1977, there have been many reports from people who claim to have spotted him alive and well and engaged in an odd variety of activities. If you want to look for Elvis, you might consider some of these locations where surprised observers say they have seen him:

- Vicksburg, Michigan, where he was exiting a supermarket
- Orlando, Florida, where he was living quietly in a remote cabin
- Denton, Texas, where he parachuted in for the opening of a local carnival
- East Lansing, Michigan, where he took his dirty clothes to the laundromat
- Philadelphia, Pennsylvania, where he stopped for a meal at a Burger King

- Encino, California, where he was enjoying the sunshine
- Albuquerque, New Mexico, ditto
- Atlanta, Georgia, where he walked through a hotel bar
- Graceland, where he was spotted lurking in his own bedroom

People magazine, in the December 26, 1988 issue, published photos supposedly taken of Elvis Presley in recent years, including one of him stuffing himself on jelly donuts, and another in which his car "is riding kind of heavy on the driver's side," with a vanity license plate that reads ELVIZ.

Where to Write About Elvis

If you have an opinion you would like to express to the Elvis Presley estate, or a comment to make, here's where to write the people who now handle Elvis's affairs:

Graceland
3717 Elvis Presley Boulevard
P.O. Box 16508
Memphis TN 38186-0508

C. Barry Ward
c/o Glanker, Brown, Gilliland, Chase,
   Robinson, and Raines
One Commerce Square
Memphis TN 38103

Priscilla Presley
1167 Summit Avenue
Beverly Hills CA 90210

White Cotton Panties

According to insider sources one thing a woman could always count on to arouse Elvis Presley sexually was a pair of white cotton underpants.

Whitehaven Music Company

Whitehaven Music Company was one of the corporations set up to administer the rights to Elvis Presley's music publishing and musical rights activities. Whitehaven was the name of the unincorporated town in which Graceland was located until it became part of the city of Memphis.

Who Really Produced Elvis's Records?

The early records Elvis Presley made for RCA were officially produced by the label's A&R man, Steve Sholes. But according to eyewitnesses Sholes was not often actively involved with the recording sessions; Presley biographer Albert Goldman suggests that Sholes did little more than stretch out on a sofa in the studio to take a nap. Guitarist Scotty Moore, who played on many of the sessions and was himself a producer, has said that Elvis himself was the real producer of his own recordings. "It was just strictly Elvis, if you had to give anybody credit. It was up to him to weed through the pile of material and the demos that were brought in for the songs, and once he found one he wanted to try, then it was just a group effort to work it out. Everybody made suggestions—sometimes a song would get thrown out even after we'd run through it two or three times, and he'd say, 'No, that's just not right.' "

Why Did Elvis Die?

According to the official autopsy report of the Shelby County Medical Examiner, Elvis Presley's death was due to cardiac arrhythmia in the course of an apparent heart attack. Elvis was, of course, surprisingly young to suffer from heart trouble, but it is well known to be a life-style disease and Elvis's high-cholesterol diet, sporadic exercise, and continual tension all added up to a high-risk profile. A spokesman for Baptist Hospital, where Elvis was admitted to the emergency room and officially pronounced dead, said, "Elvis had the arteries of an eighty-year-old man. His body was just worn out. His arteries and veins were terribly corroded."

Why Elvis Stopped Making Movies

After Elvis Presley stopped making movies he explained why. "It was getting harder and harder singing to the camera all day long. Let's face it, when you have ten different songs for each movie, well, they can't all be good. Eventually I got tired of singing to turtles and guys I'd just beaten up!"

Why Save Money?

Vernon Presley regularly lectured his son Elvis on the need to cut down expenses and save money. But Elvis never agreed to any of Vernon's money-saving plans. The superstar simply answered, "It's only money, Daddy. I just have to go out and make more." And he always did. Despite his open-handed spending and his epic generosity to friends and family Elvis was always able to earn the money he needed to support his preferred life-style.

Why a Star Wasn't Born

When Barbra Streisand coproduced and starred in the update of the classic Hollywood tear-jerker *A Star Is Born* in 1977, her first choice of a leading man was Elvis Presley. Certainly he would have been well cast in the role of the popular singer who found it hard to accept his wife's increasingly successful career, and his performance in such a role might have given him the serious acting credentials he never had with film professionals. But manager Colonel Tom Parker vetoed the proposition by Streisand, not because of money but because of issues of billing and control. She then turned to her second choice, country-and-western singer-songwriter Kris Kristofferson. The movie made Kris a respected actor—as it might have done for Elvis.

Sue Wiegert

Sue Wiegert is a shining example of the dedication of the true fans of Elvis Presley. Sue first saw Elvis in concert in St. Louis in 1957. Later, while living in Hawaii, the young woman met her idol when he was on location to film his 1967 movie, *Paradise, Hawaiian Style*. Several years later Sue moved to Memphis, right across the highway from Graceland. A subsequent relocation to Los Angeles provided the opportunity to see the star frequently as he made movies in Hollywood and appeared in Las Vegas and Lake Tahoe. Elvis rewarded her devotion by trusting her to

W

become a part of his circle. Sue is the author of *Elvis: Precious Memories*, an account of her own memories of Elvis as well as those of his friends and colleagues. She is also the president of the Elvis fan club called "Blue Hawaiians for Elvis." Sue comments fervently about her idol:

> Elvis was a gift from God. People who never met him or saw him may dispute or misunderstand that, but anybody who cared about Elvis realizes the truth of that statement.

We [fans] were privileged to share the life and talents of someone who comes through history only once in creation. Because we saw past the image and embraced the person, we were given "precious memories" that set us apart as Elvis fans and will always bind us together in a group known as the "family of Elvis."

For information about the book or the fan club, write to P.O. Box 69834, Los Angeles CA 90069.

Wild in the Country

The movie *Wild in the Country*, starring Elvis Presley, was released in 1961. One of the singer's more ambitious films, it was directed by Philip Dunne from a script written by Clifford Odets. Elvis's costars were Tuesday Weld, Hope Lange, and Millie Perkins. Much of the movie was shot on location in the wine country of California. According to insider reports, Elvis's manager, Colonel Tom Parker, was not happy about a serious movie that would demonstrate his client's acting talent; he believed fans just wanted a chance to hear Elvis sing and then buy the soundtrack album.

Thus he conspired with 20th Century-Fox studio head Spiros Skouras to insert six production numbers (two of which were eventually cut) that undermined the serious intent of the film. Director Dunne later commented, "*Wild in the Country* fell between two stools. Audiences who might have liked Clifford Odets's drama wouldn't buy Elvis and his songs; Elvis fans were disappointed in a Presley picture which departed so radically from his usual song-and-sex comedy formula." Elvis, who usually hated to watch his movies, was reported to have liked this one.

The Will

Elvis Presley signed his final will on March 3, 1976, about a year and a half before his death. Witnesses to the document were Ginger Alden, Charlie Hodge, and Ann Dewey Smith, wife of the attorney who drew up the document. The will left his estate to be held in trust for the benefit of his daughter, Lisa Marie; his grandmother, Minnie Mae Presley; his father, Vernon E. Presley; and any other family members who

in the opinion of the trustees might need financial assistance. After the death of Elvis's grandmother and father, all money was to be reabsorbed into the trust and held for Lisa Marie until she was twenty-five. The trustee appointed by Elvis was Vernon Presley, with the National Bank of Commerce in Memphis second choice, in case Vernon died or was unable to serve.

Elvis co-starred with Tuesday Weld in the 1961 movie *Wild in the Country*. This photo was a publicity shot for a teen fan-mag. (Photo from Neal Peters Collection)

William Morris Agency

Elvis Presley's official agent was the William Morris Agency, which received 10 percent of his income in return for handling the details of contracts and collecting fees and royalties due the artist. This cut was over and above the 25 percent taken by Elvis's personal manager, Colonel Tom Parker. It was Parker who introduced Elvis to the William Morris Agency, one of the biggest and most powerful in the entertainment business. During the time Parker was managing the career of Eddy Arnold, he had worked with Harry Kalcheim in the New York office; later it was Abe Lastvogel who handled Elvis's bookings and contracts. The links between Parker and the agency were so strong that in the 1980s, after Parker had lost most of his money in the lawsuits over his mismanagement of Elvis, the William Morris Agency volunteered financial support to their old colleague.

Jackie Wilson

Jackie Wilson, the famed soul singer, was sometimes called "The Black Elvis"—an ironical compliment since Elvis had adapted much of his own material and performance style from the black artists of the 1950s. Jackie and Elvis were good friends with a mutual admiration for many years. Jackie suffered a stroke in 1975 and never recovered from the resulting coma and paralysis. Elvis generously offered to help with his astronomical medical bills. Ironically, Elvis died several years later, but Jackie Wilson lingered until 1984.

The Woman at the Cadillac Dealer's

In July 1974, Elvis Presley made a shopping stop at a Cadillac dealer on Union Avenue in Memphis. A woman walking past the dealer's stopped to admire Elvis's own Cadillac, parked out by the curb. The star noticed her and warned, "You can't have that, it's mine." He then went on to say, "But never mind, I'll buy you another. Go into the showroom and pick the one you like." The astonished woman left in the new Cadillac that Elvis paid for.

"Won't Live to Be Thirty"

When Elvis Presley first became a big star, his mother Gladys, always overprotective, worried incessantly about the physical demands his career made on him—the travel, the long hours, the sheer amount of energy it took to sing the way Elvis did. She warned her son, "You're puttin' too much into your singin'. Keep that up and you won't live to be thirty."

Anita Wood

Before Elvis Presley was drafted and sent to Germany, he was dating a Memphis television hostess and former deejay at country station WHHM, Anita Wood, whom he nicknamed "Little Bit." According to her own account, the two met on a blind date when they were still teenagers, before Elvis had yet achieved any success as a performer. They went roller-skating together and saw the latest movies, in a typical teenage courtship of the 1950s. Elvis continued to see Anita even after his quick rise to fame, and he arranged for her to get a small part in a movie so she could go out to Hollywood when he was there. He also introduced her to Sam Phillips at Sun Records, where she recorded "I'll Wait Forever" in 1958. When Elvis was drafted, Anita was the girl who said goodbye to him and she later visited him frequently at Fort Hood in Texas. When he left to go overseas Elvis gave her a beautiful diamond friendship ring and he often called her from Germany. According to Priscilla Presley, Anita reciprocated by writing to Elvis at least twice a week. But when the star returned to the States early in 1960 the romance inexplicably faded.

Anita Wood later married former football player Johnny Brewer, with whom she had three children. In 1972 the Brewers filed a libel suit against a Memphis newspaper, the *Commercial Appeal*, which had run a story claiming that Anita had gone to Las Vegas for a romantic reunion with former boyfriend Elvis. She was able to prove that she'd gone nowhere more glamorous than on a camping trip with her parents and her children and thus she won her suit. Although she didn't get the $2 million in damages she asked for, she was eventually awarded $210,000.

Anita Wood can be heard singing with Elvis in a bootleg record released on the Memphis Flash label at the time of Elvis's death. The recording was made by Eddie Fadal, a friend of Colonel Tom Parker's who lived near the Texas army base where Elvis was stationed. Sometime in 1958 Elvis visited Eddie, bringing along Anita Wood; Elvis played the piano, sang along with records, and performed several duets with Anita. The album was called *Forever Young, Forever Beautiful*.

B.F. Wood Music Company

In Great Britain Elvis Presley's music is published by B.F. Wood Music Company.

Natalie Wood

When Elvis Presley went to Hollywood to make his first movie in 1956, he met teen star Natalie Wood through mutual friend Nick Adams, and the two had a brief romance. Natalie, born in 1938, visited Elvis at Graceland, riding behind him on his motorcycle as he showed her his hometown. She later described their relationship as being more like a high school date than a torrid romance. Veteran Hollywood actress Shelley Winters, however, remembers that Elvis and Natalie were deeply in love. Elvis himself told *Motion Picture* magazine that they "just stopped dating. We're usually at opposite ends of the country anyway, and we never did go steady or anything like that." Natalie Wood later married actor Robert Wagner (twice). She died in an accidental drowning in 1981.

Becky Yancy

Becky Yancy was a young Memphis fan of Elvis Presley's whose dream of being close to her idol came true when she was hired in 1962 to work as a secretary at Graceland. Becky stayed with the Presleys for twelve years, until the demands of her own growing family caused her to give up her job. She later wrote a book about her years at Graceland, called *My Life with Elvis*. It was published in 1977.

"Yisa"

"Yisa" was a nickname Elvis Presley frequently used for his daughter, Lisa Marie.

Yogi Paramahansa Yogananda

Yogi Paramahansa Yogananda was an Indian yogi who attracted a large following in California in the 1940s. He authored a book called *The Autobiography of a Yogi*, which over the years has attracted more disciples. Yogananda died in Los Angeles in 1952, and it was reported by some of his followers that his unpreserved body lay in an open casket for twenty days without any signs of decomposition.

The organization Yogananda founded in southern California, the Self-Realization Fellowship, continued to draw followers after his death. For a time, one of them was Elvis Presley. People who knew Elvis well agree that he was always interested in the spiritual side of human existence, reading books about religion, parapsychology, and the occult. The doctrine of self-realization never replaced Elvis's deep belief in Christianity but it did supplement his traditional religious faith. The star regularly donated money to the organization and in 1973 he gave them a sum big enough to worry his father Vernon, who made an effort to separate Elvis from the group. Like many of Elvis's enthusiasms, this one too waned in time.

Sandra Zancan

Sandra Zancan was a Las Vegas showgirl who dated Elvis Presley in the mid-1970s, while he was in the city for his hotel concert dates.